The Appointed Times of Jesus the Messiah

By Fred R. Coulter

York Publishing Company
Post Office Box 1038
Hollister, California 95024-1038

Unless otherwise noted,
all Scriptures used in
this book are quoted from
*The Holy Bible In Its
Original Order—A Faithful
Version With Commentary
ISBN 978-0-9675479-7-2*

ISBN 978-0-9819787-8-9

*York Publishing Company
Post Office Box 1038
Hollister, California 95024-1038*

Table of Contents

About the Author

Fred R. Coulter attended the University of San Francisco and graduated from San Mateo State College before graduating from Ambassador University (Ambassador College), Pasadena, California, with a BA in Theology in 1964. He was ordained a minister of Jesus Christ in 1965 and pastored churches of God in the Pacific Northwest, the Mountain States, the greater Los Angeles area and Monterey, including the central coast area of California. Mr. Coulter completed advanced biblical and ministerial studies in 1972-75 under the Ambassador University Master's Program. While completing these studies, he was encouraged by his professor of *Koiné* Greek to consider translating the books of the New Testament.

For the next twenty years, Mr. Coulter diligently studied, continuing to expand his knowledge of *Koiné* Greek. While undertaking a verse-by-verse study of the books of the New Testament, he was moved to translate the New Testament into clear, easy-to-read English for contemporary readers—resulting in *The New Testament In Its Original Order* (now incorporated into *The Holy Bible In Its Original Order—A Faithful Version With Commentary*).

With a ministry now spanning more than 45 years, Fred Coulter has dedicated his life and talents to *restoring original Christianity* for today's generation. Laying aside all traditions of men, he has preached the *truth* of the Scriptures as taught by Jesus Christ and the apostles—proclaiming Jesus as personal Savior for all. Since 1983, Mr. Coulter has been the president of the Christian Biblical Church of God, headquartered in Hollister, California. He has an active ministry that reaches all parts of the United States and Canada, with additional offices in Australia, New Zealand, the United Kingdom, South Africa, Ethiopia and Kenya.

Each year over 600,000 people from around the world actively utilize the church's Web sites where they find timely, inspiring weekly sermons and in-depth verse-by-verse biblical study materials covering virtually all of Scripture (see **www.cbcg.org** and **www.churchathome.org**).

Editor's note: Author Fred R. Coulter has previously written extensively about Jesus' birth, death and resurrection in *A Harmony of the Gospels in Modern English—the Life of Jesus Christ*. In this new book, however, Coulter covers the entire spectrum of the "appointed times" of Jesus the Messiah while incorporating new, unpublished material concerning the 70-week prophecy of Daniel nine and end-time prophecies of Revelation. It is truly a first-of-its-kind publication.

Acknowledgments

We first acknowledge God the Father and Jesus Christ, and thank them for preserving the Holy Bible—in spite of mankind's tumultuous history—so that today God's truth is available for everyone. It is the very Word of God that gives us the true understanding of the purpose of human existence. Jesus said, "Your Word is the truth" (John 17:17), and "you shall know the truth, and the truth shall set you free" (John 8:32).

Primarily, I give my heartfelt gratitude and appreciation to my loving, dear wife, Dolores, for her personal encouragement and assistance. A special "thank you" goes to all the faithful brethren whose freewill tithes and offerings made this book possible. Through your spirit of giving, each of you have a special part in helping to preach and spread the Gospel of Jesus Christ.

Special thanks and congratulations go to Carl Franklin for his vital content contribution. His countless hours of in-depth research into the histories and dynastic genealogies of the ancient Middle East (Persia and Babylon in particular) have been invaluable in understanding the writings of Daniel, Ezra and Nehemiah. Having dedicated a lifetime to studying Scripture and ancient history, Carl has successfully harmonized the histories of the kings of Babylon, Media and Persia with the biblical books of Ezra, Nehemiah and I and II Chronicles. His full, detailed analysis is contained in Appendix C. Because of his work, it is now possible to correctly understand the mysterious 70-week prophecy of Daniel nine as it relates to God's "appointed times."

Thanks also to Philip Neal for his editing, to Dwight Blevins for his research and writing in Appendix E, and to John and Hiedi Vogele for their proofreading and final formatting of the text. As with my other publications, many people have helped and shared in the production of this book. Their diligent work and support has made it possible.

Fred R. Coulter
February 2012

Other Works by the Author

The Holy Bible In Its Original Order—A Faithful Version With Commentary is a new translation that reflects the meaning of the original Hebrew and Greek with fidelity and accuracy—and is the only English version in which the books of the Bible are arranged in their original order. The easy-to-read translation retains the grace and grandeur of the *King James Version* while clarifying many of its problematic passages. Included are commentaries on the writing, canonization and preservation of the Scriptures. Various appendices cover numerous controversial biblical teachings, and detailed footnotes and marginal references explain hard-to-understand passages. A vital tool for all students of the Bible! See **www.restoringtheoriginalbible.com**.

A Harmony of the Gospels in Modern English brings to life the message and purpose of the true Jesus, portraying His life and ministry in their true historical setting. This easy-to-understand, step-by-step account of the life of Christ is an indispensable study aid for every Bible student.

The Christian Passover details the scriptural and historical truths of the Passover in both the Old and New Testaments, leading the reader step-by-step through every aspect of one of the most vital and fundamental teachings revealed in the Bible. With over 500 pages, the book fully explains the meaning of the Christian Passover—a remembrance of the sacrifice of Jesus Christ, the Passover Lamb of God—in a most compelling and inspiring manner. The full meaning of the body and blood of Jesus Christ is revealed, showing the magnitude of God's love for every person.

The Day Jesus the Christ Died—the Biblical Truth about His Passion, Crucifixion and Resurrection is the *only book* to present "the rest of the story"—left out by Mel Gibson in his epic movie "The Passion of the Christ." Without the true historical and biblical facts, one cannot fully understand the meaning of Jesus Christ's horrific, humiliating and gruesome death by beating, scourging and crucifixion. The author presents the full biblical account in a most compelling way. As you will see, the truth is more astounding than all of the ideas, superstitions and traditions of men!

The Seven General Epistles is designed for an in-depth verse-by-verse study of the epistles of James; I and II Peter; I, II and III John and Jude. As part of the living Word of God, these epistles are as meaningful today for personal Christian growth as when they were written.

Occult Holidays or God's Holy Days—Which? For centuries the leaders of Orthodox Christendom have sold popular holidays—Halloween, Christmas, Easter, etc.—to the masses as though they had "Christian" meaning. This book effectively demonstrates that these celebrated holidays are *not* of God, but originated from ancient religions rooted in occultism. Contrary to the false ideas of men, the *true* biblical holy days of God have vital spiritual meaning and outline God's fantastic plan of salvation for all mankind.

God's Plan for Mankind Revealed by His Sabbath and Holy Days. This first-of-its-kind, 598-page work provides a comprehensive look at God's amazing Master Plan for the human family—precisely as it is outlined by the biblical seventh-day Sabbath and annual holy days. Each chapter is a transcript of an in-depth sermon or Bible study revealing God's purpose from Genesis to Revelation. Actual sermons are included on an accompanying set of four CDs.

Lord, What Should I Do? "Christianity" is now facing an unprecedented crisis: disenchanted churchgoers are quitting by the thousands, looking for genuine spirituality *outside* of the corporate church. This new book presents *real solutions* to the problems of a dysfunctional "Christianity," emphasizing how Christians *can* and *must* take steps to recapture a faith that is authentic, relevant and applicable to modern life, even if it means leaving organized "Christianity."

Judaism—Revelation of Moses or Religion of Men? Contrary to Jewish claims, the religion of Judaism does *not* represent the way of life God gave through Moses in the Old Testament. In fact, Judaism greatly distorts the biblical Law of Moses by adding to it a massive humanly-devised "code" of laws. The result is that Jews can no longer differentiate between *God's Law* and man-made *tradition*. Using history, Scripture and the Jews' own writings, this book demonstrates that Judaism is actually a *false religion* developed by men. *Written by Philip Neal*

God's Bible Pathway for Children. *Written by Jane Spring*

Online Studies for the serious Bible student—with additional written material and in-depth Bible studies in audio and video format—can be obtained at **www.cbcg.org** and **www.churchathome.org**.

Foreword

Almost from its inception, the Bible develops its narratives, teachings and prophecies around the preeminent role of Jesus of Nazareth—the Messiah of God. In a veiled reference, the Scriptures first reveal the role of the Messiah in Genesis 3:14-15, as God is meting out judgment on the serpent, Satan the devil. "Because you have done this [in causing Adam and Eve to sin] you are cursed above all livestock, and above every animal of the field. You shall go upon your belly, and you shall eat dust all the days of your life. And I will put enmity between you [Satan] and the woman [the church], and between your seed [those who would do Satan's bidding] and her Seed [Jesus]; He [Jesus] will **bruise your head** [overcome and defeat you], and **you shall bruise His heel** [cause Him to be put to death]." Thus, from the beginning, we see foreshadowed in a single sentence the redemptive work of Christ *crucified* and the ultimate salvation wrought by His *victory*, as King of kings in the age to come, over the "god" of this present age (II Cor. 4:4)—truly, the Gospel message in a nutshell.

Numerous additional messianic prophecies are carefully woven throughout Scripture. The patriarch Abraham, for example, was promised that his *Seed* would bring blessings to all mankind. "And in your seed shall all the nations of the earth be blessed, because you have obeyed My voice" (Gen. 24:18). The apostle Paul shows clearly in Galatians 3:16 that the reference to "seed" here is messianic. Likewise, the prophet Moses told the children of Israel that God would one day raise up "a Prophet from the midst of you, of your brethren, one like me. To Him you shall hearken" (Deut. 18:15)—clearly a prophecy of Jesus Christ's first coming as well as His final return to inaugurate the age to come.

As any Bible scholar will attest, there are literally hundreds of prophetic references in the Old Testament concerning the role of Jesus the Messiah. But what is poorly understood is this: As such prophecies find fulfillment in the New Testament, they do so in a *highly organized* manner—ordered according to specific "appointed times." These "appointed times" of the Messiah range from His birth to His ministry and from His death and resurrection to His final triumphant return at the end of the age. Of primary importance, these "appointed times" are arranged according to the timeframe set by the biblical festivals and holy days—which outline God's plan of salvation. (Unfortunately, these festivals have all but been ignored by mainstream Christianity.) In fact, the biblical feasts and high days—coordinated around three "seasons" (Lev. 23:4; Ex. 23:14-16)—form a framework or substructure that God uses to fulfill prophecy.

As will be demonstrated, God has precisely designed the role of Jesus the Messiah in accordance with the "appointed times" of His holy days. Indeed, *every key event* in the life and ministry of Jesus Christ—including His second coming—has been correlated to the various aspects of the Passover, the spring festival of Unleavened Bread, the late spring festival of Pentecost, and the fall festival season featuring the Day of Trumpets, the Day of Atonement and the Feast of Tabernacles (see Appendix E for an overview of God's annual holy days).

It is the purpose of this book, *The Appointed Times of Jesus the Messiah*, to unveil the step-by-step fulfillment of all the major messianic prophecies as revealed by the "appointed times" of God's holy day Master Plan. As the reader will come to see, it is only within this unique framework that the role of Jesus as the Messiah can be fully understood.—*Philip Neal*

Introduction

God is a God of purpose, order and *design*. The prophet Isaiah describes God as one "declaring the end from the beginning, and from ancient times the things which were not yet done, saying, 'My counsel shall stand, and I will do all My pleasure' " (Isa. 46:10). As such, God works according to His carefully planned *timetable*. We see this, for example, when God promised Abraham that Sarah would conceive only at "the time appointed" (Gen. 17:21; 18:14; 21:2). The Hebrew term used here is *moed*, meaning an *appointed* or *set* time—one that had been well thought out in advance. Concerning end-time events, God shows through the prophet Daniel that He works in concert with *appointed times*: "Behold, I will make you know what shall happen in the latter time of the indignation, because it belongs to '**the appointed time**' [*moed*] of the end" (Dan. 8:19; 11:27, 35). As well, the vision given to the prophet Habakkuk was for "an appointed time" at the end (Hab. 2:3).

A vital *key* to understanding how God works according to a carefully ordered plan is the knowledge of His annual festivals—or "appointed times." In Genesis chapter one, we see that God ordained the heavens as a kind of *timepiece* to indicate the timing of His *moadim* (plural of *moed*)—literally His *appointed times*. "And God said, 'Let there be lights in the firmament of the heavens to divide between the day and the night, and let them be for signs, and **for [the] appointed [festival] seasons**, and for days and years' " (verse 14). Indeed, God "made the moon [to indicate] the appointed times" (Psa. 104:19). In Exodus 13:10 we are instructed to keep the Feast of Unleavened Bread "in its season [*moed*]" or "appointed time." In Leviticus 23, where all of God's festivals are listed together, they are called "the **appointed feasts** [*moadim*] of the LORD, holy convocations which you shall proclaim in their **appointed seasons** [*moadim*]" (verses 2, 4). Thus, God's "appointed times" *are* His set festivals and holy days.

The entire Master Plan of God revolves around His Anointed One, Jesus the Messiah. Jesus' life, ministry, sacrificial death, resurrection, and role as King of the age to come is the focal point of God's grand purpose on earth. Thus, it should come as no surprise that every aspect of Jesus' role as Messiah is ordered according to God's "appointed times." We see that Jesus was "*slain*," as it were, from the foundation of this present age (Rev. 13:8)—that is, His death would be required as a result of the sin of Adam and Eve. Thus, it was *appointed* from the beginning that Christ would have to be sacrificed for the reconciling of mankind to God. The apostle Paul tells us that "at **the appointed time** Christ died for the ungodly" (Rom. 5:6). The Greek means a definite, *fixed* time. Similarly, Paul tells the Galatians that God sent Jesus only when "the fullness of time" had come (Gal. 4:4). Again, the Greek points to a specific, *appointed* time.

But exactly *what* and *when* are the "appointed times" of Jesus the

Messiah? How can we know them? As we will see, the mystery of the "appointed times" of the Messiah can only be resolved by understanding God's feasts and holy days!

Appointed Times "Hidden" in Plain Sight

It is mind-boggling that the Orthodox Christian world—consisting of over two billion professed believers—has little or no clear understanding of the biblical "appointed times" of Jesus the Messiah. This ignorance stems primarily from the overarching *rejection* by popular Christianity of the Old Testament festivals of God—falsely labeled as "Jewish." It is precisely because of this bias that most "Christians" are *blinded* to the truth of God's plan as it revolves around the "appointed times" of the Messiah. In other words, they have thrown away the very *key* that unlocks the prophecies hidden in God's Word.

Jesus' messianic role is fundamental to the establishment of the millennial Kingdom of God. Yet mankind as a whole has been locked in the *dark* concerning that kingdom. In Jesus' day, He often intentionally spoke in parables in order to *obscure* the facts of the kingdom: "And His disciples came to Him and asked, 'Why do You speak to them in parables?' And He answered and said to them, 'Because it has been **given to you to know the mysteries** [or secrets] **of the kingdom of heaven**, **but to them** [those who do not love and obey God] **it has not been given**' " (Matt. 13:10-11). In fact, "Jesus spoke all these things [concerning the kingdom] to the multitudes in parables, and without a parable He did not speak to them, so that it might be fulfilled which was spoken by the prophet [see Psalm 78:2], saying, 'I will open My mouth in parables; **I will utter things hidden from the foundation of the world**' " (verses 34-35).

God Himself has concealed these things—howbeit, in *plain sight* in the Scriptures. As Proverbs tells us, "**The glory of God *is* to conceal a thing, but the honor of kings *is* to search out a matter**" (Prov. 25:2). Paul writes that God reveals His secrets to those who *love* and *obey* Him. "**Having made known to us the mystery of His own will, according to His good pleasure, which He purposed in Himself; that in *the divine* plan for the fulfilling of *the* times** [His appointed times], He might bring all things together in Christ, both the things in the heavens and the things upon the earth; *yes,* in Him, in Whom we also have obtained an inheritance, having been predestinated according to His purpose, Who is working out all things according to the counsel of His own will" (Eph. 1:9-11).

This *mystery*—the authentic plan of God, centered on the Gospel of the kingdom (Eph. 6:19) and organized around God's "appointed times"—"has been **hidden from ages** and from generations, **but has now been revealed to His saints**" (Col. 1:26; also Rom. 16:25-26).

We observe this concept throughout the New Testament: God has chosen to reveal the truth of the kingdom *only* to a select few *at this time.*

All others remain blinded. But why? Why is the truth of God's "appointed times" *hidden* in plain view right in the pages of the Bible?

Continuing in Matthew 13, notice Jesus' explanation: "For whoever has *understanding*, to him more shall be given, and he shall have an abundance; but whoever does not have *understanding*, even what he has shall be taken away from him. **For this *reason* I speak to them in parables, because seeing, they see not; and hearing, they hear not; neither do they understand**" (verses 12-13). Amazing! They *read* the words right in their Bibles, but "see not." They *hear* the words being preached, but "hear not." They simply do not—*cannot*—understand!

Why? Jesus answers: "And in them is fulfilled the prophecy of Isaiah, which says, 'In hearing you shall hear, and in no way understand; and *in* seeing you shall see, and in no way perceive; for **the heart of this people has grown fat**, and **their ears are dull of hearing**, and **their eyes THEY have closed**; lest they should see with their eyes, and should hear with their ears, and should understand with their hearts, and should be converted, and I should heal them' " (verses 14-15).

Indeed, modern "Christianity" has almost no knowledge of the "appointed times" of God—of His Sabbath, holy days and feasts—keys to His prophetic plan. While they profess to believe in and accept Jesus as Savior, their *rejection* of God's Word has left them spiritually blind and incapable of understanding. Notice what Isaiah writes: "Be stunned and amazed! Blind your eyes and be blind! They are drunk, but not with wine; they stagger, but not *with* strong drink, for the LORD has poured out upon you the **spirit of deep sleep**, and has **closed your eyes**; He has covered [blinded] the prophets and your rulers, *and* the seers. And the vision of all has become to you like **the words of a book that is sealed**, which they give to one who is learned saying, 'Please read this,' and he says, 'I cannot, for it is sealed.' And the book is delivered to him who is not learned, saying, 'Please read this,' and he says, 'I am not learned' " (Isa. 29:9-12).

Jesus continues the thought, quoting from the same passage. "Well did Isaiah prophesy concerning you hypocrites, as it is written, 'This people honors Me [God the Father] with their lips, but their hearts are far away from Me. **But in vain do they worship Me**, **teaching for doctrine the commandments of men**.' **For leaving the commandment of God**, **you hold fast the tradition of men**…" (Mark 7:6-7).

In other words, they are *willingly ignorant* of the truth because they prefer their humanly-devised traditions over the clear commands of God. Today, in mainstream Christianity, such "teachings of men" would include: 1) the erroneous idea that God's weekly Sabbath and annual holy days—ignorantly labeled as "Old Covenant" rituals—are now *obsolete*, and 2) that "traditions of men"—such as Easter and Christmas—are perfectly *acceptable* forms of Christian worship. However, God commands us to *not* worship Him according to the customs of the pagan world (Deut. 12:30-32)—for such an approach is tantamount to calling good evil, and evil good

(Isa. 5:20). Of those who do so, God says they have "cast away the law of the LORD of hosts, and despised the Word of the Holy One of Israel" (verse 24).

As Jesus said and Paul wrote, this *mystery* of God's plan—previously hidden for ages—has *now been revealed* to His saints (Col. 1:26). Accordingly, as Daniel brings out, "there is a God in heaven Who reveals secrets" (Dan. 2:26)—and He reveals the secrets of His plan to "those who fear Him" (Psa. 25:14). These are the mysteries of the Kingdom of God—of His plan and purpose, the deep things of God as outlined by His "appointed times."

God makes plain the secrets of His prophecies according to His *own* timetable—when it is needful for such knowledge to be given. Case in point: When Daniel wanted to know the truth of the prophecies God had given to him, he was told, "Go your way, Daniel, for the words *are* closed up and **sealed until the time of the end**. Many shall be purified, and made white, and refined. But the wicked shall do wickedly; and **none of the wicked shall understand, but the wise shall understand**" (Dan. 12:9-10). Indeed, the Scriptures are written "here a little, and there a little" so that only those who are truly *yielded* to God will be able to understand (Isa. 28:9-10).

Today, *during these latter days*, as God has promised, He has abundantly revealed the previously hidden truths of His plan. The unveiling of the book of Revelation and the knowledge of the Calculated Hebrew Calendar (CHC) are vital keys to understanding God's plan. But the first and most critical requirement is a simple desire to *believe* and *obey* what the Scriptures teach. Only with such an attitude can one hope to have their mind opened and understanding granted by God's Holy Spirit—for "God has revealed [His mysteries] to us by His Spirit, for the Spirit searches all things—even the deep things of God. For who among men understands the things of man except *by* the spirit of man which *is* in him? In the same way also, the things of God no one understands except *by* the Spirit of God" (I Cor. 2:10-11).

Will *you* understand? Or will you allow yourself to be blinded by human tradition, hindered by religious bias? God shows no favoritism, as He is no respecter of persons (Rom. 2:11; Acts 10:34). However, for those who diligently *ask*, *seek* and *knock* (Matt. 7:7-8), the truth is readily available, *in plain sight*, right in the pages of the Bible. It is "hidden" only to those who willingly reject or dismiss the *key*—the Sabbath, holy days and festivals of God (Lev. 23).

Understanding the "appointed times" of Jesus the Messiah is essential to comprehending the Master Plan of God—the very plan designed to deliver humanity from utter destruction and bring *eternal life* to all who will embrace God's way. *If you are willing*, this book will open your eyes to the truth of God's plan of salvation as it follows the "appointed times" of Jesus the Messiah along the framework of God's annual festivals.

***One final note*:** The in-depth information contained in this book is based on Scripture, the time frame of the God-given CHC, as well as substantiating historical fact. No consideration has been given to the religious teachings and traditions of men. Thus, those who are not familiar with basic biblical teachings may initially find this book to be somewhat difficult. It is our hope, however, that the reader will follow the wise example of the Bereans, who "received the Word with all readiness of mind and examined the Scriptures daily to see if these things [being taught by Paul] were so" (Acts 17:11). As a result, "a great number of them believed" (verse 12).

CHAPTER ONE

The Appointed Birth of the Messiah

An Examination of the Evidence Concerning the Appointed Time of the Messiah's Birth

The first of the "appointed times" of Jesus the Messiah relates to His human *birth* as the long-awaited Savior of mankind. Notice what the apostle Paul wrote: "But when the [appointed] time for the fulfillment [of the promise to Abraham of a "Seed" (Gal. 3:16)] came, God sent forth His own Son, born of a woman…" (Gal. 4:4). Determining exactly when Christ was born will demonstrate that God has indeed planned key elements of Jesus' life and messianic role in such a manner that they correspond to the biblical festival seasons—or God's "appointed times." As this chapter will explain, there is sufficient historical and scriptural evidence to correlate Jesus' birth with the fall festival season, and with the Feast of Trumpets in particular.

The date of Christ's birth has been a topic of controversy for centuries. Various theories place the year of His birth in a range from 6 BC to 1 AD. As to the season of the year, some claim that He was born in the spring or fall, while *most* believe He was born in the winter. Others are inclined to shrug their shoulders, declaring that they don't know and that it really doesn't matter. While some theologians claim that it is not possible to know when Jesus was born, they readily accept December 25 as the day to celebrate His birth. They reason that the correct date or season is not as important as simply "remembering" the event (via Christmas).

Although an abundance of scriptural and historical evidence proves Jesus was *not* born on December 25, the majority of professing Christians celebrate this date as His birthday. Few realize that this observance is based on ancient traditions that predate Jesus' birth by thousands of years. Age-old customs of *pagan origin* entered the Christian churches many centuries ago and are now viewed as an essential part of Christian worship. Most churches today encourage their members to freely participate in the popular customs of the Christmas season.

While supposedly honoring the birth of Christ, the traditional observance of Christmas actually distorts the biblical account of His birth and ignores the revealed purpose of His coming to earth in the flesh. **His birth is, in fact, a chief cornerstone of true Christianity.** The birth of Jesus Christ fulfilled a number of significant prophecies that are recorded in the Old Testament. A proper understanding of the true circumstances of His birth will provide deeper insight into the meaning of His life and the ultimate purpose of His coming.

The scriptural and historical facts concerning the birth of Christ are readily available to all who are willing to examine them. The combined records of the Scriptures and God's sacred Calculated Hebrew Calendar (CHC), coordinated with the Julian calendar used during Jesus' lifetime, clearly reveal the year, season and approximate day of Jesus' birth—a key "appointed time" of the Messiah.

Jesus was Born During the Reign of Herod the Great

The Gospel of Matthew records that the birth of Jesus Christ occurred during the reign of Herod the Great. When Herod heard that the prophesied king of the Jews had been born, he feared that the Jews would begin to revolt against his rule. Matthew's account follows: "Now after Jesus had been born in Bethlehem of Judea, in *the* days of Herod the king, behold, Magi from *the* east arrived at Jerusalem, saying, 'Where is the one who has been born King of the Jews? For we have seen His star in the east, and have come to worship Him.' But when Herod the king heard *this*, he was troubled, and all Jerusalem with him" (Matt. 2:1-3).

Intending to slay the infant king, Herod summoned the scribes and chief priests to Jerusalem to inquire where the Messiah would be born, according to the prophecies in the Old Testament. Hearing that the Christ was prophesied to be born in Bethlehem, Herod instructed the Magi to return and inform him when they had found Him. But God intervened, through a dream to Joseph, to prevent Herod from harming the young Jesus:

> "And after hearing the king, they departed; and behold, the star that they had seen in the east went in front of them, until it came and stood over *the house* where the little Child was. And after seeing the star, they rejoiced *with* exceedingly great joy.
>
> "And when they had come into the house, they found the little Child with Mary His mother, and they bowed down and worshiped Him; then they opened their treasures *and* presented their gifts to Him—gold and frankincense and myrrh.
>
> "But being divinely instructed in a dream not to go back to Herod, they returned to their own country by another way. Now after they had departed, behold, an angel of *the* Lord appeared to Joseph in a dream, saying, 'Arise and take the little Child and His mother, and escape into Egypt, and remain there until I shall tell you; for Herod is about to seek the little Child to destroy Him.' And he arose by night and took the little Child and His mother, and went into Egypt, and was there until the death of Herod…" (Matt. 2:9-15).

Matthew's account of these events indicates that Herod died not long after Jesus was taken to Egypt. Following the death of Herod, Joseph brought Jesus and Mary back from Egypt to Nazareth, a city in the district of Galilee:

> "Now when Herod had died, behold, an angel of *the* Lord appeared to Joseph in Egypt in a dream, saying, 'Arise and take the little Child and His mother, and go into *the* land of Israel; for those who were seeking the life of the little Child have died.' And he arose *and* took the little Child and His mother, and came into *the* land of Israel. But when he heard that Archelaus was reigning over Judea instead of Herod his father, he was afraid to go there; and after being divinely instructed in a dream, he went into the parts of Galilee. And after arriving, he dwelt in a city called Nazareth..." (Matt. 2:19-23).

This scriptural record offers conclusive evidence that the birth of Jesus Christ occurred a short time before the death of Herod the Great. Through the writings of Josephus, a noted Jewish historian, we can determine precisely when Herod reigned and when he died. Josephus reveals the specific year that Herod was crowned king at Rome: "And thus did this man receive the kingdom, having obtained it on the hundred and eighty-fourth Olympiad, when Caius Domitius Calvinus was consul the second time and Caius Asinius Pollio [the first time]" (Josephus, *Antiquities of the Jews,* 14:14:5).

An Olympiad is four years in length and is reckoned from July to July. The 184th Olympiad extended from July 1, 44 BC, to June 30, 40 BC. Records of this period show that Calvinus and Pollio were consuls in the year 714 AUC (years from the founding of Rome), which was 40 BC (Finegan, *Handbook of Biblical Chronology*, p. 96). Thus, we know that Herod became king in 40 BC. While the Olympiad was reckoned from July 1 to June 30, the calendar year for consuls was reckoned from January 1 to December 31. Since the 184th Olympiad ended on June 30, 40 BC, and the consuls did not take office until January 1 of that year, we know that Herod was made king sometime during the six-month period from January through June of 40 BC.

Although Herod was crowned at Rome in 40 BC, three years passed before he conquered Jerusalem and began to reign in that city: "When the rigour of winter was over, Herod removed his army, and came near to Jerusalem and pitched his camp hard by the city. Now this was the third year since he had been made king at Rome..." (Josephus, *Ant.*, 14:15:14).

While Herod launched his attack in the spring, it was not until the summer of that year that he was able to take the city. Josephus reveals the specific date of this event: "[For] it was summer time.... This destruction befell the city of Jerusalem when Marcus Agrippa and Canninius Gallus were consuls of Rome, on the hundred eighty and fifth Olympiad, on the third month, on the solemnity of the fast…" (Ibid., 14:16:2, 4).

The 185th Olympiad extended from July 1, 40 BC, to June 30, 36 BC. Agrippa and Gallus became consuls in 717 AUC, which corresponds to 37 BC. The fast of the third month to which Josephus refers was the 23rd of Sivan, according to the CHC, which was June 22 on the Julian Calendar. Herod completed the conquest of the city of Jerusalem in the summer of 37 BC, and began to reign as king in Jerusalem at that time.

Josephus provides additional historical records concerning the reign of Herod that enable us to determine the time of his death: "[Herod] died … having reigned since he had procured Antigonus to be slain, thirty-four years; but since he had been declared king by the Romans, thirty-seven" (Ibid., 17:8:1). Josephus records elsewhere in the same book that Antigonus was killed shortly after Herod had conquered Jerusalem (Ibid., 14:16:4).

In linking Antigonus's death with Herod's conquest of Jerusalem in 37 BC, Josephus confirms that Herod did not reign in Jerusalem until three years after his coronation at Rome. Consequently, there are two methods of reckoning the reign of Herod the Great—the Jewish method, which counts 34 years from 37 BC, and the Roman method, which counts 37 years from 40 BC. Since the first year of his reign is included in the count, both methods of reckoning arrive at 4 BC as the end of Herod's reign. This date is conclusively established by the records of history as the year that Herod died.

Josephus' detailed account of Herod's death enables us to further pinpoint the time of the year. In his account, Josephus records that Herod died after an eclipse of the moon, but *before* Passover. The lunar eclipses that occurred during this period of history have been calculated in the 1971 book *Solar and Lunar Eclipses of the Ancient Near East* by M. Kudler and E. Mickler. Here is a listing of the lunar eclipses:

7 BC - No eclipses
6 BC - No eclipses
5 BC - Total eclipse, March 23, 8:30 PM
5 BC - Total eclipse, September 15, 10:30 PM
4 BC - Partial eclipse, March 13, 2:20 AM
3 BC - No eclipses
2 BC - No eclipses

The first lunar eclipse to occur during this period was a total eclipse on March 23 in the year 5 BC. In this year the Passover, Nisan 14, was observed by the Jews on March 22. Because the scriptural reckoning of days is from sunset to sunset, the Passover day extended from sunset March 21 to sunset March 22. Since the total eclipse that occurred at 8:30 PM on the night of March 23 was *after* Passover, this was not the eclipse to which Josephus refers in conjunction with Herod's death.

The second total eclipse of the moon during this period took place on 15 September, 5 BC, which was a significant day by scriptural reckoning. According to the CHC, September 15 was the 14th of Tishri (the seventh month). The moon was totally eclipsed at 10:30 PM that night, which was the beginning of the 15th of Tishri, the first day of the Feast of Tabernacles.

Josephus' account of this period of Jewish history includes a number of events which point to this eclipse as the one that occurred shortly before the death of Herod. In recounting the final months of Herod's reign, Josephus gives us an accurate time frame for establishing the date of Jesus' birth.

Historical Records of Herod's Death Reveal the Year of Christ's Birth

Josephus gives us detailed records of some of the events that took place before the death and burial of Herod. These events are listed chronologically in the synchronized Hebrew/Roman calendar at the end of this chapter. Events that are not specifically dated by historical records have been given approximate dates based on the available evidence. This calendar accurately depicts the sequence of events that took place during that time period.

Josephus relates that shortly before his death, Herod sent ambassadors to Rome. As noted on the synchronized Hebrew/Roman calendar, this action is estimated to have occurred during the week ending August 26, 5 BC. Sometime during the next week, a group of zealots stormed the Temple and proceeded to chop down the golden idol that Herod had erected over one of its gates. Herod learned that Matthias, the high priest, had incited the zealots to undertake this action in the mistaken belief that Herod was dead. Herod punished Matthias by removing him from the office of high priest and burning him alive, as Josephus relates. In his writings, Josephus shows that these events took place in the fall of the year and were marked by an eclipse of the moon. Josephus' gives this detailed account:

> "He deprived Matthias of the high priesthood, as in part an occasion of this action, and made Joazar, who was Matthias' wife's brother, high priest in his stead. Now it happened, that during the time of the high priesthood of this Matthias, there was another person made high priest for a single day, that very day which the Jews observe as a fast day [the day of Atonement, the 10th day of Tishri, the seventh month] 'the great day of expiation.' The occasion was this: Matthias the high priest, on the night before the day when the fast was to be celebrated, seemed in a dream to have conversation [sexual relations] with his wife: and because he could not officiate

> himself on that account, Joseph, the son of Ellemus, his kinsman, assisted him in that sacred office. But Herod deprived this Matthias of the high priesthood, and [later] burnt the other Matthias [on Tishri 14], who had raised the sedition, with his companions, alive. And that very night there was an eclipse of the moon [Tishri 15]" (*Ant.*, 17:6:4).

This eclipse was obviously an autumnal eclipse, as it occurred in Tishri, the seventh month of the CHC, which corresponds to September/October on the Julian Calendar. As documented in the record of lunar eclipses by Kudler and Mickler, only one autumnal eclipse occurred during that period of history. This was the eclipse of 15 September, 5 BC, on the evening beginning the Feast of Tabernacles—the 15th day of Tishri.

Josephus records the decline of Herod's health after this autumnal eclipse and the state of insanity that preceded his death. Shortly after the Feast of Tabernacles, Herod's "distemper" increased, and he sought the help of the warm mineral baths at Callirrhoe, which was located beyond the Jordan River. It has been estimated that he went there the week ending November 4. There is no record of the exact length of his stay; but since his funeral procession and burial took place after the winter, he must have stayed there approximately eight or nine weeks. He then went to Jericho, probably arriving by January 13. Josephus describes Herod's deplorable mental state at that time: "[Herod] came again to Jericho, where he grew so choleric, that it brought him to do all things like a madman; and though he was near his death, he contrived the following wicked designs" (Ibid., 17:6:5).

Herod commanded the principal men of his government to come to Jericho, intending to have them killed after his death. It is estimated that these men arrived at Jericho by January 20 to 27. A few days later, Herod received letters from Rome brought by the ambassadors he had sent. Although the news was good and seemed to revive him, he attempted suicide soon afterward. His attempt was not successful, as he was restrained by Achiabus. In his rage he ordered his son Antipater to be killed, and he himself died five days later. Josephus records, "When he had done these things, he died, the fifth day after he had caused Antipater to be slain; having reigned, since he had procured Antigonus to be slain, thirty-four years; but since he had been declared king by the Romans, thirty-seven" (Ibid., 17:8:1).

Herod died thirty-seven years from the time of his coronation at Rome in the spring of 40 BC. Although his reign began near the end of the 184th Olympiad, it is included as the first year in Josephus' count. Based on the records of Josephus and other historical evidence, Herod's death is estimated to have occurred during the week ending February 17, 4 BC.

After Herod's death, Archelaus succeeded him as king. He carried out Herod's wishes for an extended period of mourning and a long funeral before his burial. The time needed for these ceremonies was approximately

25 days, not counting Sabbaths. The chronology of these events is laid out step-by-step in the synchronized Hebrew/Roman calendar (see pp. 13-16). As illustrated in this calendar, the funeral procession finished its journey with the arrival of Herod's body in Jerusalem during the week ending March 24, 4 BC, at which time Archelaus began his rule in Jerusalem.

The records of Josephus clearly contradict the commonly held theory that the eclipse of March 13, 4 BC, was the eclipse before Herod's death. If Herod had died after March 13, the extended mourning and funeral procession could not possibly have been completed by March 24. As Josephus shows, these extended ceremonies began many weeks before the Passover day and ended with Herod's burial in the middle of the Feast of Unleavened Bread, which followed the Passover. To further substantiate the time of Herod's burial, Josephus records that at that time Archelaus slaughtered 3,000 people who had crowded into the Temple area to celebrate the Feast of Unleavened Bread. This slaughter occurred during the week which ended April 14, 4 BC, confirming that Herod's burial took place about two months after his death.

As recorded in the Gospel of Matthew, Jesus was born in Bethlehem of Judea during the reign of Herod the Great. Sometime after His birth, Jesus was taken to Egypt and remained there for a period of time before Herod died. Matthew's record of these events indicates that the birth of Jesus occurred several months before the death of Herod. Since Herod's death occurred very early in 4 BC—approximately mid-February—it is evident that Jesus was born sometime during the preceding year. **Thus, Herod's death places Christ's birth in the year 5 BC.** The Gospel of Luke provides additional evidence that enables us to know the *specific season* of the year in which Christ was born.

Scriptural Evidence of the Season of Jesus' Birth

In his account of the birth of Jesus, Luke records a major historical event of that time. He writes, "Now it happened in those days *that* a decree went out from Caesar Augustus that all the world should be registered. (This registration first occurred when Cyrenius was governor of Syria.) Then all went to be registered, each to his own city" (Luke 2:1-3).

The taxation and census decree by Caesar Augustus was carried out according to the Jewish custom which required that such taxes be collected after the fall harvest (See *Unger's Bible Dictionary*, Chronology, New Testament, pp. 199-200). Luke's record of this taxation reveals that the birth of Jesus took place during the autumn. When we combine Luke's record with Matthew's account of Herod's death, it is evident that **Jesus was born in the fall of 5 BC**.

Luke gives us additional evidence that **Jesus was born during the fall festival season** by recording that there were no guest rooms available at the inn when Joseph and Mary arrived in Bethlehem. The scarcity of room was due not only to the taxation but also to the festival days that followed the fall harvest. Many thousands of people were already in the Jerusalem area to observe the fall festival season. Bethlehem was extremely crowded because of its proximity to Jerusalem. Since there was no room at the inn, Joseph and Mary were forced to lodge in a barn. Jesus was born there and was laid in a manger.

In addition, Luke makes it clear that Jesus was not born in the winter by recording that shepherds were tending their flocks in the fields that night (Luke 2:8). The shepherds in that region of Palestine always brought their flocks out of the fields before the onset of winter. The flocks were never left to graze in the pastures during the winter months because the cold weather prevented the grass from growing. There is much discussion in Bible commentaries for those who desire to study these points further.

Records of John's Ministry Confirm Jesus' Birth in the Fall of 5 BC

In his account of the beginning of John the Baptist's ministry, Luke gives another historical reference that helps to verify the date of Jesus Christ's birth: "Now in *the* fifteenth year of the government of Tiberius Caesar … *the* word of God came unto John, the son of Zacharias, in the wilderness. And he went into all the country around the Jordan, proclaiming *the* baptism of repentance for *the* remission of sins" (Luke 3:1-3).

Luke tells us that John the Baptist began his ministry in the fifteenth year of Tiberius Caesar. A dispute has existed over which year of Tiberius' reign was reckoned by Luke as the fifteenth year because the first two years of Tiberius' reign were a co-rulership with Augustus. Consequently, there are conflicting opinions as to whether the scriptural record includes Tiberius' co-reign or counts from the beginning of his sole reign.

The dispute is settled when Luke's record is linked with other scriptural and historical records of that time. The reign of Tiberius is firmly established by historical records dating the death of Augustus. Augustus died August 19 in the year that Sextus Apuleius and Sextus Sillus were consuls. The year of the consuls' rule was 767 AUC, which was 14 AD. This date is confirmed by the fact that Augustus died 44 years, lacking 13 days, after the battle of Actium (*Dio's Roman History*, Loeb ed., Book LVI: 29-30, vol. 7, pp. 65, 69).

Josephus records that the battle of Actium took place during the 187th Olympiad in the seventh year of the reign of Herod (*Ant.*, 15:5:1-2; *Wars*, 1:20:3). The 187th Olympiad was the four-year period from July 1, 32 BC, to June 30, 28 BC. The battle of Actium took place during the second year of the Olympiad, which was July 1, 31 BC, to June 30, 30 BC. This was the seventh year of Herod's reign by Jewish reckoning, but the tenth year of his reign by Roman reckoning. Counting forward 44 years from the battle of Actium, which ended in September, 31 BC, we arrive at 14 AD as the year of Augustus' death.

Records of the reign of Augustus reveal that during his final years "the consuls caused a law to be passed ... that he [Tiberius] should govern the provinces jointly with Augustus and hold the census with him" (*Seutonius*, Ed. J.C. Rolfe, LCL, vol. 1, p. 323).

Tiberius began his co-rulership with Augustus in 12 AD, two years before the death of Augustus. Counting from this date, we arrive at 26 AD as the 15th year of Tiberius and the beginning of John the Baptist's ministry. Other scriptural and historical records confirm that John the Baptist began his ministry in the spring of 26 AD and that Jesus began His ministry six months later in the fall of 26 AD.

Major supporting evidence is found in the Gospel of John, which records the words of the Jews at the time of the first Passover of Christ's ministry. During this Passover season, the Jews stated that the Temple had been 46 years in building (John 2:20). We can determine the date of this Passover, and the first year of Christ's ministry, by counting from the year that the building of the Temple began.

Josephus records that the building of the Temple was begun during the 18th year of Herod's reign: "And now Herod, in the eighteenth year of his reign [that is, the eighteenth in Jerusalem, but the twenty-first year from his coronation in Rome] ... undertook a very great work, that is to build of himself the Temple of God" (*Ant.*, 15:11:1).

The 18th year of Herod's reign in Jerusalem, which was the first year of building the Temple, was from the summer of 20 BC to the summer of 19 BC. Counting forward, the 46th year of building was from the summer of 26 AD to the summer of 27 AD. The only Passover that occurred during this period of time was the Passover of 27 AD. Thus, scriptural and historical records place the first Passover of Christ's ministry in the spring of 27 AD. Since His ministry began in the fall of the year, we can date its beginning to the autumn of 26 AD.

The Birth of John the Baptist Provides Key to the Day of Christ's Birth

In the first chapter of the Gospel of Luke, we find a detailed account of the circumstances and events that preceded the birth of Christ. In this account, Luke reveals that the conception of Jesus by the virgin Mary occurred *six months after* the conception of John by Mary's aunt, Elizabeth, the wife of Zacharias. Zacharias, a priest of God, served in the Temple at Jerusalem.

At the beginning of his account, Luke records, "There was in the days of Herod, the king of Judea, a certain priest of *the* course of Abijah, Zacharias by name.... And it came to pass *that* in fulfilling his priestly service before God in the order of his course, according to the custom of the priestly service, it fell to him by lot to burn incense when he entered into the temple of the Lord" (Luke 1:5, 8-9).

Zacharias was executing his priestly duties according to the order and course of Abijah. This information is most helpful in establishing the time frame of Luke's account. In ancient Israel, King David divided the duties of the priests into 24 working courses, or shifts (I Chron. 24:7-19). Each course or shift was assigned to work one full week, from noon Sabbath to noon Sabbath (*Talmud*, Sukkah). The Old Testament records the exact rotation and time order of the priestly courses, which continued down to New Testament times. Zacharias was of the course of Abijah, which was the eighth course or shift in the series of yearly assignments for the priesthood.

The Jewish historian Josephus was a priest of the first course or shift. Josephus confirms that the priestly courses established by King David were still functioning in New Testament times. He records, "He [King David] divided them also into courses ... and he found [or established] of these priests, twenty-four courses ... and he ordained that one course should minister to God eight days, from Sabbath to Sabbath ... and this partition hath remained to this day" (*Ant.*, 7:14:7). This record confirms that the courses of priests remained in effect down to the time of Zacharias and the birth of Christ. These courses undoubtedly continued until the Temple was destroyed in 70 AD.

The *Talmud* reveals that the first priestly course, or shift, began in the first full week of the first month of the CHC. The second course worked the second week. This rotation continued on a week-by-week basis through all 24 courses. Each priestly course served a one-week shift twice each year. In addition, all courses were required to work during the three weeks in the year that coincided with the three festival seasons: Passover, Pentecost and Tabernacles. Thus, all the priests shared equally in the priestly responsibilities for the entire year.

We know that the angel Gabriel delivered the promise of John's birth while Zacharias was serving in his priestly course in the Temple. The Gospel of Luke reveals that John was born six months before Jesus (Luke 1:35-36). Our examination of both the scriptural and historical records has established that Jesus was born in the fall of 5 BC. Accordingly, John the Baptist was born in the spring of 5 BC and was conceived six months earlier in the summer of 6 BC. Knowing the year that John was conceived enables us to determine the exact period of time that Zacharias was serving in the Temple.

In the year 6 BC, the first day of the first month (the month of Nisan according to the CHC) was a weekly Sabbath. According to calculations synchronizing the CHC and the Julian Calendar, this Sabbath was March 20. Projecting forward, the assignments course by course, or week by week, were: Course 1, the first week; Course 2, the second week; all courses for the Passover and Feast of Unleavened Bread, the third week; Course 3, the fourth week; Course 4, the fifth week; Course 5, the sixth week; Course 6, the seventh week; Course 7, the eighth week; Course 8, the ninth week; and all courses the tenth week, which was the week of Pentecost.

Because Zacharias was of the course of Abijah, the eighth course, he was assigned the ninth and tenth weeks from the beginning of the year.

These weeks of service were counted from noon Sabbath to noon Sabbath. The ninth week was from Iyar 27 through Sivan 5, which corresponds to May 15 through May 22 on the Julian Calendar. The tenth week, Sivan 5 through Sivan 12, or May 22 through May 29, was the week of Pentecost. Sometime during these two weeks, the angel Gabriel appeared to Zacharias in the Temple and prophesied the birth of John.

Although the exact time of Gabriel's appearance is not recorded, it is reasonable to conclude that Gabriel delivered this message from God on the day of Pentecost. The announcement that Zacharias's wife Elizabeth would bear a son came during the two weeks in which Zacharias served at the Temple; the day of Pentecost occurred on Sivan 6, in the middle of that two-week period. Since John the Baptist's birth was a major fulfillment of prophecy, it is appropriate that God would send Gabriel on a holy day to announce the promise of his conception to Zacharias. Luke records Gabriel's message to Zacharias as he was in the Temple offering incense:

> "According to the custom of the priestly service, it fell to him [Zacharias] by lot to burn incense when he entered into the temple of the Lord. And all the multitude of the people outside were praying at the hour of the *burning of* incense. Then an angel of *the* Lord appeared to him, standing at *the* right side of the altar of incense. And when he saw *the angel*, Zacharias was troubled, and fear fell upon him.
>
> "But the angel said to him, 'Fear not, Zacharias, because your supplication has been heard; and your wife Elizabeth shall bear a son to you, and you shall call his name John. And he shall be a joy and exultation to you; and many shall rejoice at his birth. For he shall be great before the Lord. And he shall never drink wine or strong drink in any form, but he shall be filled with *the* Holy Spirit even from his mother's womb. And many of the children of Israel shall he turn to *the* Lord their God. And he shall go before Him in *the* spirit and power of Elijah, to turn *the* hearts of the fathers to *the* children, and *the* disobedient to *the* wisdom of *the* righteous, to make ready a people prepared for *the* Lord' " (Luke 1:9-17).

Because Zacharias did not believe God's promise, Gabriel pronounced a sign from God. Zacharias would be unable to speak until the child was born and given the name John, which God had chosen (Luke 1:13, 19-20). After completing his service at the Temple, Zacharias returned to his house, and John was conceived in the following days: "Now it came to pass *that* when the days of his service were fulfilled, he departed to his house. And after those days, Elizabeth his wife conceived, but hid herself *for* five months..." (Luke 1:23-24).

The account indicates that Elizabeth became pregnant shortly after Zacharias returned home. Since he returned on May 29, it is reasonable to conclude that she became pregnant between May 30 and June 12 (Sivan 13-26) in the year 6 BC. This estimated time allows a two-week conception period.

Luke was inspired to record that **Elizabeth was in the sixth month of her pregnancy when the virgin Mary was miraculously impregnated through the power of the Holy Spirit** and conceived Jesus: "Now behold, Elizabeth your kinswoman has also conceived a son in her old age; and **this is *the* sixth month** for her who *was* called barren" (Luke 1:36). Based on the estimated time of conception, the sixth month of Elizabeth's pregnancy was November/December by Roman reckoning.

Luke gives additional details that indicate Mary was impregnated in the last two weeks of Elizabeth's sixth month. Mary was told by the angel Gabriel that Elizabeth was already in the sixth month of her pregnancy. Mary then visited Elizabeth and stayed with her almost three months (Luke 1:39-40, 56). Soon after Mary left, Elizabeth reached her full term of nine months, and John was born sometime between Adar 19 and Nisan 3, or February 27 and March 11, in 5 BC.

As illustrated by the synchronized Hebrew/Roman calendar on the following pages, Mary's probable conception period coincides with the last two weeks of Elizabeth's sixth month. That two-week period was Keslev 17-30, or November 28-December 11. Projecting forward nine months from the estimated time of Mary's conception, we arrive at the two-week period during which Christ was probably born. This two-week time period was Elul 24-Tishri 8, or August 27-September 9. **As the synchronized calendar shows, the Feast of Trumpets was the middle day of this two-week period**.

Why *Trumpets* as "the Appointed Time" of Jesus' Birth?

Many passages in the Bible show that the Feast of Trumpets pictures the second coming of Christ (Joel 2:1; Zeph. 1:14-18; etc.). The Day of the Lord and the angelic trumpets in the book of Revelation clearly project this symbolism and meaning. Is it not reasonable to conclude that God also chose the Feast of Trumpets as the day of Jesus' birth? The apostle Paul reveals that the prophesied birth of Jesus was fulfilled *at a set time*. Paul wrote, "But when the [appointed] time for the fulfillment came, God sent forth His own Son, born of a woman…" (Gal. 4:4). While the Gospels do not reveal the specific day, **the birth of Jesus on the Feast of Trumpets would be in harmony with God's great plan as portrayed through His annual holy days—His "appointed times."**

The Calculated Hebrew Calendar with the Julian Roman Calendar

This synchronized calculated Hebrew/Julian calendar illustrates the time period from March 6 BC to April 4 BC. The sequence of scriptural, historical and astronomical events depicted in this calendar reveals the actual year, season, and the most likely day of Jesus Christ's birth. **Note: The columns read downward—left column first**.

6 B.C.

NISAN

MARCH — APRIL

S	M	T	W	T	F	SAB	
						20	1st Course begins - noon Sabbath
						1	
21	22	23	24	25	26	27	1st Course works - 2nd Course begins noon Sabbath
2	3	4	5	6	7	8	
28	29	30	31	1	2	3	2nd Course works - All courses begin at Passover
9	10	11	12	13	*14	15	
4	5	6	7	8	9	10	All work - 3rd Course begins noon Sabbath
16	17	18	19	20	21	22	
11	12	13	14	15	16	17	3rd Course works - 4th Course begins noon Sabbath
23	24	25	26	27	28	29	
18							
30							

*14th - Passover
15th-21st - Feast of Unleavened Bread

6 B.C.

IYAR

APRIL — MAY

S	M	T	W	T	F	SAB	
	19	20	21	22	23	24	4th Course works - 5th Course begins noon Sabbath
	1	2	3	4	5	6	
25	26	27	28	29	30	1	5th Course works - 6th Course begins noon Sabbath
7	8	9	10	11	12	13	
2	3	4	5	6	7	8	6th Course works - 7th Course begins noon Sabbath
14	15	16	17	18	19	20	
9	10	11	12	13	14	15	7th Course works - 8th Course begins noon Sabbath
21	22	23	24	25	26	27	
16	17						8th Course works
28	29						

6 B.C.

SIVAN

MAY — JUNE

S	M	T	W	T	F	SAB	
		18	19	20	21	22	8th Course works - All courses begin at noon Sabbath
		1	2	3	4	5	
23	24	25	26	27	28	29	9th Course begins noon Sabbath
*6	7	8	9	10	11	12	Zacharias leaves
30	31	1	2	3	4	5	Elizabeth's probable two-week conception period ends
13	14	15	16	17	18	19	
6	7	8	9	10	11	12	
20	21	22	23	24	25	26	
13	14	15	16				
27	28	29	30				

*6th - Day of Pentecost (probably day that Gabriel appeared to Zacharias)

6 B.C.

TAMMUZ

JUNE — JULY

S	M	T	W	T	F	SAB	
				17	18	19	
				1	2	3	
20	21	22	23	24	25	26	
4	5	6	7	8	9	10	
27	28	29	30	1	2	3	
11	12	13	14	15	16	17	
4	5	6	7	8	9	10	
18	19	20	21	22	23	24	
11	12	13	14	15			End of 1st month of Elizabeth's pregnancy
25	26	27	28	29			

6 B.C.

AB

JULY — AUGUST

S	M	T	W	T	F	SAB	
					16	17	
					1	2	
18	19	20	21	22	23	24	
3	4	5	6	7	8	9	
25	26	27	28	29	30	31	
10	11	12	13	14	15	16	
1	2	3	4	5	6	7	
17	18	19	20	21	22	23	
8	9	10	11	12	13	14	End of 2nd month of Elizabeth's pregnancy
24	25	26	27	28	29	30	

6 B.C.

ELUL

AUGUST — SEPTEMBER

S	M	T	W	T	F	SAB	
15	16	17	18	19	20	21	
1	2	3	4	5	6	7	
22	23	24	25	26	27	28	
8	9	10	11	12	13	14	
29	30	31	1	2	3	4	
15	16	17	18	19	20	21	
5	6	7	8	9	10	11	End of 3rd month of Elizabeth's pregnancy
22	23	24	25	26	27	28	
12							
29							

Chapter One

6 B.C.

TISHRI

SEPTEMBER — OCTOBER

S	M	T	W	T	F	SAB
	13	14	15	16	17	18
	1	2	3	4	5	6
19	20	21	22	23	24	25
7	8	9	10	11	12	13
26	27	28	29	30	1	2
14	*15	16	17	18	19	20
3	4	5	6	7	8	9
21	22	23	24	25	26	27
10	11	12				
28	29	30				

1st of Tishri - Feast of Trumpets

10th of Tishri - Day of Atonement

End of 4th month of Elizabeth's pregnancy

**15th-21st - Feast of Tabernacles*

22nd - Last Great Day

6 B.C.

HESHVAN

OCTOBER — NOVEMBER

S	M	T	W	T	F	SAB
			13	14	15	16
			1	2	3	4
17	18	19	20	21	22	23
5	6	7	8	9	10	11
24	25	26	27	28	29	30
12	13	14	15	16	17	18
31	1	2	3	4	5	6
19	20	21	22	23	24	25
7	8	9	10	11		
26	27	28	29	30		

End of 5th month of Elizabeth's pregnancy

6 B.C.

KISLEV

NOVEMBER — DECEMBER

S	M	T	W	T	F	SAB
					12	13
					1	2
14	15	16	17	18	19	20
3	4	5	6	7	8	9
21	22	23	24	25	26	27
10	11	12	13	14	15	16
28	29	30	1	2	3	4
17	18	19	20	21	22	23
5	6	7	8	9	10	11
24	25	26	27	28	29	30

The angel Gabriel is sent to the virgin Mary. The power of the Holy Spirit overshadows her and she is impregnated. Then Mary visits Elizabeth.

End of 6th month of Elizabeth's pregnancy

6 B.C. / 5 B.C.

TEBETH

DECEMBER — JANUARY

S	M	T	W	T	F	SAB
12	13	14	15	16	17	18
1	2	3	4	5	6	7
19	20	21	22	23	24	25
8	9	10	11	12	13	14
26	27	28	29	30	31	1
15	16	17	18	19	20	21
2	3	4	5	6	7	8
22	23	24	25	26	27	28
9						
29						

End of 1st month of Mary's pregnancy

End of 7th month of Elizabeth's pregnancy

5 B.C.

SHEBAT

JANUARY — FEBRUARY

S	M	T	W	T	F	SAB
	10	11	12	13	14	15
	1	2	3	4	5	6
16	17	18	19	20	21	22
7	8	9	10	11	12	13
23	24	25	26	27	28	29
14	15	16	17	18	19	20
30	31	1	2	3	4	5
21	22	23	24	25	26	27
6	7	8				
28	29	30				

End of 2nd month of Mary's pregnancy

End of 8th month of Elizabeth's pregnancy

5 B.C.

ADAR

FEBRUARY — MARCH

S	M	T	W	T	F	SAB
			9	10	11	12
			1	2	3	4
13	14	15	16	17	18	19
5	6	7	8	9	10	11
20	21	22	23	24	25	26
12	13	14	15	16	17	18
27	28	29	1	2	3	4
19	20	21	22	23	24	25
5	6	7	8			
26	27	28	29			

End of 3rd month of Mary's pregnancy

End of 9th month of Elizabeth's pregnancy

John the Baptist born

5 B.C.

NISAN

MARCH — APRIL

S	M	T	W	T	F	SAB
				9	10	11
				1	2	3
12	13	14	15	16	17	18
4	5	6	7	8	9	10
19	20	21	22	(23)	24	25
11	12	13	*14	15	16	17
26	27	28	29	30	31	1
18	19	20	21	22	23	24
2	3	4	5	6	7	
25	26	27	28	29	30	

(23) Total eclipse on March 23 at 8:30 PM

**14th-Passover*

15th-21st-Feast of Unleavened Bread

End of 4th month of Mary's pregnancy

5 B.C.

IYAR

APRIL — MAY

S	M	T	W	T	F	SAB
						8
						1
9	10	11	12	13	14	15
2	3	4	5	6	7	8
16	17	18	19	20	21	22
9	10	11	12	13	*14	15
23	24	25	26	27	28	29
16	17	18	19	20	21	22
30	1	2	3	4	5	6
23	24	25	26	27	28	29

End of 5th month of Mary's pregnancy

5 B.C.

SIVAN

MAY — JUNE

S	M	T	W	T	F	SAB	
7	8	9	10	11	12	13	
1	2	3	4	5	6	7	
14	15	16	17	18	19	20	
*8	9	10	11	12	13	14	**Day of Pentecost*
21	22	23	24	25	26	27	
15	16	17	18	19	20	21	
28	29	30	31	1	2	3	End of 6th month of Mary's pregnancy
22	23	24	25	26	27	28	
4	5						
29	30						

5 B.C.

TAMMUZ

JUNE — JULY

S	M	T	W	T	F	SAB	
		6	7	8	9	10	
		1	2	3	4	5	
11	12	13	14	15	16	17	
6	7	8	9	10	11	12	
18	19	20	21	22	23	24	
13	14	15	16	17	18	19	
25	26	27	28	29	30	1	
20	21	22	23	24	25	26	
2	3	4					End of 7th month of Mary's pregnancy
27	28	29					

5 B.C.

AB

JULY — AUGUST

S	M	T	W	T	F	SAB	
			5	6	7	8	
			1	2	3	4	
9	10	11	12	13	14	15	
5	6	7	8	9	10	11	
16	17	18	19	20	21	22	
12	13	14	15	16	17	18	
23	24	25	26	27	28	29	
19	20	21	22	23	24	25	
30	31	1	2	3			End of 8th month of Mary's pregnancy
26	27	28	29	30			

5 B.C.

ELUL

AUGUST — SEPTEMBER

S	M	T	W	T	F	SAB	
					4	5	
					1	2	
6	7	8	9	10	11	12	
3	4	5	6	7	8	9	
13	14	15	16	17	18	19	
10	11	12	13	14	15	16	
20	21	22	23	24	25	26	
17	18	19	20	21	22	23	
27	28	29	30	31	1		End of 9th month of Mary's pregnancy
24	25	26	27	28	29		

5 B.C.

TISHRI

Probable two-week period for the birth of Jesus

SEPTEMBER — OCTOBER

S	M	T	W	T	F	SAB	
						2	Feast of Trumpets, Tishri 1, middle day of two-week period
						*1	
3	4	5	6	7	8	9	**Probable day of Jesus' circumcision
2	3	4	5	6	7	**8	
10	11	12	13	14	(15)	16	(15) Total eclipse on September 15, at 10:30 PM.
9	10	11	12	13	14	15	
17	18	19	20	21	22	23	**1st - Feast of Trumpets*
16	17	18	19	20	21	22	*10th - Day of Atonement*
24	25	26	27	28	29	30	*15th-21st - Feast of Tabernacles*
23	24	25	26	27	28	29	*22nd - Last Great Day*
1							
30							

5 B.C.

HESHVAN

OCTOBER

S	M	T	W	T	F	SAB	
	2	3	4	5	6	7	Wise men arrive and meet with Herod.
	1	2	3	4	5	6	
8	9	10	11	12	13	14	Probable two-week period for the presentation and blessing of Jesus at the Temple. Wise men find Jesus and present their gifts. Joseph, Mary and Jesus escape into Egypt.
7	8	9	10	11	12	13	
15	16	17	18	19	20	21	
14	15	16	17	18	19	20	
22	23	24	25	26	27	28	
21	22	23	24	25	26	27	Herod orders the slaughter of all male children two years and younger.
29	30	31					
28	29	30					

5 B.C.

KISLEV

NOVEMBER

S	M	T	W	T	F	SAB
			1	2	3	4
			1	*2*	*3*	*4*
5	6	7	8	9	10	11
5	*6*	*7*	*8*	*9*	*10*	*11*
12	13	14	15	16	17	18
12	*13*	*14*	*15*	*16*	*17*	*18*
19	20	21	22	23	24	25
19	*20*	*21*	*22*	*23*	*24*	*25*
26	27	28	29	30		
26	*27*	*28*	*29*	*30*		

Herod goes beyond Jordan

5 B.C.

TEBETH

DECEMBER

S	M	T	W	T	F	SAB
					1	2
					1	*2*
3	4	5	6	7	8	9
3	*4*	*5*	*6*	*7*	*8*	*9*
10	11	12	13	14	15	16
10	*11*	*12*	*13*	*14*	*15*	*16*
17	18	19	20	21	22	23
17	*18*	*19*	*20*	*21*	*22*	*23*
24	25	26	27	28	29	
24	*25*	*26*	*27*	*28*	*29*	

Herod still beyond Jordan

5 B.C. / 4 B.C.

SHEBAT

DECEMBER JANUARY

S	M	T	W	T	F	SAB
						30
						1
31	1	2	3	4	5	6
2	*3*	*4*	*5*	*6*	*7*	*8*
7	8	9	10	11	12	13
9	*10*	*11*	*12*	*13*	*14*	*15*
14	15	16	17	18	19	20
16	*17*	*18*	*19*	*20*	*21*	*22*
21	22	23	24	25	26	27
23	*24*	*25*	*26*	*27*	*28*	*29*
28						
30						

Herod orders principal men to come to Jericho.

4 B.C.

ADAR I

JANUARY FEBRUARY

S	M	T	W	T	F	SAB
	29	30	31	1	2	3
	1	*2*	*3*	*4*	*5*	*6*
4	5	6	7	8	9	10
7	*8*	*9*	*10*	*11*	*12*	*13*
11	12	13	14	15	16	17
14	*15*	*16*	*17*	*18*	*19*	*20*
18	19	20	21	22	23	24
21	*22*	*23*	*24*	*25*	*26*	*27*
25	26	27				
28	*29*	*30*				

Herod locks up principal men in Hyppodrome.

Letters come from Rome. Herod attempts suicide. Antipater is killed.

Herod dies. Principal men released from Hyppodrome.

Herod's funeral preparations and 7 days of mourning in Jericho.

Archelaus becomes king. Herod's funeral procession begins.

4 B.C.

ADAR II

FEBRUARY MARCH

S	M	T	W	T	F	SAB
			28	1	2	3
			1	*2*	*3*	*4*
4	5	6	7	8	9	10
5	*6*	*7*	*8*	*9*	*10*	*11*
11	12	13	14	15	16	17
12	*13*	*14*	*15*	*16*	*17*	*18*
18	19	20	21	22	23	24
19	*20*	*21*	*22*	*23*	*24*	*25*
25	26	27	28			
26	*27*	*28*	*29*			

Funeral procession slowly heads from Jericho to Jerusalem.

Herod's body arrives at Herodium in Bethlehem via Jerusalem.

Archelaus begins reign in Jerusalem.

4 B.C.

NISAN

MARCH APRIL

S	M	T	W	T	F	SAB
				29	30	31
				1	*2*	*3*
1	2	3	4	5	6	7
4	*5*	*6*	*7*	*8*	*9*	*10*
8	9	10	11	12	13	14
11	*12*	*13*	**14*	*15*	*16*	*17*
15	16	17	18	19	20	21
18	*19*	*20*	*21*	*22*	*23*	*24*
22	23	24	25	26	27	
25	*26*	*27*	*28*	*29*	*30*	

Revolt by Jews over the lack of mourning for Mathias, the high priest who was burned to death by Herod on September 15, 5 BC.

Revolt grows as thousands of Jews arrive for Passover and the Feast of Unleavened Bread.

Archelaus orders the slaughter of 3,000 in the middle of the Feast of Unleavened Bread. Herod's burial takes place.

**14th - Passover,*
15th-21st - Feast of Unleavened Bread.

CHAPTER TWO

The Appointed Time of the Anointing of the Messiah

How Daniel's Seventy-Week Prophecy Pinpoints the Appointed Time of the Messiah's Coming

The second of the "appointed times" of Jesus the Messiah relates to His ministry—to its beginning and to His anointing. Pinpointing exactly when Jesus began His ministry will confirm once again that God has planned Jesus' all-important role around the festival seasons—or God's "appointed times." The key to establishing the beginning of Jesus' ministry lies in understanding Daniel's mysterious 70-week prophecy (Dan. 9:24-27). This prophecy places Jesus' anointing and the beginning of His ministry in the fall of 26 AD. In fact, as we will see, Daniel's prophecy points to the *fall festival season*—and specifically the Day of Atonement—as the time Jesus' ministry began. As will also be demonstrated, Jesus intentionally declined to announce the fact that He was the Messiah at the onset of His ministry. Rather, He waited until the late spring festival of Pentecost to publicly reveal His identity as God's Anointed. Why the delay? The answer is astonishing!

The 70-week prophecy of Daniel chapter nine has intrigued scholars and sages down through the centuries. A succession of differing views and interpretations of this prophecy can be found in historical writings dating back to antiquity. Verses 20-23 introduce the prophecy:

> "And while I was speaking, and praying, and confessing my sin, and the sin of my people Israel, and presenting my supplication before the LORD my God for the holy mountain of my God; yea, while I was speaking in prayer, even the man Gabriel, whom I had seen in the vision at the beginning, being caused to fly swiftly, came to me, about the time of the evening sacrifice. And he made me to understand, and talked with me, and said, 'O Daniel, I have now come forth to give you insight and understanding. At the beginning of your supplications the word went forth, and I have come to declare it, for you are greatly beloved; therefore **consider the word**, and **understand the vision**.' "

These words of Gabriel show that the 70-week prophecy was given to *impart understanding* to Daniel. This was not a prophecy to remain "sealed" until the end of the age (Dan. 12:9-10). In fact, its fulfillment would begin to take place in *that very year*. The following verses in Daniel nine describe the sequence of events that would come to pass during its fulfillment. Note that these events are all centered at Jerusalem and the Temple. Verses 24-27:

> "**Seventy weeks are decreed** upon your people and upon your holy city to finish the transgression and to make an end of sin, and to make reconciliation for iniquity, and to bring in everlasting righteousness, and to seal up the vision and prophecy, and to anoint the Most Holy. Know therefore and understand that from the going forth of the commandment to restore and to build Jerusalem, to Messiah the Prince, shall be **seven weeks**, and **sixty-two weeks**. It shall be built again with streets and the wall, even in troublous times. And **after sixty-two weeks Messiah shall be cut off**, but not for Himself. And the people of the prince who shall come shall destroy the city and the sanctuary. But his end shall be with a flood, and unto the end of the war desolations are determined. And he shall confirm a covenant with many for **one week**. And in the midst of the week he shall cause the sacrifice and the offering to cease, and upon the wing of abominations shall come one who makes desolate even until the consummation. And the fully determined end which is decreed shall be poured out upon the desolator."

In verse 24, the 70-week prophecy is summed up as a whole. The following verses describe the division of the 70 weeks into *three distinct periods*: **seven weeks**, **62 weeks** and **one week**. The words "weeks" and "week" in these verses are translated from the Hebrew *shabua*, which is a unit of time composed of seven years. **These units of time, known today as *heptads*, were used by ancient Israel to calculate the *sabbatical years*. The use of *shabua* in the Hebrew text signifies that the 70 weeks are not literal weeks of seven days' duration, but are each composed of seven years**. Thus, the three divisions of weeks in the prophecy **add up to a total of 490 years**. Since the structure of the Hebrew text divides the 70-week prophecy into three distinct periods, each segment is to be considered separately. As we will see, the three periods are *separated from each other* by intervening years. This division is conveyed by the Hebrew verbs. Moreover, the historical fulfillment of the first two periods (of 7 weeks and 62 weeks) establishes that idea as factual. Indeed, when these divisions with the intervening years between them are ignored, and the 70 weeks are considered as a continuous, single unit, it becomes impossible to reconcile the prophecy's fulfillment with history.

As verse 24 states, the 490 years are "decreed" in order for specific events to take place in the city of Jerusalem in preparation for the coming of the Messiah. The Hebrew verb translated as "decreed" may also be rendered as "determined" (*KJV*) or "divided." In modern terminology, this verb might be translated as "marked out." The basic meaning is that these prophetic "weeks" are time periods of years "marked out" or *set apart* by God in the course of history. Thus, it becomes clear that the 70-weeks prophecy deals with *periods of time* that have been *appointed* and *decreed* by God. Indeed, the prophecy points to one of the key "appointed times" in Jesus' life and work—His anointing and the beginning of His ministry as the Messiah. Of the three divisions of time that make up the 70-week prophecy, the first two—the 7 weeks and the 62 weeks—are relevant to Jesus' ministry and anointing. The final *heptad*, the one week, relates to future end-time events.

Period One: Seven Weeks, or 49 Years—539 BC to 490 BC

The first period—of seven weeks, or 49 years—was prophesied to begin with "the going forth of the commandment to restore and to build Jerusalem." That proclamation was issued by Cyrus the Great in **539 BC**, the same year Daniel received the vision. The vision of the 70 weeks announced the intervention of God to bring a remnant of Judah back to their land to rebuild Jerusalem and the Temple and to dwell again in the land. All these events were necessary in order for the birth of the Messiah to take place in Bethlehem as foretold by the prophets (Isa. 9:6-7; Micah 5:2).

The book of Ezra begins with a description of the proclamation of Cyrus, which marked the beginning of the fulfillment of the first division of the 70-week prophecy. In his account of Cyrus' decree, Ezra focuses on the rebuilding of the Temple. As a descendant of the high priests, his principle concerns were the preservation of the law of God and the restoration of the Temple service. In reading the account in Ezra chapter one, it is important to remember that the decree also included the restoration of the city of Jerusalem, as noted by the prophet Isaiah (Isa. 44:28).

> "And in the first year of Cyrus king of Persia, that the Word of the LORD by the mouth of Jeremiah [Jer. 25:11-12; 29:10] might he fulfilled, the LORD stirred up the spirit of Cyrus king of Persia, so that he made a proclamation throughout all his kingdom, and put it also in writing, saying, 'Thus says Cyrus king of Persia, "The LORD God of heaven has given me all the kingdoms of the earth. And **He has charged me to build Him a house at Jerusalem, which is in Judah**. Whoever there is among you of all His people, may his God be with him, and let him go up to Jerusalem, which is in Judah, and build the house of the LORD God of Israel—He is the God Who is in Jerusalem" ' " (Ezra 1:1-3).

The first year of Cyrus II (the Great) by Persian reckoning was 539 BC. That same year, Cyrus appointed Zerubbabel governor of Judah and commissioned him to go to Jerusalem to rebuild the Temple. The materials that were needed were ordered upon his arrival in Jerusalem, and the laying of the foundation began in the spring of 538 BC. The prophecies of Haggai and Zechariah show that Zerubbabel was still serving as governor of Judah in 515 BC when the Temple was completed (Hag. 1:1, 14; 2:1-4; Zech. 4:9).

The scriptural accounts show that Nehemiah came to Jerusalem to succeed Zerubbabel as governor of Judea. Nehemiah's governorship actually ran from 502 BC to 490 BC. As the end of Nehemiah's governorship approached, the Temple was in service and the city was protected by a secure wall, but the restoration of Jerusalem was not yet complete. The houses that were destroyed by Nebuchadnezzar and his army had not been rebuilt. Nehemiah chapter seven describes the condition of Jerusalem. "**And the city was large and great, but the people in it were few, and the houses not built**" (verse 4).

When those who were selected to dwell in Jerusalem had built their houses, the restoration of the city was complete. This event was the final act in the fulfillment of Cyrus' proclamation as prophesied by Isaiah. "[I am the LORD] Who makes the word of His servant sure, and makes good the counsel of His messengers; Who says to Jerusalem, '**She shall have people**;'… Who says of Cyrus, 'He is My shepherd, and shall do all My pleasure; even saying to Jerusalem, "**You shall be built**;" and to the temple, "**Your foundation shall be laid**" ' " (Isa. 44:26, 28).

When Nehemiah returned to the king of Persia at the end of his governorship in 490 BC, the first division of the 70-week prophecy was complete. The fulfillment of the "seven weeks" (seven *heptads*, which equates to 7 x 7 years, or 49 years) had begun in 539 BC with Cyrus' decree and had ended in 490 BC when Nehemiah's governorship ended—exactly 49 years.

The Fulfillment of the 49 Years — 539 BC - 490 BC

PROCLAMATION OF CYRUS II TO REBUILD JERUSALEM	539
COMPLETION OF TEMPLE	515
NEHEMIAH APPOINTED GOVERNOR OF JUDEA	502
WORK ON THE WALL BEGINS	502
WALL COMPLETED	492
JERUSALEM REPOPULATED, HOUSES REBUILT	491
NEHEMIAH LEAVES JERUSALEM	490

With the fulfillment of the "seven weeks," the *physical* stage was set for the appearing of the Messiah. But problems of corruption and complacency soon developed in the priesthood. In fact, twelve years *after* the completion of the first division of the prophecy—in 478 BC—Ezra made a final journey to Jerusalem to deal primarily with such problems. The second part of the prophecy—the 62 weeks or 434 years—was to begin the countdown to the appearing of the Messiah. As we will see, this key time period would begin in the fall of 409 BC and end in the fall of 26 AD with the beginning of Jesus Christ's ministry.

Meanwhile, God sent the final Old Testament prophet, Malachi, to deal with problems in the priesthood and deliver prophecies concerning the Messiah. Moreover, the tiny nation of Judah would undergo tremendous cultural and religious changes in the interim period known as the time "between the Testaments"—from the close of the age of the prophets (with Malachi being the last) to the work of John the Baptist, as the messenger who would herald the coming of the Messiah as foretold of by Malachi (Mal. 3:1).

The Book of Malachi and John the Baptist

God's warnings to His people—and especially the priests who had violated His laws—are recorded in the book of Malachi, which pronounced a curse upon those who failed to take heed and repent of their evil ways (Mal. 1:6-8; 2:1-3).

Although the book of Malachi is dated to the 400s BC, there is no historical record of the specific year that it was written. In fact, there is sound scriptural basis for concluding that the book of Malachi was written in 409 BC and marked the *beginning* of the 62 weeks division (434 years)—the second part of the 70-week prophecy.

Since the book of Malachi contains a prophecy of the ministry of John the Baptist, which took place at the *end* of the 434 years (26 AD), it is fitting that God would inspire it to be written at the *beginning* of the 434 years, in 409 BC. The title of the book itself points to the work of John the Baptist as the one who would herald the promised Messiah. The name Malachi means "My messenger." The book begins with a call to repentance and ends with the prophecy of the messenger who would come in the spirit of Elijah to turn the hearts of the people back to their God. The Messiah Himself declared that this prophecy was fulfilled by John the Baptist (Matt. 17:12-13).

There is additional support in Scripture for dating the prophecy of Malachi to the beginning of the 62 weeks. Malachi's prophecy was, in effect, a decree from God: "Behold, **I will send My messenger**…" (Mal. 3:1). As this decree was *fulfilled* at the *end* of the 62 weeks, a parallel is established with the fulfillment of the first segment of the 70 weeks (the seven weeks or 49 years), which began with a decree and ended with the fulfillment of that decree. This parallelism is illustrated below.

> **First segment:** The seven weeks began with **the decree of Cyrus** and ended with the rebuilding of Jerusalem under Nehemiah, which completed **the fulfillment of the decree.**
>
> **Second segment:** The 62 weeks began with **the decree of God** in the book of Malachi—"Behold, I will send My messenger"—and ended with **its fulfillment through the ministry of John the Baptist and the appearance of the Messiah.**

The book of Malachi reveals that the time span between the end of the seven weeks in 490 BC and the beginning of the 62 weeks in 409 BC was a period of increasing corruption within the priesthood after it was restored by Ezra and Nehemiah. Ezra's visit to Jerusalem in 478 BC had helped to reinforce and complete the reforms that Nehemiah had begun, but the repentance of the people at that time did not end the pattern of disobedience that had stained the history of the house of Israel and the house of Judah since their Exodus from Egypt.

Malachi's message is directed to a priesthood that had lost its reverence for God and defiled His altar by sacrificing diseased and defective animals (Mal. 1:6-8, 12-14). This is the decadent condition that moved God to issue His warnings in the book of Malachi at the beginning of the 62 weeks. The failure of the priests and the people to heed these warnings and repent led God to forsake His Temple in Jerusalem and allow the city to be overrun by foreign armies several times during the 62 weeks, or 434 years, which extended from 409 BC to 26 AD.

Indeed, the first division of 49 years was a period of *restoration* after 70 years of desolation; but the second division of 434 years was a period of *judgment* marked by invasion and foreign domination after the people and the priests fell back into sin.

Period Two: 62 Weeks, or 434 Years—409 BC to 26 AD Ends with "the Appointed Time" of Jesus' Anointing And the Beginning of His Ministry

Since the 70-week prophecy declares that the 62-week period ends with the *coming* of the Messiah—"to Messiah the Prince"—we can establish the *beginning* of the 62 weeks (or 434 years) by counting *backwards* from the beginning of Jesus' ministry. Moreover, pinpointing the beginning of Jesus' ministry is also simply a matter of counting backwards 3 and 1/2 years from the date of His crucifixion in 30 AD—a key historical marker. This brings us to the fall of 26 AD.

However, many biblical scholars and theologians teach that the 62 weeks of Daniel's prophecy ended in 27 AD. This chronology is based on counting backward 3 and 1/2 years from a crucifixion in the spring of 31 AD. However, a crucifixion in 31 AD is contradicted by the Gospel accounts and by the intercalary cycle of the Calculated Hebrew Calendar (CHC). The Gospel writers reveal that the Passover day, Nisan 14 (CHC), fell on Wednesday in the year that Christ was crucified; but according to the CHC, the Passover of 31 AD fell on Monday, which eliminates any possibility that the crucifixion occurred in that year. The only years during Christ's ministry in which the Passover fell on Wednesday were 27 AD and 30 AD. Since 27 AD was in the early phase of His ministry, it is excluded as a possibility, leaving **30 AD as the only historically valid date for the crucifixion**. Other scriptural and historical records confirm that the Passover of 30 AD fell on Wednesday, April 5, according to the Roman Julian Calendar.

In addition to the error of dating the crucifixion to 31AD, some commit a second error in calculating the 62 weeks. Instead of counting backward from the crucifixion to the beginning of Christ's ministry, they *include* the 3 and 1/2 years of His ministry as part of the 62 weeks and reckon the end of the 62 weeks to the Passover day—the date of His crucifixion—in the spring of the year.

But in reckoning the 62-week segment to *end in the spring* at the Passover (the 14th day of the first month, Nisan, CHC) with the crucifixion of the Messiah, they overlook the fact that each week of Daniel's prophecy is a **7-year Sabbatical cycle** (*heptad*). Thus, in each *heptad* the 7th year is a *land Sabbath.* Since land Sabbaths are declared on the Day of Atonement (the 10th day of the 7th month, Tishri, CHC) in the fall of the year, this means that **Daniel's "weeks" must run from fall to fall. Consequently, the Hebrew text and the CHC absolutely rule out any reckoning of the 62 weeks to end in the spring of the year.**

Furthermore, the prophecy in **Daniel nine states that the Messiah would be "cut off"** ***AFTER*** **the 62 weeks—not during** (verse 26). The Hebrew preposition that is translated "after" does not allow the "cutting off" to be included as part of the 62 weeks.

Below is an illustration of the meaning of this Hebrew proposition as diagrammed by Waltke in *An Introduction to Biblical Hebrew Syntax.* The line and the space between the circle and the preposition represent a *space of time* between the preposition and its object, ruling out any link between the ending of the 62 weeks and Messiah's being "cut off," which occurred **after 62 weeks.**

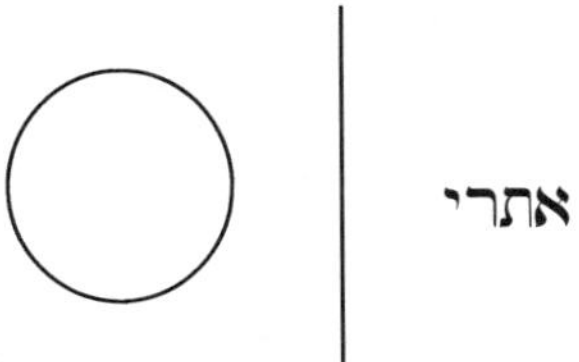

Jesus' Ministry Began in the Fall of 26 AD At the Beginning of a Jubilee Year

In addition to the above evidence from the Hebrew text, the prophecy states that the 62 weeks would *end* with "**the coming** of an anointed one" (see Owens, Dan. 9:25)—not with His being "cut off." **Furthermore, every Sabbatical year begins on the 10th day of the 7th month, which is the Day of Atonement, and is reckoned from Atonement to Atonement. The 62-week segment of the 70-week prophecy** ***ended*** **on the Day of Atonement in 26 AD and ended the Sabbatical year which ran from 25/26 AD. It was also the end of 49 years (seven Sabbatical years). Thus, the next year—26/27 AD, from Atonement to Atonement—was the 50th year, or a Jubilee year (Lev. 25:8-13). This was the first year of Jesus'**

ministry. In fact, Christ's ministry was a *Jubilee* ministry proclaiming release from sin and Satan. **Hence, His ministry had to commence at the beginning of a Jubilee year on the Day of Atonement—"the appointed time" for the Messiah to come, according to Daniel 9:25.**

Additional supporting evidence for Jesus' ministry starting in the fall of 26 AD is found in the Gospel of John, which records the words of the Jews at the time of the first Passover of Christ's ministry. During this Passover season, the Jews stated that the Temple had been 46 years in building (John 2:20). Thus, we can determine the date of this Passover—and the first year of Christ's ministry—by counting from the year that the building of the Temple began.

Josephus records that the building of the Temple was begun during the 18th year of Herod's reign: "And now Herod, in the eighteenth year of his reign [that is, the 18th in Jerusalem, but the 21st year from his coronation in Rome] … undertook a very great work, that is to build of himself the temple of God" (*Ant.*, 15:11:1).

The 18th year of Herod's reign in Jerusalem, which was the first year of building the Temple, was from the summer of 20 BC to the summer of 19 BC. Counting forward, the 46th year of building was from the summer of 26 AD to the summer of 27 AD. **The only Passover that occurred during this period of time was the Passover of 27 AD. Thus, scriptural and historical records place the first Passover of Christ's ministry in the spring of 27 AD. Since His ministry began in the *fall* of the year, we can firmly establish that it began in the autumn of 26 AD**.

Although a Jubilee year begins in the fall on the Day of Atonement, Jesus did not *publicly announce Himself* as the Anointed One until well *after* the Jubilee year had begun. Rather, this proclamation coincided with His public reading of the prophecy of Isaiah 61 at the synagogue in Nazareth during the Jubilee year 26/27 AD:

> "And He came to Nazareth, where He had been brought up; and according to His custom, He went into the synagogue on the Sabbath day and stood up to read. And there was given Him the book of the prophet Isaiah; and when He had unrolled the scroll, He found the place where it was written, '**The Spirit of the Lord is upon Me**; for this reason, **He has anointed Me** to preach the gospel to the poor; **He has sent Me** to heal those who are brokenhearted, **[He has sent Me]** to proclaim pardon to the captives and recovery of sight to the blind, **[He has sent Me]** to send forth in deliverance those who have been crushed, **[He has sent Me]** to proclaim the acceptable year of the Lord.' And after rolling up the scroll and delivering it to the attendant, He sat down; and the eyes of everyone in the synagogue were fixed on Him. Then He began to say to them, '**Today, this scripture is being fulfilled in your ears**' " (Luke 4:16-21).

Some scholars speculate that this particular Sabbath was the Day of Atonement, because the Jubilee year is reckoned from Atonement to Atonement. However, in verse 16, the Greek words translated, "the Sabbath day" actually reveal that this particular Sabbath was neither a regular weekly Sabbath nor the Day of Atonement. The phrase *en te hemera toon sabbatoon* (εν τη ημερα των σαββατων) is literally translated "on the day of the Sabbaths" or "on the day of the weeks." **The *only* Sabbath day called the "day of the Sabbaths" or the "day of the weeks" is the annual holy day of Pentecost** (the Feast of Weeks).

Since the Jubilee year is reckoned fall to fall (from Atonement to Atonement), why did Jesus *wait until Pentecost* in the spring to make this proclamation? Why didn't He make this announcement on the Day of Atonement—at the *beginning* of His ministry—instead of Pentecost? The answers to these questions are found when we examine Jesus' anointing and the beginning of His ministry. **As we will see, Jesus did, indeed, commence His ministry in the fall of 26 AD, on the Day of Atonement—at "the appointed time"—the very day that began the Jubilee year of 26/27 AD** (the 10th day of the 7th month, Tishri, CHC; on the Julian Roman Calendar, it was Wednesday, September 11, 26 AD). But He waited until Pentecost to announce that He was the Messiah because of the *special meaning* attached to that holy day.

From the Gospel accounts, it is clear that Jesus' ministry did not begin in Galilee on the day of Pentecost in the spring of 27 AD. Rather, it actually began in the fall of 26 AD, at the beginning of the Jubilee year, after Jesus was baptized by John the Baptist:

> "Then Jesus came from Galilee to the Jordan to John, to be baptized by him. But John tried to prevent Him, saying, 'I have need to be baptized by You, and You come to me?' Then Jesus answered and said to him, 'You must permit *it* at this time; for in this manner it is fitting for us to fulfill all righteousness.' Then he permitted Him *to be baptized.*
>
> "And after He was baptized, Jesus came up immediately out of the water; and behold, the heavens were opened to him, and he saw **the Spirit of God descending as a dove, and coming upon Him**. And lo, a voice from heaven said, 'This is My Son, the Beloved, in Whom I have *great* delight' " (Matt. 3:13-17).

John the Baptist further testifies concerning Jesus' baptism: "I myself beheld the Spirit descending as a dove out of heaven, and it remained upon Him. And I did not know Him *before*; but He Who sent me to baptize with water said to me, 'Upon Whom you shall see the Spirit descending, and remaining on Him, He is the one Who baptizes with *the* Holy Spirit.' And I have seen, and have borne witness that this is the Son of God" (John 1:32-35). Since Jesus was filled with the Holy Spirit from conception, **His baptism and receiving of the Holy Spirit as described in this passage was His *anointing* by God the Father as the prophesied Messiah of Daniel nine.**

The Scriptures do not disclose the exact date Jesus was baptized. However, from the context of the Gospel accounts we can determine that it took place in the fall of 26 AD, just before the Day of Atonement, the day which began the Jubilee year of 26/27 AD.

Immediately after Jesus was baptized by John, He was led of the Spirit into the wilderness to face Satan the devil and to be tempted by him for 40 days—the number of severe trial (Matt. 4:1-11; Luke 4:1-13). Although the Gospel accounts do not designate the specific date, Satan's 40-day temptation of Jesus must have begun on the Day of Atonement—the fast day. **That Day of Atonement brought an end to the second segment of 62 weeks, totaling 434 years, and simultaneously began the first day of Jesus' ministry**. **Furthermore, that day of Atonement began a 50th year, a Jubilee year—the exact "appointed time," to the very day, for the Messiah to begin His ministry.** Thus, there is no question that Jesus' extended 40-day fast and temptation was the fulfillment of "the appointed time" for the Messiah to begin His ministry. The first thing Jesus Christ had to do—as God manifested in the flesh, the true Messiah of God—was to spiritually overcome Satan the devil.

Jesus' baptism and anointing with the Holy Spirit, 40-day fast and temptation were the key events that marked the actual *beginning* of His ministry. That Day of Atonement, which began the Jubilee year of 26/27 AD, was the beginning of the first year of Jesus' ministry, thus fulfilling—to the very day—the prophecy of the decreed or "appointed" time the Messiah would come: "Know therefore and understand that from the going forth of the commandment to restore and to build Jerusalem, to [unto] Messiah the Prince, shall be **seven weeks** [the first segment of 49 years], and **sixty-two weeks** [the second segment of 434 years]" (Dan. 9:25).

The Gospel accounts of Matthew and Luke give the appearance that Jesus went into Galilee after recovering from His 40-day fast. However, that was not the case. The Gospel of John, chapters 1-4, records the chronology of events after Jesus' baptism and 40-day temptation until He and His disciples came to Nazareth, where He announced that He was the Messiah of God. We will summarize the sequence of those events concerning the first part of His ministry.

In John *chapter one*, verses 35-52, Jesus first meets some of His disciples. *Chapter two* covers the marriage in Cana and the miracle of turning water into wine, verses 1-12. Next, Jesus first shows Himself at the Temple in Jerusalem during the Passover and the Feast of Unleavened Bread, 27 AD—casting out the money changers and performing miracles, verses 13-25. This fulfilled Malachi 3:1, " 'Behold, I will send My messenger and he will prepare the way before Me. **And the Lord, Whom you seek, SHALL**

SUDDENLY COME TO HIS TEMPLE, even the Messenger of the covenant, in Whom you delight. Behold He comes, says the LORD of hosts.' " Yet, when Jesus suddenly came to His Temple, He did not declare Himself to be the Messiah.

The chronology continues in *chapter three* with Nicodemus the Pharisee coming to Jesus by night, verses 1-13; Jesus teaches, verses 14-24; John the Baptist testifies of Jesus, verses 25-34; and, John was not yet in prison, verse 34. In *chapter four*, Jesus and the disciples go to Samaria; Jesus talks to a woman at a well and teaches the people, verses 1-42.

After that, Jesus and the disciples depart from Samaria and return to Galilee, verses 43-54. (The Gospel of Luke records that John was put into prison while Jesus and His disciples were in Samaria—Luke 3:19-20.) Finally, they returned to Galilee where Jesus began "proclaiming the gospel of the kingdom of God, and saying, 'The time has been fulfilled, and the kingdom of God is near at hand; repent, and believe in the gospel' " (Mark 1:14-15).

Jesus and His disciples later traveled to Nazareth. There, on the day of Pentecost, "the day of the weeks," Jesus entered the synagogue to make His public declaration that He was the Messiah—the Anointed One of God—by reading from a prophecy of Isaiah 61: " 'The Spirit of the Lord is upon Me; for this reason, **He has anointed Me** [as the Messiah] **to preach the gospel** to the poor; He has sent Me to heal those who are brokenhearted, to proclaim pardon to the captives and recovery of sight to the blind, to send forth in deliverance those who have been crushed, to proclaim the acceptable year of the Lord [a Jubilee year].' And after rolling up the scroll *and* delivering *it* to the attendant, He sat down; and the eyes of everyone in the synagogue were fixed on Him. **Then He began to say to them, 'Today, this scripture is being fulfilled in your ears**' " (Luke 4:18-21). Thus, His announcement was made public—and they should have *known* Who He was: THE MESSIAH OF GOD.

Jesus Announced He was the Messiah On the Day of Pentecost

Since Jesus was being tempted by Satan, beginning on the Day of Atonement—which actually began the Jubilee year—He was not able to publicly announce His anointing as Messiah at that time. However, He *did* make that proclamation *during* the Jubilee year on the day of Pentecost. But why did He wait until then to do so? Why didn't He make His announcement during the Passover-Unleavened Bread feast when He was in Jerusalem at the Temple? The answers to these questions are found in the unique way the day of Pentecost is determined or counted, plus the New Testament meaning of that special feast day.

First: Pentecost is like a mini-jubilee because it is reckoned by counting 50 days *beginning with* the day *after* the weekly Sabbath during the Feast of Unleavened Bread (or the first day of the week), which is the first day of the 50-day count. The first day is the wave sheaf offering day, when the special sheaf of the "first of the firstfruits" is waved by the priest to be accepted by the Lord. Then the harvest of the barley and wheat would begin. After seven complete weeks (or 49 days) with each week ending on a weekly Sabbath, the feast of Pentecost is the *next* day, the 50th day—and signifies the end of the firstfruit grain harvest (Lev. 23:10-21). The Jubilee year is similarly reckoned by counting seven sabbatical years, or 49 years, *plus* one year, which equals 50 years. The 50th year is the Jubilee year (Lev. 25:8-13).

Second: After Jesus' resurrection from the grave toward the end of the weekly Sabbath (see Chapter Five), the chronology of the Gospels shows that on the morning of the next day—the wave sheaf offering day, the first day of the count toward Pentecost—Jesus ascended into heaven to be *accepted* by God the Father as the perfect sacrifice for the sins of the world (John 20:17). As the firstborn from the dead (Rev. 1:5; Col. 1:18), Jesus fulfilled another key "appointed time" as the *first* of the firstfruits resurrected from the dead (I Cor. 15:12-23). After being accepted by God the Father, He returned later that same day and showed Himself to His disciples (John 20:19-21; Luke 24:36-48). Jesus continued to teach them and reveal Himself to them for an additional 40 days. Then, on the 40th day, He ascended into heaven for the second and final time (Acts 1:1-11). Thus, Jesus *began* His ministry with a 40-day fast and temptation by Satan, and, after His resurrection, He *finished* with a 40-day ministry of personally appearing to the disciples, teaching them of God's way.

Third: On the Day of Pentecost, 30 AD, God sent the Holy Spirit, the power of God, upon the apostles and disciples; immediately they began preaching the truth about the resurrected Jesus Christ at the Temple in Jerusalem. Peter proclaimed repentance, baptism and the receiving of the Holy Spirit. The New Testament shows that it is only through the power of the Holy Spirit—with belief in the Gospel and full faith in the sacrifice and resurrection of Christ—that people can be released from being held captive by Satan the devil and sin, just as Jesus proclaimed on that day of Pentecost in Nazareth in 27 AD. **Thus, on the *spiritual* mini-jubilee of Pentecost, during the Jubilee year that began Jesus' ministry, He declared that He was the prophesied Christ—the appointed Messiah of God.**

Fourth: The New Testament teaches that those true believers who have received the Holy Spirit and die in the faith, or are alive when Jesus returns, will be harvested as the spiritual firstfruits to God the Father on the Day of Pentecost by the power of the resurrection (James 1:18; Rev. 14:14-16; I Thess. 4:13-18; I Cor. 15:20-23, 49-54). As resurrected, immortal spirit beings—sons and daughters of God—those in the first resurrection will be totally free from the body of flesh, sin and Satan the devil—**an everlasting spiritual Jubilee indeed!**

Jesus made His proclamation that He was the Messiah sent from God *on the day of Pentecost* because He was *pointing toward the final result* of conversion and salvation. Salvation for the firstfruits will be completed at "the appointed time" of the first resurrection—on the Day of Pentecost when Christ returns. Thus, Jesus declared Himself to be the Messiah on the *spiritual* Jubilee of Pentecost, during the Jubilee year that began on the Day of Atonement (which ended the second segment of 62 weeks or 434 years).

This was an official proclamation that the Messiah had come—*why?* —"**to preach the gospel**." There is abundant evidence proving that the coming of the Anointed One is directly linked to the beginning of Christ's ministry. Since Jesus Christ, the Anointed One of Isaiah 61, is also the Anointed One of Daniel nine, it is evident that the 62 weeks ended on the Day of Atonement in the fall of 26 AD—which began a Jubilee year.

As each of the 62 weeks was a *heptad* composed of seven sabbatical years, this division of Daniel's prophecy extended over a period of 434 years (62 x 7 = 434). Counting backward from the fall of 26 AD, we can determine that the 434 years began in the fall of 409 BC. (Since there is no year zero, one year must be subtracted when calculating from AD to BC.)

Why a Jubilee Year?

It is significant that Jesus began to reveal Himself as the Messiah during a jubilee year. The scriptural passage which He selected for His opening message in the synagogue at Nazareth has traditionally been reserved by the Jews to be read in the synagogues on the Day of Atonement, and to this day is acknowledged to be a direct reference to the proclamation of a jubilee. However, Jesus read this passage on the Day of Pentecost—**a mini-jubilee within a jubilee year**. In Appendix Four of his publication *The Star of Bethlehem*, Dr. Ernest L. Martin emphasizes the obvious connection of Luke 4:16 with the jubilee year: "**These terms that Jesus was using** in His discourse at the synagogue at Nazareth **were those associated with Sabbatical Years (and with the Jubilee** which was a type of Sabbatical Year)...."

Dr. Ernest Martin also discusses the Jubilee in his book *The Teachings of Pentecost*:

> "Back in Leviticus 25 we read of the Jubilee. It is most interesting to read what would happen every 50th year: 'And you shall number seven sabbaths of years unto you, seven times seven years; and the space of the seven sabbaths of years shall be unto you forty and nine years. Then shall you cause the trumpet of the jubilee to sound on the tenth day of the seventh month, in the day of atonement shall you make the trumpet sound throughout all your land' (Leviticus 25:8-9).
>
> "Immediately someone would say this is the Day of Atonement, this is not Pentecost. You would be correct.... What is this year of Jubilee all about...? 'And you shall **hallow the fiftieth year, and proclaim liberty** throughout all the land

> unto all the inhabitants thereof: **it shall be a jubilee** unto you; and you shall return every man unto his possession, and you shall return every man unto his family' (Leviticus 25:10)."

Jesus' reading of Isaiah's prophecy includes the words "to set at liberty" and "the acceptable year of the Lord"—both of which are direct references to a Jubilee. The exegete Albert Vanhoye wrote the following about Luke 4:16 in an essay titled *The Jubilee Year in the Gospel of Luke*, in which he dogmatically states that Jesus *was* proclaiming a jubilee:

> Saint Luke is not the only evangelist who records Jesus' visit to Nazareth "where he had been brought up" (Luke 4:16). Saint Mark and Saint Matthew also refer to this episode, although without mentioning the name of the town, referred to simply as "his home town" (Mark 6:1; Matt. 13:54). There are, however, several differences between the story told by Luke and those of Mark and Matthew. We have already implicitly indicated one, when we observed that Luke is the only one who gives the contents of Jesus' preaching. The other two evangelists limit themselves to saying that Jesus "began to teach in the synagogue" (Mark 6:2; cf. Matt. 13:54); but they do not say what he taught. Luke, on the other hand, tells how Jesus "stood up to read, and they handed him the scroll of the prophet Isaiah. Unrolling the scroll he found the place where it is written: The spirit of the Lord has been given to me...!" (Luke 4:16-18; Isa. 61:1). Very significantly, the last line of Isaiah read by Jesus says: "to proclaim *the Lord's year of favor*" (Luke 4:19; Isa. 61:2), and immediately afterwards Jesus' message was a declaration that precisely "this text" was being fulfilled on that day. The expression of Isaiah 61:2, "year of the Lord's favor," clearly refers to the prescriptions in the Book of Leviticus on the *jubilee year* (Lev. 25:10-13). **Therefore at Nazareth, Jesus was proclaiming a Jubilee year**.

Historical records in the works of Josephus provide additional evidence that Jesus' ministry began during a Jubilee. In Book XIV, Chapter XV, Paragraph 14, Josephus states that Herod's attack on Jerusalem took place in the third year after his coronation at Rome:

> When the rigour of winter was over, Herod removed his army, and came near to Jerusalem, and pitched his camp hard by the city. **Now this was the third year since he had been made king at Rome**; and as he removed his camp, and came

> near that part of the wall where it could be most easily assaulted, he pitched that camp before the temple, intending to make his attacks in the same manner as did Pompey. So he encompassed the place with three bulwarks, and erected towers, and employed a great many hands about the work, and cut down the trees that were round about the city; and when he had appointed proper persons to oversee the works, even while the army lay before the city, he himself went to Samaria, to complete his marriage, and to take to wife the daughter of Alexander, the son of Aristobulus; for he had betrothed her already, as I have before related.

The Romans made Herod king of Jerusalem in 40 BC. By Roman count "the third year since he [Herod] had been made king at Rome" was 38 BC. In Book XV, Chapter 1, Paragraph 2, Josephus reveals that the battle for Jerusalem occurred **in the spring of a sabbatical year**:

> At this time Herod, now he had got Jerusalem under his power, carried off all the royal ornaments, and spoiled the wealthy men of what they had gotten; and when, by these means, he had heaped together a great quantity of silver and gold, he gave it all to Antony, and his friends that were about him. He also slew forty-five of the principal men of Antigonus's party, and set guards at the gates of the city, that nothing might be carried out together with their dead bodies. They also searched the dead, and whatever was found, either of silver or gold, or other treasure, it was carried to the king; nor was there any end of the miseries he brought upon them; and this distress was in part occasioned by the covetousness of the prince regent, who was still in want of more, **and in part by the sabbatic year, which was still going on**, and forced the country to lie still uncultivated, since we are forbidden to sow our land in that year.

The events discussed by Josephus occurred in the spring of 38 BC, a sabbatical year that began on Atonement of 39 BC and extended to Atonement of 38 BC. A study of sabbatical cycles from Herod's battle for Jerusalem down to the ministry of Christ will demonstrate that 25/26 AD was a sabbatical year (See next page). This chronology adds historical support to the scriptural evidence in Luke 4:16-18 that the following year, 26/27 AD, which was the first year of Jesus' ministry, was a 50th year Jubilee. It was "the appointed time" for the Messiah to appear—fulfilling the 62 weeks division of the prophecy of Daniel nine to the exact day!

The Gospel accounts reveal that throughout Jesus' ministry He experienced far more persecution from the Jewish religious leaders than from the

Roman authorities. In fact, the laws of Rome prevented the Jewish officials of His day from putting Him to death. To accomplish their purpose, the Jews brought false charges of political crimes against Him, knowing that Rome imposed the death penalty for such crimes. They succeeded in convincing the Roman authorities of His guilt by hiring false witnesses to testify against Him. Their evil plot led to His crucifixion on the Passover day in 30 AD.

As we will see in the next chapter, the crucifixion of Jesus fulfilled the prophecy in Daniel 9:26 that **the Messiah would be "cut off"** ***after*** **the completion of the 62 weeks.** Thus, Daniel's prophecy sets the stage for the next "appointed time" of the Messiah—His preordained death by crucifixion for the sins of all mankind.

Land Sabbatical/Jubilee Cycles			
39-38	**BC**	**7**	**Sabbatical Year — 35**
38-37	BC	1	
37-36	BC	2	
36-35	BC	3	
35-34	BC	4	
34-33	BC	5	
33-32	BC	6	
32-31	**BC**	**7**	**Sabbatical Year — 42**
31-30	BC	1	
30-29	BC	2	
29-28	BC	3	
28-27	BC	4	
27-26	BC	5	
26-25	BC	6	
25-24	**BC**	**7**	**Sabbatical Year — 49**
24-23	**BC**	**1**	**Jubilee Year — 50**
23-22	BC	2	
22-21	BC	3	
21-20	BC	4	
20-19	BC	5	
19-18	BC	6	
18-17	**BC**	**7**	**Sabbatical Year — 7**
17-16	BC	1	
16-15	BC	2	
15-14	BC	3	
14-13	BC	4	
13-12	BC	5	
12-11	BC	6	
11-10	**BC**	**7**	**Sabbatical Year — 14**
10-9	BC	1	
9-8	BC	2	
8-7	BC	3	
7-6	BC	4	
6-5	BC	5	
5-4	BC	6	
4-3	**BC**	**7**	**Sabbatical Year — 21**

Land Sabbatical/Jubilee Cycles			
3-2	BC	1	
2-1	BC	2	
1-1	BC/AD	3	
1-2	AD	4	
2-3	AD	5	
3-4	AD	6	
4-5	**AD**	**7**	**Sabbatical Year — 28**
5-6	AD	1	
6-7	AD	2	
7-8	AD	3	
8-9	AD	4	
9-10	AD	5	
10-11	AD	6	
11-12	**AD**	**7**	**Sabbatical Year — 35**
12-13	AD	1	
13-14	AD	2	
14-15	AD	3	
15-16	AD	4	
16-17	AD	5	
17-18	AD	6	
18-19	**AD**	**7**	**Sabbatical Year — 42**
19-20	AD	1	
20-21	AD	2	
21-22	AD	3	
22-23	AD	4	
23-24	AD	5	
24-25	AD	6	
25-26	**AD**	**7**	**Sabbatical Year — 49**
26-27	**AD**	**1**	**Jubilee Year — 50** **First year of Jesus Christ's ministry**

Jesus' Ministry Begins with the 40-Day Temptation

26 AD

A Jubilee Year—Begins on Atonement

September - Julian Calendar
7th month - Calculated Hebrew Calendar

Days of Week

One	Two	Three	Four	Five	Six	Sabbath
1	*2* Trumpets 1	*3* 2	*4* 3	*5* 4	*6* 5	*7* SAB 6
8 Jesus Baptism 7	*9* Journey Into 8	*10* Wilderness 9	*11* Temptation ***1*** Began Atonement 10	*12* ***2*** 11	*13* ***3*** 12	*14* SAB ***4*** 13
15 ***5*** 14	*16* ***6*** FOT 15	*17* ***7*** FOT 16	*18* ***8*** FOT 17	*19* ***9*** FOT 18	*20* ***10*** FOT 19	*21* SAB ***11*** FOT 20
22 ***12*** FOT 21	*23* ***13*** LGD 22	*24* ***14*** 23	*25* ***15*** 24	*26* ***16*** 25	*27* ***17*** 26	*28* SAB ***18*** 27
29 ***19*** 28	*30* ***20*** 29					

Roman Dates—in small bold italics
Hebrew Dates—in bold
FOT—Feast of Tabernacles/LGD—Last Great Day
40 Days of Temptation—Large Bold Italics within ☐

October - Julian Calendar
8th month - Calculated Hebrew Calendar

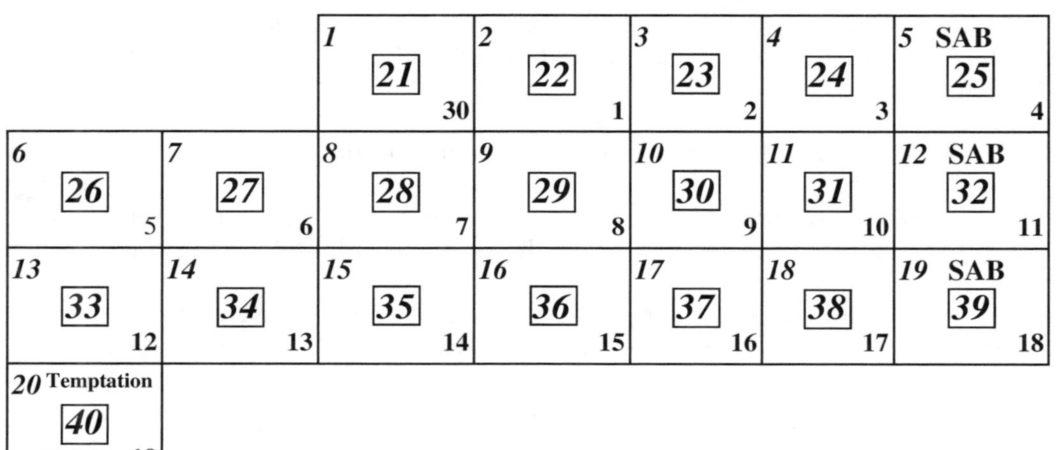

		1 ***21*** 30	*2* ***22*** 1	*3* ***23*** 2	*4* ***24*** 3	*5* SAB ***25*** 4
6 ***26*** 5	*7* ***27*** 6	*8* ***28*** 7	*9* ***29*** 8	*10* ***30*** 9	*11* ***31*** 10	*12* SAB ***32*** 11
13 ***33*** 12	*14* ***34*** 13	*15* ***35*** 14	*16* ***36*** 15	*17* ***37*** 16	*18* ***38*** 17	*19* SAB ***39*** 18
20 Temptation ***40*** Ended 19						

CHAPTER THREE

The Appointed Time of the Death of the Messiah

The Pivotal Role of Passover in the Plan of God—The Day Jesus the Christ Died

After the creation of the world, God planned a *momentous event*: At "the appointed time," a member of the very God Family would divest Himself of His glory and manifest Himself as a human being—the Messiah of God. After completing His ministry, God's Anointed One would voluntarily lay down His life at "the appointed time"—to die "the death" by crucifixion for the sins of man (Rom. 5:6). That Being was the One Who became Jesus Christ, "the Lamb [of God], slain from *the* foundation of *the* world" (Rev. 13:8).

Indeed, the greatest event since the creation of the world was the death of Jesus Christ. As God manifested in the flesh (I Tim. 3:16), He chose to give His life as the supreme sacrifice for the sins of all mankind. John the Baptist understood this when he said of Jesus: "Behold the [Passover] Lamb of God, Who takes away the sin of the world" (John 1:29).

"The appointed time" of His death—the *Passover day*—was a pivotal benchmark in the plan of God. In fact, God the Father had planned every key element of Jesus' life and messianic role in such a manner that they parallel the biblical festival seasons—or God's "appointed times." As this chapter will show, the Spring festival of the Passover—the appointed day of Jesus' death—pictures the divine deliverance of mankind from the grip of certain eternal death. That specific "appointed time" was the Passover day, Nisan 14, according to God's sacred Calculated Hebrew Calendar (CHC), or April 5, 30 AD, according to the Julian Roman Calendar. This vital "appointed time" had been predetermined "from the foundation of the world."

Mankind Becomes Captive to Sin and Death

When and how did sin enter the world? Why was it imperative for Jesus Christ to lay down His life for the sins of mankind? How can His one sacrifice purge all sin?

The sin of Adam and Eve was not the first transgression against God. The original sin was committed by Lucifer and the angels who followed him. *Lucifer* (Latin, "Light Bringer" or "Shining Star") was the first created being to commit sin—therefore he is the author of sin. He boasted that he would become like the Most High and sit on God's throne (Isa. 14:14-15; Ezek. 28:12-18). One third of the angels followed him in his rebellion (Rev. 12:3-4). At that time, Lucifer became Satan the devil, the adversary of God, and the rebelling angels who followed him became demons—or devils.

When Satan and the demons attempted to seize the throne of God, they were cast back down to the earth (Luke 10:18). That war left the earth in ruin and parts of the heavens in shambles. Everything that Lucifer and his angels had established on earth before the rebellion was destroyed, and the earth was covered with a flood (Gen. 1:2). Then the Creator God, the One Who became Jesus Christ, recreated the surface of the earth and filled it with life.

On the sixth day of creation, God made man in His own image and likeness, male and female (Gen. 1:26-27). God gave Adam and Eve free moral agency. He set before them the way of eternal life, as symbolized by the "tree of life." He also set before them the "tree of the knowledge of good and evil," which represented the way that seemed right to them, under the sway of Satan the devil. But God commanded them not to eat of the fruit of that tree, and warned them that if they ate of it they would surely die.

Under the influence of Satan the devil, Adam and Eve chose to disobey God by eating the fruit from "the tree of the knowledge of good and evil." As I Timothy 2:14 shows, Adam was not deceived, whereas Eve "came to be in transgression by being deceived." Paul describes the tragic consequences: "Therefore, as by one man sin entered into the world, and by means of sin *came* death; and in this way, death passed into all mankind; *and it is* for this reason that all have sinned" (Rom. 5:12). Thus, every man and woman has inherited a carnal, sinful *nature*. The result is that nearly all of humanity has followed the dictates of human nature under Satan's sway, cut off from God. Although God set limits on Satan, He has not yet removed him and his evil influence. However, in a future "appointed time," God will bring *all mankind* out from subjection to sin and Satan. Through His plan of redemption, initiated by His Son's perfect sacrifice, God has made it possible for all mankind to be delivered from sin and the penalty of death (I John 2:1-2).

God as Lawgiver and Creator decreed that the wages of sin for all human beings is death (Rom. 6:23). Sin is the transgression of God's holy, spiritual laws and commandments (I John 3:4). All have sinned and have come short of the glory of God, so all face death unless they accept the way of salvation that God has provided (Rom. 3:23). The ultimate death that is decreed for sin is the second death in the lake of fire. From that death there is no resurrection (Rev. 20:13-15; 21:8).

After Adam and Eve sinned, God pronounced His judgment upon them. Within His sentence, we find the *first prophecy* of the death of the Messiah: "And I will put enmity between you [the serpent, Satan the devil] and the woman [a type of Israel, and later, the Church of God], and between your seed [the followers of Satan] and her Seed [Jesus Christ, the coming Messiah]; He will bruise your head [Satan], and you [Satan], shall *bruise His heel* [the crucifixion of Christ]" (Gen. 3:15).

This prophecy was spoken by the Lord God Himself, the One Who would become Jesus Christ. As the God of the Old Testament, He prophesied of His own death to atone for the sins of Adam and Eve and all their descendants to come. This prophecy was spoken more than 4,000 years before His beating, scourging and crucifixion on the Passover day. According to the CHC, that "appointed" day was Nisan 14, 30 AD (or April 5 on the Julian Roman Calendar).

The Promised Seed of the Covenant With Abraham

The promise of a Seed who would conquer sin and banish Satan was confirmed by the covenant that God made with Abraham. The words of the covenant were a prophecy of His own *future birth* as the fleshly Seed of Abraham. Let us examine the account in the book of Genesis: "And behold, the Word of the LORD *came* to him [Abraham], saying, 'This man [his steward, Eliezer] shall not be your heir; but he that shall come forth out of your own loins shall be your heir' " (Gen. 15:4).

The birth of Isaac, the son of Abraham and Sarah, was only the beginning of the fulfillment of this promise to Abraham. The promise was not only for Isaac, but also for his future descendant, the coming Messiah. The birth of Jesus was the ultimate fulfillment of the promise, the Seed to whom the promises were given: "Now to Abraham and to his Seed were the promises spoken. He does not say, 'and to *your* seeds,' as of many; but as of one, 'and to your Seed,' which is Christ" (Gal. 3:16). Christ is the promised Seed and true Heir of the promises God made to Abraham.

The account in Genesis 15 reveals that evening had already come when God began to give the promises to Abraham. On that night, God took Abraham outside and showed him the stars of heaven. Then He gave Abraham another promise: "And He brought him outside and said, 'Look now toward the heavens and number the stars—if you are able to count them.' And He said to him, 'So shall your seed be' " (Gen. 15:5). The New Testament shows that these words of God do not refer to Abraham's physical descendants through Isaac and Jacob, but to those who would become the children of Abraham through faith in Jesus Christ. The apostle Paul wrote: "Because of this, *you should* understand that those who *are* of faith are the *true* sons of Abraham.... Because you are all sons of God through faith in Christ Jesus. For as many *of you* as were baptized into Christ did put on Christ. There is neither Jew nor Greek; there is neither bond nor free; there is neither male nor female; for you are all one in Christ Jesus. And if you *are* Christ's, then you are Abraham's seed, and heirs according to *the* promise" (Gal. 3:7, 26-29).

The true children of Abraham are not counted by physical lineage. They are a spiritual nation, composed of individuals of every race and bloodline who follow in the faith of Abraham (Gal. 3:8, 14). At the return of Christ, they will be resurrected to eternal life as glorified spirit beings and will shine as the stars forever (Dan. 12:3; Matt. 13:43; I Cor. 15:40-44).

Next, God promised to give to Abraham and his physical seed the land of the Canaanites: "And He said unto him, 'I *am* the LORD that brought you out of Ur of the Chaldees, to give you this land to inherit it' " (Gen. 15:7). This promise was for his physical descendants, the children of Israel. Numerous generations would pass before the promised Seed, Jesus Christ, would come to prepare a spiritual people for a spiritual kingdom—the sons of God in the Kingdom of God. Abraham received the promises with complete faith that God would fulfill them: "And he believed in the LORD. And He accounted it to him for righteousness" (verse 6).

The Covenant Confirmed by a Maledictory Oath

When God established His covenant with Abraham, He confirmed it with a maledictory oath, which was a pledge and prophecy of His own future death. On the morning after giving Abraham the promises, God spoke to him and instructed him to prepare a special sacrifice to seal the covenant: "And He said to him, 'Take Me a heifer of three years old, and a she-goat of three years old, and a ram of three years old, and a turtledove, and a young pigeon.' And he took all these to himself, and divided them in the middle, and laid each piece opposite the other; but he did not divide the birds. And when the birds of prey came down upon the carcasses, Abram drove them away" (verses 9-11). The bloody carcasses of the sacrificial animals were laid on the ground to represent the symbolic death of the one who would confirm the covenant. By passing between the parts, God would pledge His *own life* to fulfill the covenant. By the time Abraham had finished preparing the covenant sacrifice, it was late in the day:

> "And it came to pass, as the sun was going down, that a deep sleep fell upon Abram. And, behold, a horror of great darkness fell upon him" (verse 12). While Abraham lay sleeping, God appeared to him in a vision and promised that his physical descendants would inherit the land. However, this would not happen until they had lived in another land for four generations: "And He said to Abram, 'You must surely know that your seed shall be sojourners in a land *that is* not theirs, (and shall serve [their captors] *and they shall* afflict [your seed]) four hundred years. And also I will judge that nation whom they shall serve. And afterward they shall come out with great substance. And you shall go to your fathers in peace. You shall be buried in a good old age. But in the fourth generation they shall come here again, for the iniquity of the Amorites is not yet full' " (verses 13-16).

After prophesying these events, God bound Himself to fulfill His promises by passing between the sacrificial animals to seal the covenant: "And it came to pass—**when the sun went down** [beginning the next day], and it was dark—behold, a smoking furnace and a burning lamp passed between those pieces. In the same day the LORD made a covenant with Abram…" (verses 17-18).

After the sun had gone down, God passed between the parts; He walked a death walk, pledging His future death. Apparently, the smoking furnace wholly consumed the sacrificial animals. That is how God ratified His unilateral covenant with Abraham.

The full account in Genesis 15 reveals that the making of the covenant took place during two consecutive days. When God first spoke to Abraham, it was night because the stars could be seen (verse 5). In the morning, God gave Abraham instructions for preparing the covenant sacrifice. Abraham prepared the sacrifice that same day. We know that he completed the preparations while the sun was still high because the birds of prey were flying about and attempting to land on the sacrifice (verse 11). The next verse records the end of the day: "And it came to pass, as the sun was going down, that a deep sleep fell upon Abram " (verse 12). After the sun had gone down, God appeared to Abraham and ratified the covenant (verse 18).

There is great significance in the fact that the covenant was established over a two-day period, with the promises being given on the first night and the covenant being ratified on the second night. The timing of these events has an exact parallel in the chronology of the Passover and the beginning of the Exodus, which were the first acts in the fulfillment of God's promises for the physical seed—the descendants of Abraham through Isaac and Jacob, the 12 tribes of the children of Israel.

Israel's First Passover and the Exodus from Egypt

As Exodus 12 records, the children of Israel kept the Passover on the 14th day of the first month, or Abib (this month was later known as Nisan). The Passover lamb, a type of the coming Messiah, was killed immediately after sunset at the beginning of the 14th. The people took some of the blood and put it on the side posts and lintel of the doors of their houses so that God would pass over their houses and spare their firstborn. Then they roasted the lamb with fire and ate it with bitter herbs.

At midnight on the 14th, God executed His final judgment on the Egyptians and their gods by killing all the firstborn of men and beasts. When God saw the blood of the Passover lambs on the houses of the children of Israel, He passed over them, sparing their firstborn.

Then, as the day portion of Nisan 14 began at sunrise, the children of Israel left their houses to assemble at Rameses for the Exodus. As they journeyed to Rameses, they completely spoiled the Egyptians, fulfilling God's promise to Abraham that his descendants would depart from the land of their servitude with great substance. God commanded the children of Israel to observe this day, the 14th day of the first month, as the feast of the Passover for all generations to come, in commemoration of His final judgment against the Egyptians and their gods and His sparing of the firstborn of Israel (Ex. 12:3-14, 21-28; Lev. 23:5).

After the children of Israel had assembled in Rameses, the Exodus from Egypt began. The people departed from Rameses as the 14th day was ending at sunset and the 15th day was beginning. The timing of this event fulfilled another promise that God had made to Abraham: "Now the sojourning of the children of Israel in Egypt *was* **four hundred and thirty years**, and it came to pass at the end of the **four hundred and thirty years, it was EVEN ON THAT VERY SAME DAY, all the armies of the LORD went out from the land of Egypt. It *is* a night to be much observed to the LORD for bringing them out from the land of Egypt**..." (Ex. 12:40-42).

The phrase "**the selfsame day**" (*KJV*) refers to **a specific day exactly four hundred and thirty years before the Exodus**. What day was this? The Scriptures reveal that it was the "selfsame day" that God established His covenant with Abraham. On that day, God promised that He would bring his descendants out of bondage with great substance. On that "selfsame day," the 15th day of the first month, God fulfilled His promise. Therefore, God established the 15th day of the first month as a holy day to commemorate the beginning of the Exodus (Ex. 12:37-42; 13:3-10; Lev. 23:6-8).

The Foundation of the Christian Passover in the Covenant with Abraham

Four hundred and thirty years after establishing His covenant with Abraham, God brought the children of Israel out of Egypt. After bringing them out, He established a covenant with them—which we now call the Old Covenant. In his epistle to the Galatians, the apostle Paul confirms that the Old Covenant was established four hundred and thirty years after God's covenant with Abraham: "Now this I say, *that the* covenant ratified beforehand by God to Christ [Abraham's true Heir] cannot be annulled by the law [the physical requirements of the Old Covenant], which was *given* four hundred and thirty years later, so as to make the promise of no effect" (Gal. 3:17).

The Old Covenant with the children of Israel did not fulfill God's promise to Abraham of a multitude of spiritual seed that would shine as the stars forever. This promise did not begin to be fulfilled until the coming of the New Covenant, the covenant of everlasting life, which was established nearly 2,000 years later by Christ. As God manifested in the flesh, Jesus Christ, the promised Seed of Abraham, instituted the New Covenant on the Passover night, the 14th day of the first month (CHC). The Passover that initiated the New Covenant was not a supper of lamb and bitter herbs, as was the Passover of the children of Israel under the Old Covenant. When Jesus instituted the new Christian Passover, He changed the symbols of the Passover to be symbols of His own body and blood, which He sacrificed as the true Passover Lamb of God to ratify the New Covenant. Although He changed the symbols, He did not change the day, or the time of day, on which the Passover was to be observed.

The New Covenant Christian Passover, as instituted by Jesus, is to be observed on the night of Nisan 14. The new ceremony consists of three parts: 1) foot washing (John 13:2-17); 2) partaking of the broken unleavened bread, symbolizing Jesus' broken body (Matt. 26:26; Mark 14:22; Luke 22:19; I Cor. 11:23-24); and 3) partaking of the wine, symbolizing the blood of Jesus shed for the remission of sins so that all who accept His sacrifice may enter the New Covenant (Matt. 26:27-29; Mark 14:23-25; Luke 22:17-20; I Cor. 11:25-26).

Why Did God Have to Die?

As we have learned, God ratified His promises to Abraham with a maledictory oath. By passing between the parts of the covenant sacrifice, He pledged that He would give His own life to fulfill the promises. The bloody slaughter of these sacrificial animals symbolized the brutal suffering and crucifixion of Jesus Christ, which occurred in 30 AD on the Passover day. The deep sleep and horror of great darkness that Abraham experienced was symbolic of Christ's death at the 9th hour (approximately 3 PM) on the Passover day and His subsequent burial in the tomb as Nisan 14 was ending at sunset. Thus, 2,000 years later, on the very same day that God ratified His covenant with Abraham, His lifeless body was in the tomb. He had carried out His pledge that He would die in order to fulfill the promises—precisely at "the appointed time."

Before we can appreciate the death of God manifested in the flesh, we need to understand a fundamental truth about God. The Scriptures reveal that the Godhead is composed of more than one divine Being. In the first chapter of Genesis, the Hebrew name *Elohim* is used to describe God. In the Hebrew language, the suffix *im* added to a word makes it plural. Thus, *Elohim* is a plural noun, meaning that there is more than one Being in the Godhead. When God created Adam and Eve, He said, "Let **Us** make man in **Our** image, after **Our** likeness…" (Gen. 1:26).

John begins his Gospel by revealing this fundamental truth:

> "**In *the* beginning was the Word, and the Word was with God, and the Word was God. He was in *the* beginning with God**. All things came into being through Him, and not even one *thing* that was created came into being without Him. In Him was life, and the life was the light of men…. **He**

> **was in the world, and the world came into being through Him, but the world did not know Him.... And the Word became flesh, and tabernacled** [temporarily dwelt] **among us** (and we ourselves beheld His glory, *the* glory as of *the* only begotten with the Father), full of grace and truth" (John 1:1-4, 10, 14).

Jesus Himself testified that He was with the Father in glory before the world existed. In His final prayer to God the Father before He was arrested, tried and crucified, He said, "I have glorified You on the earth. I have finished the work that You gave Me to do. And now, **Father, glorify Me with Your own self, with the glory that I had with You before the world existed**" (John 17:4-5).

The Scriptures of the Old Testament and the New Testament consistently reveal that from the beginning there were two Beings Who existed together as God, or *Elohim*. The one of Elohim Who created all things was the one Who became Jesus Christ, the Messiah and the Savior of the world. The other one of Elohim became the Father. We find a prophecy of this in the book of Psalms: "I [the one of Elohim Who became the Son, Jesus Christ] will declare the decree of the LORD. He [the one of Elohim Who became the Father] has said to Me, '**You are My Son; this day I have begotten You** [the day He was begotten in the womb of the virgin Mary]" (Psa. 2:7).

The one of Elohim Who became Jesus Christ, the Son of God, had to divest himself of His power and glory as God. He had to become a pinpoint of life in order to be begotten by the Father in the womb of the virgin Mary. Paul reveals how this was accomplished: "Let this mind be in you, which *was* also in Christ Jesus; Who, although He existed [Greek, *huparchoon*, to exist or pre-exist] in *the* form of God, did not consider it robbery to be equal with God, but emptied Himself [of His power and glory], *and* was made in *the* likeness [Greek, *homoioma*, the same existence] of men, *and* took the form of a servant [Greek, *doulos*, a slave]; and being found in *the* manner of man, He humbled Himself, *and* became obedient unto death, even *the* death of *the* cross" (Phil. 2:5-8).

These inspired words of Paul confirm that before Jesus became human He was, in fact, *Jehovah Elohim*, the Lord God of the Old Testament. Existing as God, He was composed of ever-living Spirit. In this existence, it was impossible for Him to die. The only way for God to die was to become fully human—to be "manifested in the flesh." The God Who had created man in His image and likeness took on the same flesh and nature as man in order to redeem man from sin.

Jesus Christ voluntarily became a man in order to give His life as an offering for the sin of the world. The Father gave Him authority to lay down His life and to receive it back, as Jesus Himself testified: "Just as the Father knows Me, I also know the Father; and **I lay down My life for the sheep**.

And I have other sheep that are not of this fold. I must bring those also, and they shall hear My voice; and there shall be one flock *and* one Shepherd. **On account of this, the Father loves Me: because I lay down My life, that I may receive it back again. No one takes it from Me, but I lay it down of Myself. I have authority to lay it down and authority to receive it back again. This commandment I received from My Father**" (John 10:15-18).

Jesus Christ came to do the will of the Father and to give His life as the sacrifice for sin. In his epistle to the Hebrews, Paul quotes the words of the prophecy of Psalm 40:6-8: "For this reason, when He comes into the world, He says, 'Sacrifice and offering You did not desire, but You have prepared a body for Me [Christ's human body of flesh]. You did not delight in burnt offerings and *sacrifices* for sin. Then said I, "**Lo, I come** (*as* it is written of Me in *the* scroll of *the* book) **to do Your will, O God**" ' " (Heb. 10:5-7).

It was the purpose of the two God Beings Who were Elohim that one of them would be made fully human in order to die, so that through His sacrifice all mankind might be granted grace unto salvation. Paul makes this absolutely clear: "But we see Jesus, **Who *was* made a little lower than *the* angels**, crowned with glory and honor on account of suffering **the death**, in order that **by *the* grace of God He Himself might taste [partake of] death for everyone**; because it was fitting for Him, for Whom all things *were created*, and by Whom all things *exist*, in bringing many sons unto glory, to make the Author of their salvation perfect through sufferings" (Heb. 2:9-10).

The Scriptures reveal that Jesus Christ was a mortal human being. He was not an angelic being that appeared to be a man. Nor was He a spirit being (the Christ) inhabiting a physical, human body (Jesus the man). Paul states very clearly that He shared the same flesh and blood as all human beings:

> "**Therefore, since the children are partakers of flesh and blood, in like manner He also took part in the same**, in order that through death He might annul him who has the power of death—that is, the devil; and *that* He might deliver those who were subject to bondage all through their lives by *their* fear of death.
>
> "For surely, He is not taking upon Himself to help *the* angels; but He is taking upon Himself to help *the* [spiritual—Gal. 3:29] seed of Abraham. For this reason, it was obligatory for *Him* to be made like *His* brethren in everything [sharing the same flesh and nature], that He might be a merciful and faithful High Priest *in* things pertaining to God, in order to make propitiation for the sins of the people. For because He Himself has suffered, having been tempted *in like manner*, He is able to help those who are being tempted" (Heb. 2:14-18).

What a magnificent expression of God's love! The Creator of all mankind temporarily gave up His eternal existence as God and lowered Himself to the level of mortal man, with human nature, so that He could suffer and die for every human being at "the appointed time." By the grace and love of God, through the power of the Holy Spirit, He willingly took upon Himself the death penalty that He had pronounced upon Adam and Eve and their descendants.

Jesus voluntarily chose to lay down His life to reconcile mankind to God so that all who accept His sacrifice may have the opportunity to receive salvation and eternal life. Jesus endured all His suffering in the flesh so that He might become the Author of eternal salvation, "Who, in the days of His flesh, offered up both prayers and supplications with strong crying and tears to Him Who was able to save Him from death, and was heard because *He* feared *God.* Although He was a Son, *yet* He learned obedience from the things that He suffered; and having been perfected, He became *the* Author of eternal salvation to all those who obey Him" (Heb. 5:7-9).

The death of the Creator God, manifested in the flesh, was the perfect sacrifice for the forgiveness of human sin. No other sacrifice could bring forgiveness of sin to mankind. All the animal sacrifices and the shedding of their blood could never bring full spiritual forgiveness for human sin before God. Paul makes this truth clear: "For the law, having *only* a shadow of the good things that are coming *and* not the image of those things, with the same sacrifices which they offer continually year by year, is never able to make perfect those who come *to worship.* Otherwise, would they not have ceased to be offered? For once those who worship had been purified, *they would* no longer be conscious of sin. On the contrary, in *offering* these *sacrifices* year by year, *there is* a remembrance of sins; **because *it is* impossible *for the* blood of bulls and goats to take away sins**" (Heb. 10:1-4).

Only God Can Save Mankind

No other fleshly human being could have sacrificed his life to redeem mankind. Even if it were possible for a man to live perfectly in the letter of the law and never sin, his perfect human life, if sacrificed for sin, would not be sufficient to redeem even one human life. Redemption from sin and death requires *greater obedience* than the letter of the law. This is the whole lesson of Job's trials and suffering. Although he was blameless in the letter of the law, His own righteousness could not save him:

> "And the LORD answered Job and said, 'Shall he who contends with the Almighty instruct *Him*? He who reproves God, let him answer it.'
>
> "And Job answered the LORD and said, 'Behold, I am vile [all human beings have a sinful nature, regardless of perfect

behavior in the letter of the law]! What shall I answer You? I will lay my hand on my mouth. Once I have spoken; but I will not answer; yea, twice, but I will proceed no further.' And the LORD answered Job out of the whirlwind, and said, 'Gird up your loins now like a man. I will demand you, and you declare unto Me. Will you even annul My judgment? Will you condemn Me so that you may be righteous?

" 'And *have* you an arm like God? Or can you thunder with a voice like His? Deck yourself now with majesty and excellency, and array yourself with glory and beauty. Cast abroad the rage of your wrath; and behold everyone who is proud, and abase him. Look on everyone *who is* proud, *and* bring him low; and tread down the wicked in their place. Hide them in the dust together; *and* bind their faces in darkness. Then I will also confess to you that your own right hand can save you' " (Job 40:1-14).

As God told Job, it is impossible for *any man* to save himself from sin—much less all of humanity.

On the other hand, is it possible for angels to save man from sin? God created angels to be ministering spirits. Angels are in a completely different category than human beings or God. While God created them out of spirit, they do not have the potential to enter into the God Family, as do humans, who will be transformed into immortal spirit beings at the first resurrection. Neither are the angels like the One of Elohim Who became the Son, as Paul wrote:

"God, Who spoke to the fathers at different times in the past and in many ways by the prophets, has spoken to us in these last days by *His* Son, Whom He has appointed heir of all things, by Whom also He made the worlds; Who, being *the* brightness of *His* glory and *the* exact image of His person, and upholding all things by the word of His own power, when He had by Himself purged our sins, sat down at *the* right hand of the Majesty on high; **having been made so much greater than *any of* the angels, inasmuch as He has inherited a name exceedingly superior to them**.

"**For to which of the angels did He ever say, 'You are My Son; this day have I begotten You**'? And again, 'I will be a Father to Him, and He will be a Son to Me'? And again, when He brought the Firstborn into the world, He said, 'Let all *the* angels of God worship Him.' Now on one hand, of the angels He says, 'Who makes His angels spirits, and His ministers a flame of fire.'... But unto which of the angels did He

> ever say, 'Sit at My right hand, until I make Your enemies a footstool for Your feet'? **Are they not all ministering spirits, sent forth to minister to those who are about to inherit salvation**?" (Heb. 1:1-7, 13-14).

Indeed, even if an angel could be sacrificed, it would not be possible for such a sacrifice to pay for the sins of all mankind. The only Being whose life could purchase redemption from sin for all humanity is the Creator God. If the One Who had created man died, complete and total payment for human sin could be made, and reconciliation with God would be possible for all humanity. God's mercy could then be extended to all who repent and accept the death of Jesus Christ, God manifested in the flesh, as payment for their sins. This is why God had to die!

The One of Elohim Who created the heavens and the earth became Jesus Christ—God manifested in the flesh. He was divinely begotten by God the Father and the firstborn of the virgin Mary, His physical mother. He was the same as any ordinary human being, except that He had the Holy Spirit from conception. Only the death of God could reconcile man and God. Thus, Jesus had to be God in the flesh—human, as well as divine.

While He lived in the flesh, Jesus was subject to every type of temptation that a human being can experience, but He never yielded to a single temptation of the flesh or of Satan. Jesus never sinned. His obedience was perfect in the full spirit of the law. By living a sinless life, He alone was qualified to become not only the Savior and Redeemer of mankind, but also the High Priest and Mediator between God and man: "Having therefore a great High Priest, *Who* has passed into the heavens, Jesus the Son of God, we should hold fast the confession *of our faith*. **For we do not have a high priest who cannot empathize with our weaknesses, but *one Who* was tempted in all things according to *the* likeness of *our own temptations*, yet *He was* without sin**. Therefore, we should come with boldness to the throne of grace, so that we may receive mercy and find grace to help in time of need" (Heb. 4:14-16).

Jesus' life in the flesh was able to purchase redemption from sin for all humanity because:

1) He was the Creator of all human beings.
2) He was divinely begotten by God the Father.
3) He was God manifested in the flesh.
4) He was the only human to live His entire life according to the will of God.
5) He was the only human never to sin.
6) He was the only human never to yield to a single temptation of the flesh or of Satan the devil.
7) He was the only human not to come under the death penalty for sin.

Only the precious blood of the Lamb of God could atone for all human sin. The death of God in the flesh was complete and perfect as a sacrifice and an atonement because His life in the flesh encompassed the full scope of human experience. On the human level, He suffered every type of temptation possible. He suffered the vilest of human indignities and excruciating tortures, enduring a violent beating, scourging, and crucifixion, and the shame of public death. He suffered rejection by His own people and injustice at the hands of religious and civil authorities. He was the victim of political expediency and religious hypocrisy. He overcame all, gaining total victory over Satan the devil and the pulls of the flesh through His perfect love and obedience to God the Father. The sacrifice of His perfect life opened the way for all mankind to receive salvation through faith: "For God so loved the world that He gave His only begotten Son, so that everyone who believes in Him may not perish, but may have everlasting life. For God sent not His Son into the world that He might judge the world, but that the world might be saved through Him" (John 3:16-17).

God the Father accepted the death of Christ once for all time as full payment for human sin. But before Jesus' sacrifice can be applied to an individual, he or she must first repent of sin, accept Jesus as personal Savior and be baptized by full immersion in water. At baptism, he or she is conjoined into Christ's death by symbolic burial in a watery grave. Each one who is raised out of that baptismal burial is to walk in newness of life, learning to love God the Father and Jesus Christ with all the heart and to keep their commandments in the full spirit of the law. This is the way of life that Jesus established for those who enter the New Covenant through faith in His sacrifice for sin.

All who enter the New Covenant are commanded to observe the Passover year by year as a renewal of the covenant of everlasting life. By partaking of the Passover as Jesus taught, they acknowledge that they have accepted the body and blood of Christ as full payment for their sins and have dedicated their lives to live by Him (John 6:57). When they partake of the broken unleavened bread, they acknowledge that they are healed of their diseases by the broken body of Christ—"by Whose stripes you were healed" (I Pet. 2:24). When they partake of the wine, they acknowledge that they trust in His shed blood "for the remission of sins" (Matt. 26:28).

All true Christians have been bought with a great price. They belong to Jesus Christ, Who paid with His own blood to release them from the power of Satan and the bondage of sin, and to reconcile them to God the Father. "Christ our Passover was sacrificed for us" (I Cor. 5:7). This is the meaning of the "appointed time" Jesus the Messiah died for the sins of the world.

CHAPTER FOUR

The Agony of the Crucifixion

The Sacrifice of the "Lamb of God"
On the Appointed Passover Day

The prophecy of Daniel nine confirms that *after* 62 weeks the Messiah would be "cut off, but not for Himself." This prophecy does not give us specific details of how, when, or for what reason the Messiah would be "cut off." However, in the Old Testament there are scores of prophecies that give us precise details concerning the agony of the crucifixion—the *appointed death* of Jesus the Messiah. When we examine the New Testament, we find these fulfilled prophetic details documented by Matthew, Mark, Luke and John (see Appendix B, "Twenty-Eight Prophecies Fulfilled on the Crucifixion Day").

God's "appointed times" are the vital *keys* that unlock the understanding of God's precise *timing* in the fulfillment of His prophecies and covenants concerning Israel, Judah, and the New Testament Church. Of primary importance are the prophecies of Jesus the Messiah. We have seen that Jesus was born at "the appointed time"—the Feast of Trumpets, in 5 BC. In accordance with the 70-week prophecy, Jesus began His ministry exactly at "the appointed time" on the Day of Atonement, beginning a Jubilee year, Wednesday, September 11, 26 AD. In this chapter, we will research "the appointed time" of His crucifixion on the Passover day, the 14th day of the first month of the Calculated Hebrew Calendar (CHC) in 30 AD—the day of destiny determined from the foundation of the world before Adam and Eve were created.

Just before Jesus began His three and one-half year ministry, He was baptized by John the Baptist by full immersion in water in the Jordan River. Shortly after He began His ministry, Jesus told His disciples, "My meat [the purpose of His coming] is to do the will of Him Who sent Me, and **to finish His work**" (John 4:34).

In Jesus' final prayer to the Father before His arrest, He said, "**I have glorified You on the earth. I have finished the work that You gave Me to do**" (John 17:4). Here Jesus must have been referring to the work of His ministry—which He actually *finished* through that final prayer. But there was something else He had yet to finish—the ignominy of being falsely accused and tried, the suffering of being beaten and scourged, and the agony of death by crucifixion. Indeed, this was *a separate work that had to be finished.* Jesus explained this to His disciples while they were on their way to Jerusalem to observe the Passover: " '**Behold, we are going up to**

Jerusalem, and the Son of man shall be betrayed to the chief priests and scribes, and they shall condemn Him to death; and they shall deliver Him up to the Gentiles to mock *Him*, and to scourge *Him*, and to crucify *Him*; but He shall rise again the third day' " (Matt. 20:18-19).

Remarkably, just as Jesus *began* His ministry with a baptism, He also *ended* His ministry with a baptism—but not of water. Jesus told His disciples, "**For I have a baptism to be baptized *with*, and how burdened I am until it be accomplished** [finished]!" (Luke 12:50; also see Matt. 20:22-23; Mark 10:38-39). What was that baptism? It was the beating, scourging, and final crucifixion. Why did Jesus call it a baptism? Through this brutal, gruesome ordeal, Jesus was figuratively baptized in His own blood—truly a baptism of His shed blood unto death. It was His *final work*, carried out at "the appointed time" on the Passover day, 30 AD. **Jesus had to finish this final work—a bloody baptism of death**—as God's eternal plan hinged on its completion. He had to endure to the end! He could not fail. In fact, Jesus Himself confirmed that He *did finish* this final work. While hanging on the cross, Jesus' last words before He died were, " '**IT IS FINISHED!**' **And bowing His head He yielded up *His* spirit**" (John 19:30).

We will now examine the major prophecies that describe the agony of the crucifixion, as well as their *fulfillment* as documented in the New Testament. A careful study of the Gospel accounts allows us to reconstruct the six days leading up to Jesus' final Passover. Accordingly, the Gospel of John records events that occurred on Nisan 10, the "appointed day" the Passover lambs were to be *selected* (Ex. 12:3-6). While Jesus was teaching the people, He said, "Now My soul is troubled, and what shall I say? Father, save Me from this hour [this "appointed time"]? **But for this *very* purpose I have come to this hour**. Father, glorify Your name." Then a voice from heaven responded: "I have both glorified *it* and will glorify *it* again" (John 12:27-28). This occurred on the 10th day of the first month (according to the CHC), which was the day the children of Israel were commanded to select their lambs for the Passover.

With this announcement from heaven, God the Father publicly confirmed Jesus as the ultimate Passover Lamb of God. This is why Jesus said, "My soul is troubled." He knew that His bloody baptism unto death was but a few days away. Four days later, at His last Passover with the apostles, Jesus said, "Behold, even *now* the hand of him who is betraying Me *is* with Me at the table" (Luke 22:21). Although Jesus knew that Judas would betray Him, He washed Judas' feet along with the other apostles' feet (John 13:2-5, 11). Then Judas left.

As Jesus administered the symbols of His body and His blood to the eleven apostles who were with Him, He knew that the time of His betrayal was at hand. When He departed with the apostles to the Mount of Olives, walking into the darkness of that dreaded night, Jesus began to feel the melancholy oppressiveness of the sins of the whole world weighing on Him, and His mind was filled with thoughts of the suffering, pain and agony that lay ahead. Though His apostles were with Him, an overwhelming feeling of isolation penetrated every cell of His being. He could not share His sorrow with them, for they did not understand what the rest of that Passover night and day would bring. He had spoken to them in the days leading up to the Passover, forewarning them of His betrayal and death, but they did not grasp the meaning of His words. They did not comprehend that His life was about to end with a gruesome death on the cross as the TRUE PASSOVER SACRIFICE OF GOD—THE SIN OFFERING FOR THE WORLD—**an agonizing baptism in His own blood unto death!**

The "appointed time" had come! His rendezvous with destiny drew closer and closer to its decisive climax! The Lord God of the Old Testament, Who had come to earth in the flesh, was about to die the ultimate, horrific death that He and the prophets had foretold. This was the reason He had come into the world. He had come in the flesh in order to die—to give His body to be beaten, scourged and crucified, and to offer His blood for the sins of mankind. But no human being desires to die a slow, torturous death in great pain and agony. As Jesus anticipated His suffering, His flesh cried out to be spared. Only the love of God, which had sustained Him and brought Him to this day, could give Him the strength to endure the suffering that was appointed to Him.

He had manifested the love of God during His days in the flesh, setting a perfect example for His disciples. Now the love of God would be manifested by His death. As they were walking to the Mount of Olives, He charged His apostles, "LOVE ONE ANOTHER, AS I HAVE LOVED YOU." He spoke from the depths of His innermost being, desiring to indelibly etch these words into their minds: "If you keep My commandments, you shall live in My love; just as I have kept My Father's commandments and live in His love.

"These things I have spoken to you, in order that My joy may dwell in you, and *that* your joy may be full. **This is My commandment: that you love one another, as I have loved you.** No one has greater love than this: that one lay down his life for his friends" (John 15:10-13).

Jesus was about to manifest the greatest love of all by laying down His life for them, as well as for the whole world. But the apostles did not know this yet, nor did they know that some of them would also lose their lives for His name's sake in the days ahead. Jesus warned the disciples that the world would hate them and persecute them, just as the world had hated and persecuted Him:

> "If the world hates you, you know that it hated Me before *it hated* you. If you were of the world, the world would love its own. **However, because you are not of the world, but I have personally chosen you out of the world, the world hates you for this. Remember the word that I spoke to**

> **you: a servant is not greater than his master. If they persecuted Me, they will persecute you also. If they kept My word, they will keep your *word* also.** But they will do all these things to you for My name's sake, because they do not know Him Who sent Me.
>
> "If I had not come and spoken to them, they would not have had sin; but now they have nothing to cover their sin. The one who hates Me hates My Father also. If I had not done among them the works that no other man has done, they would not have had sin; but now they have both seen and hated both Me and My Father. But this has happened so that the saying might be fulfilled which is written in their law, 'They hated Me without *a* cause.' But when the Comforter has come, which I will send to you from the Father, *even* the Spirit of the truth, which proceeds from the Father, that one shall bear witness of Me. Then you also shall bear witness, because you have been with Me from *the* beginning. I have spoken these things to you so that you will not be offended" (John 15:18-16:1).

Jesus continued to warn them, telling them that they, too, would be killed for preaching the truth of God:

> "They shall cast you out of the synagogues; furthermore, **the time is coming that everyone who kills you will think that he is rendering service to God.** And they shall do these things to you because they do not know the Father, nor Me. But **I have told you these things so that when the time comes, you may remember** that I said *them* to you. However, I did not say these things to you at *the* beginning because I was with you…. These things I have spoken to you, so that in Me you may have peace. **In the world you shall have tribulation. But be courageous! I have overcome the world**" (John 16:2-4; 33).

When they arrived at the Mount of Olives, Jesus told His apostles, "My soul is deeply grieved, even to death. Stay here and watch with Me" (Matt. 26:38). Then, taking Peter, James and John, He went into the Garden of Gethsemane. "And when He arrived at the place, He said to them, 'Pray *that you* do not enter into temptation.' And He withdrew from them about a stone's throw; and falling to *His* knees, He prayed, saying, 'Father, if You are willing to take away this cup from Me—nevertheless, NOT MY WILL, BUT YOUR *WILL* BE DONE' " (Luke 22:40-42).

Jesus Knew He Could Not Escape Death

Even as He prayed to the Father, Jesus knew that the prophecies of His suffering and death must be fulfilled. As the Lord God of the Old Testament, He had given the first prophecy of His suffering to Adam and Eve in the presence of Satan, who would actually instigate His death (Gen. 3:15).

Jesus knew He was the Lamb of God, "slain"—already deemed as good as dead—from the "foundation" or beginning of this world (Rev. 13:8). He knew from the beginning that He was destined to die on this Passover day—Nisan 14, April 5, 30 AD. As the Lord God of the Old Testament, He had entered into a covenant with Abraham by passing between the parts of the sacrificial animals to pledge His own death (Gen. 15:5-18). At the beginning of the 14th, during the dark hours of the night, He had delivered to Abraham the promises of the covenant, foreshadowing the time when, as Jesus Christ, He would deliver the promises of the New Covenant. On the day portion of the 14th, the animals for the covenant sacrifice were slaughtered and their bodies were split asunder, allowing their blood to spill on the ground. During those same hours, the body of Jesus Christ would be beaten and broken open, and His blood would be poured out unto death. In the late afternoon of the 14th, the slaughtered animals lay still on the ground, and Abraham watched and waited. In like manner, Jesus' body would remain on the cross as the end of the 14th drew near, while his followers watched and waited (Luke 23:49). Although Jesus died at the "ninth hour," or approximately 3 PM, His body was not placed in the tomb until the 14th was ready to end at sunset.

At the exact time that Jesus would be buried, nearly 2000 years before, Abraham experienced a type of His death and burial: "And it came to pass, as the sun was going down, that **a deep sleep fell upon Abram. And, behold, a horror of great darkness fell upon him**" (Gen. 15:12). Abraham remained in this symbolic burial after the sun had gone down. When the darkness of night had come, the Lord God passed between the parts of the sacrifice: "And it came to pass—when the sun went down and it was dark—behold, a smoking furnace and a burning lamp passed between those pieces" (verse 17).

By this maledictory oath, God Himself confirmed that He would fulfill the covenant through His own death and burial. This event, which took place during the time of Abraham's "horror of great darkness," had a parallel fulfillment in Christ on the same day, at the same time of day, nearly two thousand years later. In fact, Jesus' burial was pictured by this "great darkness." Moreover, the only *sign* Jesus gave that He was the true Messiah of God was the length of time He would be "in the heart of the earth" (Matt. 12:40). Jesus was the only one Who actually foretold exactly how long He would be in the tomb. That "appointed" time period was specific, patterned after the prophet Jonah's time in the belly of a whale—**three *full* days and three *full* nights** (Matt. 12:39-40. Anything less meant that Jesus was not the Messiah. Indeed, as He lay in the "great darkness" of the tomb *for three days and three nights*, He was confirming that He was the Messiah Who would fulfill the promises of the New Covenant.

Jesus Knew That the Words of the Prophets Would All be Fulfilled

As the covenant sacrifice had foreshadowed and the prophets had foretold, the suffering and death that were appointed to Jesus would surely come to pass. Every detail would be fulfilled, exactly as recorded in Scripture. When Judas left His presence on that Passover night, Jesus knew that Judas was on his way to the authorities to betray Him, as it was written: "Even a man, my friend in whom I trusted, who ate of my bread, has lifted up his heel against me" (Psa. 41:9). Jesus also knew that the elders and the chief priests would pay Judas thirty pieces of silver to betray Him: "And I said to them, 'If *it is* good, give me my price; and if not, let it go.' So **they weighed my price—thirty *pieces* of silver**" (Zech. 11:12). Thirty pieces of silver was the price of a dead slave (Ex. 21:32).

Jesus also remembered the prophecy of Isaiah, that He would be led as a lamb to the slaughter:

> "***He is* despised and rejected of men**; a Man of sorrows, and acquainted with grief; and we hid as it were our faces from Him. He was despised, and we esteemed Him not. Surely He has borne our infirmities, and carried our sorrows; yet we esteemed Him stricken, smitten of God, and afflicted.
>
> "**But He *was* wounded for our transgressions; *He was* crushed for our iniquities; the chastisement of our peace *was* upon Him; and with His stripes we ourselves are healed**. All we like sheep have gone astray; we have turned each one to his own way; and **the LORD has laid on Him the iniquity of us all. He was oppressed, and He was afflicted; yet He opened not His mouth. He is brought as a lamb to the slaughter; and as a sheep before its shearers is dumb, so He opened not His mouth**.... He was cut off out of the land of the living; for the transgression of My people He *was* stricken.... **Yet the LORD willed to crush Him and He has put Him to grief: You shall make His life an offering for sin**.... He shall see of the travail of His soul. He shall be fully satisfied. By His knowledge shall My righteous Servant justify many; and He shall bear their iniquities... because He has poured out His soul to death; and He was counted among the transgressors; and He bore the sin of many, and made intercession for transgressors" (Isa. 53:3-12).

Jesus was fully aware that He would be mocked, beaten and spit upon, and would suffer a terrible scourging. The whip that would inflict His scourging would have tips of nails and glass and would literally rip the flesh off His body. After forty lashes—now **baptized in His own blood** streaming out of His back, chest and arms—He would be near death. He knew that this torturous ordeal would leave Him so horribly disfigured that He would be almost unrecognizable. Isaiah prophesied all of these things: "**I gave My back to the smiters, and My cheeks to them that plucked off the hair**; I did not hide My face from shame and spitting.... Many were astonished at Him—for ***His body was*** **so disfigured—even His form beyond that of the sons of men**" (Isa. 50:6; 52:14).

Jesus knew that the prophecy of David in Psalm 22 was about to be fulfilled. He would cry out these very words while He was hanging on the cross:

> "**My God, my God, why have You forsaken me**, and *why are You so* far from helping me, and from the words of my groaning? O my God, I cry in the daytime, but You do not answer; and in the night season, and am not silent.... But I am a worm, and no man; **a reproach of men and despised by the people**. All who see Me mock Me; they shoot out the lip; they shake the head, saying, 'He trusted on the LORD; let Him deliver Him; let Him rescue Him, since He delights in Him' " (Psa. 22:1-2, 6-8).

Even during the mocking and jeering of the people, priests and Pharisees, Jesus—**with His mind set like flint**—would trust God the Father as He had from His earliest days in the flesh:

> "For You are He Who took Me out of the womb, causing Me to trust while on My mother's breasts. I was cast upon You from birth; You are My God from My mother's womb. Be not far from Me; for trouble is near, for there is none to help. Many bulls have encircled around Me; strong bulls of Bashan have surrounded Me. They opened wide their mouths at Me, like a ravening and a roaring lion" (verses 9-13).

The next prophecies of David reveal the excruciating agony Jesus would suffer as His physical life drained away while hanging on the cross:

> "I am poured out like water, and all My bones are out of joint [from the jolt of the cross falling into its hole]; My heart is like wax; it is melted in the midst of My bowels [from loss of blood]. My strength is dried up like a potsherd, and My tongue clings to My jaws.

> "Dogs [the soldiers] have surrounded Me; a band of evildoers [the priests and Pharisees] have encircled me; **they have pierced My hands and My feet** [nailing Him to the cross]; and You have brought Me into the dust of death. **I can count all My bones** [because the flesh had been ripped open]; they look and gloat over Me [in astonishment because He was so disfigured]. **They divide My garments among them and cast lots upon My vesture**" (verses 14-18).

In the midst of this agonizing ordeal, Jesus would pray to God the Father for strength to endure His *baptism unto death* in His own blood:

> "But You, O LORD, be not far from Me; **O My strength, hasten to help Me!** Deliver My soul from the sword, My precious *life* from the power of the dog. Save Me from the lion's mouth; yea, and from the wild ox's horns. **You have answered Me**.... For He has not despised nor abhorred the affliction of the afflicted [Jesus Christ]; **and He has not hidden His face from Him, but when He cried to Him, He heard**" (verses 19-24).

These prophetic words of David show that God the Father would not absolutely forsake His Son at any time during His suffering and crucifixion, but would be with Him as He bore the sins of all mankind.

In Psalm 69, God inspired David to write more of the thoughts that Jesus would have while on the cross. Although He had lived a perfect life in the flesh and had never committing a single sin, Jesus would be hated and condemned to die by crucifixion, which was the fate of criminals. His death would bring certain danger to His disciples, and for a time He would even be rejected by His own physical brothers and sisters:

> "**Those who hate Me without a cause are more than the hairs of My head**; those who would cut Me off are mighty, being wrongfully My enemies.... Do not let those who wait on You, O Lord God of hosts, be ashamed for My sake; **let not the ones who seek You be ashamed for My sake**, O God of Israel, because **for Your sake I have borne reproach, shame has covered My face**. I have become a stranger to My brothers and a alien to My mother's children" (Psa. 69:4-8).

Jesus would endure all the shame and agony of the crucifixion, baptized in His own blood unto death, because of His deep love and zeal for God the Father:

> "**For the zeal of Your house has eaten Me up, and the reproaches of those who reproached You have fallen upon Me**.... Hear me, O LORD, for Your steadfast love is good; turn unto Me according to the multitude of Your tender mercies. And hide not Your face from Your servant, for I am in trouble; answer Me speedily. Draw near unto My soul and redeem it; deliver Me because of My enemies. **You have known My reproach, and My shame, and My dishonor** [being executed like a criminal]; My enemies are all before You. **Reproach has broken My heart, and I am full of heaviness; and I looked for some to take pity, but there was none; and for comforters, but I found none**. They also gave Me gall for My food; and in My thirst they gave Me vinegar to drink" (verses 9, 16-21).

Jesus knew He would have to bear this shameful and agonizing ordeal to the end. He knew His suffering would become so unbearable that He would feel as if the Father had abandoned Him. He knew that a spear would be thrust into the side of His body, as the prophet Zechariah was inspired to write: "And **they shall look upon Me Whom they have pierced**, and they shall mourn for Him, as one mourns for his only *son*, and shall be in bitterness over Him, as the bitterness over the firstborn" (Zech. 12:10).

Knowing that every one of these prophecies must be fulfilled, Jesus was in great anguish as He prayed to the Father. The thought of suffering such a hideous and merciless death was nearly overwhelming. Luke records, "Then an angel from heaven appeared to Him, strengthening Him. **And being in AGONY** [in His mind and spirit, knowing that all eternity hinged on this "appointed" day], **He prayed more earnestly. And His sweat became as great drops of blood falling down to the ground**" (Luke 22:43-44).

Jesus Looked Forward to the Kingdom of God

Throughout His suffering, Jesus would focus His mind on His coming resurrection and the Kingdom of God. He never doubted that He would be raised from the dead by the power of God the Father, and He looked forward to the time when He would give praise and glory to Him at the future resurrection of the saints, when His kingdom would be established over all the earth:

> "From You comes my praise in the great congregation; I will pay my vows before those who fear Him [the resurrected saints]. The meek shall eat and be satisfied; those who seek the LORD shall praise Him; may your heart live forever. All the ends of the earth shall remember and turn to the LORD [because of Jesus Christ's sacrifice for sin]; and all the families of the nations shall worship before You [at

His return], for the kingdom is the LORD'S and He rules over the nations.

"All the rich of the earth shall eat and worship; all those who go down to the dust shall bow before Him; even he who cannot keep his own soul alive. A seed shall serve Him; it shall be told of the LORD to the coming generation. They shall come and shall declare His righteousness unto a people that shall yet be born, that He has done this [through the crucifixion and resurrection of Jesus Christ]" (Psa. 22:25-31).

In the final words of His prayer before He was arrested, Jesus asked God the Father to restore Him to the glory that He had with the Father before the world existed. He also prayed for His disciples and for those who would become His disciples through the preaching of the Gospel, that they all might be one with Him and the Father:

"Jesus spoke these words, and lifted up His eyes to heaven and said, 'Father, **the hour has come** [the appointed time]; glorify Your own Son, so that Your Son may also glorify You; since You have given Him authority over all flesh, in order that He may give eternal life to all whom You have given Him. For this is eternal life, that they may know You, the only true God, and Jesus Christ, Whom You did send. **I have glorified You on the earth. I have finished the work that You gave Me to do.**

"And now, **Father, glorify Me with Your own self, with the glory that I had with You before the world existed.** I have manifested Your name to the men whom You have given Me out of the world. They were Yours, and You have given them to Me, and they have kept Your Word. Now they have known that all things that You have given Me are from You. For I have given them the words that You gave to Me; and they have received *them* and truly have known that I came from You; and they have believed that You did send Me.

"I am praying for them; I am not praying for the world, but for those whom You have given Me, for they are Yours. All Mine are Yours, and all Yours *are* Mine; and I have been glorified in them. **And I am no longer in the world, but these are in the world, and I am coming to You. Holy Father, keep them in Your name, those whom You have given Me, so that they may be one, even as We *are one.*** When I was with them in the world, I kept them in Your name. I protected those whom You have given Me, and not one of them has perished except the son of perdition, in order that the Scriptures might be fulfilled.

"But now I am coming to You; and these things I am speaking *while yet* in the world, that they may have My joy fulfilled in them. **I have given them Your words, and the world has hated them** because they are not of the world, just as I am not of the world. I do not pray that You would take them out of the world, but that You would **keep them from the evil one**. They are not of the world, just as I am not of the world. **Sanctify them in Your truth; Your Word is the truth.**

"Even as You did send Me into the world, I also have sent them into the world. **And for their sakes I sanctify Myself, so that they also may be sanctified in *Your* truth.** I do not pray for these only, but also for those who shall believe in Me through their word; that **they all may be one, even as You, Father, *are* in Me, and I in You; that they also may be one in Us**, in order that the world may believe that You did send Me.

"And I have given them the glory that You gave *to* Me, in order that they may be one, in the same way *that* We are one: I in them, and You in Me, that they may be perfected into one; and that the world may know that You did send Me, and have loved them as You have loved Me. Father, I desire that those whom You have given Me may also be with Me where I am, so that they may behold My glory, which You have given Me; because **You did love Me before *the* foundation of *the* world**. Righteous Father, the world has not known You; but I have known You, and these have known that You did send Me. **And I have made known Your name to them, and will make *it* known** [through His death and resurrection]; **so that the love with which You have loved Me may be in them, and I in them**" (John 17:1-26).

When Jesus finished this prayer, He arose and returned to His disciples. "After saying these things, Jesus went out with His disciples *to a place* beyond the winter stream of Kidron, where *there* was a garden into which He and His disciples entered. Judas, who was already in the process of betraying Him, also knew of the place, for Jesus had often gathered there with His disciples" (John 18:1-2).

The "appointed time" had come for Jesus to be betrayed into the hands of sinners, and to give His life for their sins and for the sins of the world. It was the death of God manifested in the flesh—*the Creator God!* **His death and only His death could pay for the sins of all mankind.**

Because of God's profound love for mankind, He personally and willingly took upon Himself the penalty for sin, which is death. Though He was made in the likeness of sinful flesh (Rom. 8:2-3), He never sinned. Thus, when He laid down His life, He could offer Himself as the perfect sacrifice for sin.

He would experience a cruel, vicious death not only at the hands of wicked and treacherous men, **but at the hands of Satan the devil, the author of sin and the enemy of God and man!** Could God manifested in the flesh conquer sin and overcome Satan by enduring the suffering and shame of the cross?

The truth is, there was no question about whether He would be able to endure the pain and agony of the beating, scourging and crucifixion. Why? What was Jesus' mindset? Notice this prophecy of Isaiah: "**I gave My back to the smiters, and My cheeks to them that plucked off the hair; I did not hide My face from shame and spitting, for the Lord GOD will help Me; therefore I have not been disgraced. On account of this I HAVE SET MY FACE LIKE A FLINT, and I know that I shall not be ashamed**" (Isa. 50:6-7).

In the book of Hebrews, the apostle Paul also wrote of Jesus' attitude: "[Jesus] Who **for the joy that lay ahead of Him endured *the* cross, *although* He despised *the* shame**, and has sat down at *the* right hand of the throne of God" (Heb. 12:2).

The very fact that Jesus was to die in this manner was the ultimate purpose for His coming in the flesh. He was to taste death for every person because He alone was the Savior of mankind:

> "But we see Jesus, Who *was* made a little lower than *the* angels, crowned with glory and honor **on account of suffering THE DEATH, in order that by *the* grace of God He Himself might taste death for everyone**; because it was fitting for Him, for Whom all things *were created*, and by Whom all things *exist*, in bringing many sons unto glory, to make the Author of their salvation perfect through sufferings. For both He Who is sanctifying and those who are sanctified *are* all of one; for which cause He is not ashamed to call them brethren, saying, 'I will declare Your name to My brethren; in *the* midst of *the* church I will sing praise to You.' And again, 'I will be trusting in Him.' And again, 'Behold, I and the children whom God has given Me' " (Heb. 2:9-13).

This is what Jesus must have been thinking as He finished His prayer. The moment had arrived! The time of His betrayal was at hand. Judas was coming. Jesus was ready.

The Ordeal Begins

His fervent prayers in the Garden of Gethsemane had brought Jesus strength from the Father (Luke 22:43). Determined to do His Father's will,

Jesus said to His apostles, "Behold, the hour has drawn near, and the Son of man is betrayed into *the* hands of sinners. Arise! Let us be going. Look, the one who is betraying Me is approaching" (Matt. 26:45-46).

Without hesitation, Jesus stepped forward to meet Judas, who was now possessed of Satan. The prophecy of His arrest was being fulfilled: "And immediately, while He was speaking, Judas, being one of the twelve, came up with a great multitude with swords and clubs, from the chief priests and the scribes and the elders. Now the one who was betraying Him had given them a sign, saying, '**Whomever I shall kiss, He is *the one*. Arrest Him** and take Him securely away.' And as soon as he came up to Him, he said, 'Master, Master,' and kissed Him earnestly. Then they laid their hands on Him and arrested Him" (Mark 14:43-46).

Jesus was arrested like a common criminal, exactly as the Scriptures had prophesied: "At that point Jesus said to the crowd, 'Have you come out to take Me with swords and clubs, as against a robber? I sat day after day with you, teaching in the temple, and you did not arrest Me. **But all this has happened so that the Scriptures of the prophets might be fulfilled**.' Then all the disciples forsook Him and fled [fulfilling the prophecy in Zechariah 13:7]" (Matt. 26:55-56).

As the chain of agonizing events unfolded—the false accusations and unjust trials, the cruel beatings, the humiliating mocking and spitting, the brutal scourging and a slow death by crucifixion—Jesus Christ remained steadfast in His love and loyalty to God the Father. But the disciples and women who looked upon Jesus' mutilated and bloodied body did not understand what they were witnessing. They stood afar off, watching His crucifixion in stunned bewilderment and disbelief that this could be happening to Jesus, Whom they believed to be the Son of God, their Savior. How could the promised Messiah be nailed to the cross in naked shame, dying before their very eyes? They had hoped that He would save them from the Roman oppression and establish the Kingdom of God. As they witnessed Jesus drawing His last breath, they must have thought, *There will be no salvation, not at this time or ever.* But they did not realize until after the resurrection that **the outpouring of Jesus' blood was the *beginning* of the salvation of the world!**

At precisely "the appointed time" planned from the very beginning, the Son of God died to atone for the sins of the world! As the God Who had created man, His death paid the penalty for the sins of every human being, opening the way for all mankind to receive the gift of eternal life. This was the beginning of the New Covenant, sealed with the body and the blood of Jesus Christ, which would bring salvation to all the world—at God's "appointed time."

Jesus the Messiah was **baptized in His own blood unto "THE DEATH**." This was His greatest work as God manifested in the flesh. Jesus Himself proclaimed with His last words, "**IT IS FINISHED!**" (John 19:30).

CHAPTER FIVE

The Appointed Time of the Messiah's Entombment and Resurrection

Jesus' Three Days and Three Nights in the Grave Set the Stage for His Resurrection

Scores of prophecies in the Old Testament foretold of the death and resurrection of Jesus Christ. The prophet Daniel foresaw that Jesus' life would be taken (Dan. 9:26), and both David and Isaiah described the suffering and humiliation that He would endure before His death (Psa. 22; Isa. 53). Other prophecies pointed to His resurrection to immortality (Psa. 16:10-11; Dan. 7:13 -14; Isa. 9:6-7). However, there is no passage in the Old Testament that foretells the length of time that the Messiah would be in the tomb before He was resurrected. This prophecy is found only in the Gospel accounts, spoken by Jesus Himself: "Then some of the scribes and Pharisees answered, saying, 'Master, we desire to see a sign from You.' And He answered and said to them, 'A wicked and adulterous generation seeks after a sign, but no sign shall be given to it except the sign of Jonah the prophet. For just as Jonah was in the belly of the whale three days and three nights, in like manner the Son of man shall be in the heart of the earth three days and three nights' " (Matt. 12:38-40). **Thus, Jesus *defined* His coming "appointed time" of being in the tomb. The fulfillment of this sign—the only sign Jesus gave that He was the Messiah—was a testimony not only to that generation, but to all future generations that He was, and is, the Christ.**

Nearly all churches within Christendom have misinterpreted or rejected the scriptural record. The majority of Christians today believe that Jesus was crucified and laid in a tomb on a Friday, and that He was resurrected on Sunday morning. Indeed, according to their reasoning, He was not actually in the tomb for three days and three nights, as He had prophesied, but for two nights and one full day—which, if true, would discredit Him as our Savior.

However, the Gospel accounts do not support the traditional belief in a "Good Friday" crucifixion and an "Easter Sunday" morning resurrection. The facts recorded by the Gospel writers reveal a significantly different time frame for the death and resurrection of Jesus Christ.

The Scriptural Definition of a Day

Almost universally, Orthodox Christian scholars claim Jesus was using an idiomatic expression when He declared that He would remain in the tomb for "three days and three nights"—suggesting that His words should be interpreted as referring to parts of days rather than to whole days. But when the scriptural use of the term "day" is examined, one finds that it is very specific. The Old Testament shows that a day consists of an evening and a morning (Gen. 1). An entire day has two portions—the night portion, which begins at evening or sunset, and the day portion, which begins at sunrise or morning. These consecutive periods are identified as one complete day, reckoned from sunset to sunset, or evening to evening (Lev. 23:32).

According to Scripture, each day has an average of 12 hours in the night portion and 12 hours in the day portion, making a complete day of 24 hours. Jesus Himself verified that the day portion is about 12 hours long (John 11:9.) This scriptural method of reckoning time had been used by the Hebrews for centuries.

"Three Days and Three Nights" in the Book of Jonah

Christ's own prophecy that He would be in the grave for three days and three nights is a direct reference to Jonah 1:17, which speaks of Jonah's symbolic entombment in the belly of a great fish: "Now the LORD had prepared a great fish to swallow up Jonah. And Jonah was in the belly of the fish three days and three nights."

The construction of the Hebrew text does not allow the expression "three days and three nights" to be interpreted in any manner except the literal sense of three 24-hour days. In Hebrew, the phrase "a day and a night" defines a full day as 24 hours. In the same way, the expression "three days and three nights" refers to three whole days of 24 hours each.

The Hebrew terminology cannot be interpreted as an idiomatic expression characterizing part of a day and part of a night. To delineate incomplete units of time, the Hebrew uses a word that means "to divide"—such as in Daniel 12:7, where the term is translated "half a time." However, this word is not found in the expression "three days and three nights" recorded in Jonah 1:17. It is evident that the text is describing three complete 24-hour periods of time. Fully aware of this fact of Scripture, Jesus declared to the Jews that He would be in the heart of the earth for "three days and three nights" (Matt. 12:40).

Jesus Said He Would Rise Three Days After His Death

The Gospel writers record that Jesus made specific statements to His disciples concerning the length of time that He would be in the tomb and when He would be resurrected: "And He began to teach them that it was necessary for the Son of man to suffer many things, and to be rejected by the elders and chief priests and scribes, and to be killed, but **after three days** to rise from the dead" (Mark 8:31; see also Matt. 16:21 and Mark 9:31). Jesus explained to His disciples that He would not rise from the dead until three days after He had been killed.

Jesus' statement that He would rise three days after He had died is acutely significant. According to Jewish law, to be declared legally dead, a person must be dead for three full days or more. Therefore, if Jesus had risen from the dead before 3 PM on the afternoon of Nisan 17, a weekly Sabbath, He would not have been considered legally dead. Consequently, His return to life would not have been considered a true resurrection from the dead.

If He had been crucified on a Friday and restored to life on Sunday morning at sunrise, His death would not have been "valid" since only two nights and one day would have passed between Friday sunset and Sunday morning. In order for His death to be publicly recognized and acknowledged, it was necessary for Jesus to remain in the grave for three complete nights and three complete days before He was raised from the dead.

The Scriptures reveal that Jesus died at the ninth hour of the day, or 3 PM, on the Passover day, Nisan 14, which fell on Wednesday, April 5, in 30 AD (Matt. 27:46; Mark 15:34). He was placed in the tomb just before sunset at about 6 PM. Matthew describes His burial by Joseph of Arimathea: "And when evening was coming on, a rich man of Arimathea came, named Joseph, who was himself a disciple of Jesus. After going to Pilate, he begged to have the body of Jesus. Then Pilate commanded the body to be given over to him. And after taking the body, Joseph [with the help of Nicodemus (John 19:39)] wrapped it in clean linen cloth, and placed it in his new tomb, which he had hewn in the rock; and after rolling a great stone to the door of the tomb, he went away" (Matt. 27:57-60). Luke records that "a Sabbath was coming on" (Luke 23:54), which means that by the time they had closed the entrance of the tomb with a huge stone—at about 6 PM—a Sabbath was nearly upon them. Since all Sabbaths are reckoned from sunset to sunset, it is clear that the sun was about to set.

Jesus was resurrected from the dead exactly three days and three nights later, when the sun was setting at the end of the weekly Sabbath, or Saturday, Nisan 17. As He had prophesied, He remained in the tomb for three full days and three full nights. Jesus Christ was raised from the dead just before sunset on the weekly Sabbath, the seventh day of the week. He had already been resurrected for nearly twelve hours when the sun rose on Sunday, the first day of the week.

Two Sabbaths During the Three Days and Three Nights

According to Orthodox Christian tradition, Jesus was crucified on a Friday—which appears to be supported by the statement in John 19:31 that the day of His death "was the preparation [day]." Most have assumed that this statement refers to the Jews' preparation on Friday for the weekly Sabbath. However, they fail to realize that the Passover day, on which Jesus died, has always been a preparation day for the Feast of Unleavened Bread, which immediately follows (Lev. 23:4-6). The first day of this feast, Nisan

15, is observed as a high day—an annual Sabbath. The day portion of the Passover (Nisan 14) is always used as a day of preparation for this yearly holy day. It is erroneous to interpret "the preparation day" in John 19:31 as evidence that the day of the crucifixion was a Friday.

The Scriptures clearly demonstrate that during the crucifixion week there were *two* Sabbaths. The first Sabbath was an annual holy day, the first day of Unleavened Bread, which fell on Thursday that year. The second Sabbath was the weekly Sabbath, the seventh day of the week, or Saturday. Thus, during that week there were two preparation days. The day portion of Nisan 14, the Passover day, was the preparation day for the first day of the Feast of Unleavened Bread, the 15th, which was an annual Sabbath. The following day, the 16th, which was a Friday, was the preparation day for the weekly Sabbath, the 17th.

In reading the Gospel of John, it is "clear-cut" that the Sabbath following the day Jesus died was an annual Sabbath. "The Jews therefore, so that the bodies might not remain on the cross on the Sabbath, because it was a preparation day (for that Sabbath was a high day)..." (John 19:31). The term "high day" is never used to refer to the weekly Sabbath, but only to annual Sabbaths. John's use of this term makes it clear that the Sabbath which was about to begin was the first day of the Feast of Unleavened Bread, Nisan 15.

Mindful of the annual Sabbath, the women who followed Jesus could not purchase spices on that day because all the businesses were closed in observance of the command to rest (Lev. 23:6-7). At the conclusion of the high day, they bought spices and aromatic oils to anoint Jesus. "Now when the Sabbath had passed, Mary Magdalene and Mary, the mother of James, and Salome bought aromatic oils, so that they might come and anoint Him" (Mark 16:1).

The women bought the spices "when the Sabbath had passed" and prepared them on the same day. When they had finished, they observed a second Sabbath. "And they returned to the city, and prepared spices and ointments, and then rested on the [weekly] Sabbath according to the commandment" (Luke 23:56). The Gospel accounts note clearly the observance of two Sabbaths during the crucifixion week.

"Today Is the Third Day Since These Things Took Place"

Those who embrace a Sunday resurrection point to Luke 24:21 as evidence that Jesus rose from the dead at sunrise on the first day of the week. This statement was made by two of Jesus' disciples as they walked along with a "stranger"—not knowing that the stranger was actually the resurrected Christ. As Jesus listened to their conversation, He asked what "things" they were talking about. They answered, "Concerning Jesus of Nazareth, which was a prophet mighty in deed and word before God and all the people: and how the chief priests and our rulers delivered him to be con-

The Three Days and Three Nights In After Three Days

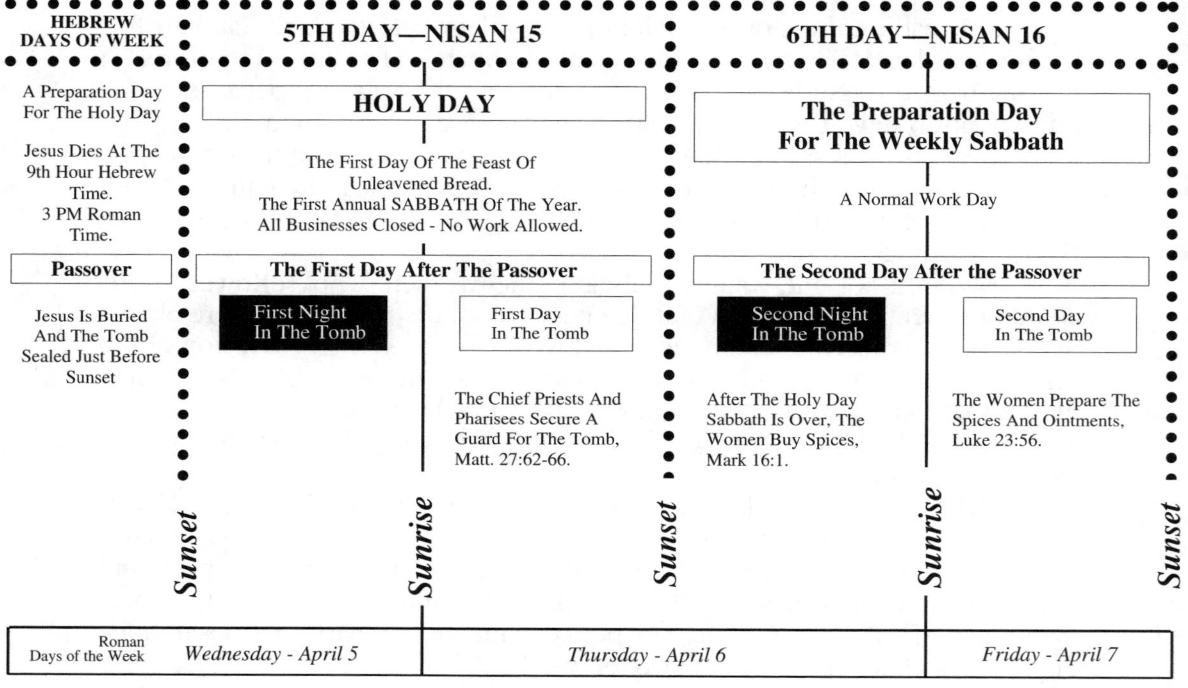

The Key To The Time Period From The Burial To The Resurrection:
Jesus Said He Would Be In The Heart Of The Earth (The Tomb)
Three Days And Three Nights, A Complete 72-Hour Period.

Matt. 12:38-40; 27:63
Mark 8:31; 9:31
Luke 13:32; 18:33; 24:7, 46

John 2:18-22
Acts 10:40
1 Cor. 15:4

the Tomb and the Resurrection and Three Nights

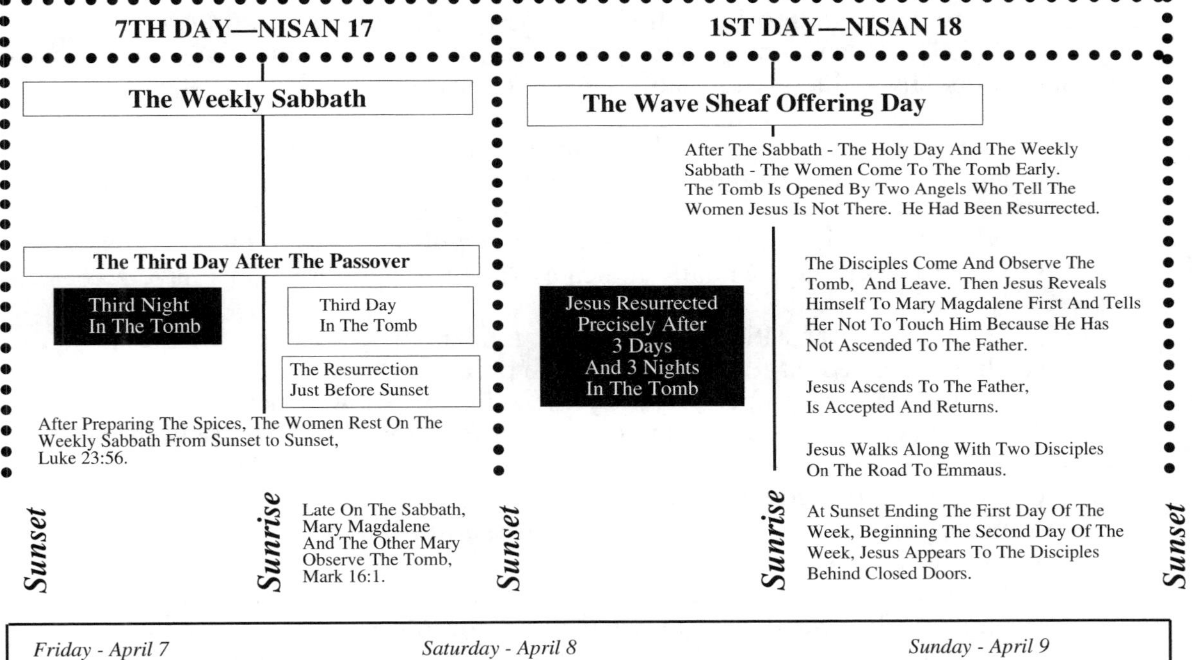

Knowledge of a Wednesday crucifixion was passed down for at least three centuries after the founding of the apostolic church. The *Didascalia*, which dates from the third century, offers historical evidence that the belief in a Friday crucifixion was a change from the original teaching. The following description of the day of Jesus' crucifixion appears in Book V of the *Apostolic Constitutions*, which contains the original words of the *Didascalia*:

"**For they began to hold a council against the Lord on the second day of the week**, in the first month, which is Xanthicus; and the deliberation continued on the third day of the week; **but on the fourth day [Wednesday] they determined to take away His life by crucifixion**" (*Apostolic Constitutions—Didascalia Apostolorum*, book V, section I, paragraph xiv). A church historian explains the significance of this record in the *Didascalia*: "...the only reason can have been that **Jesus' passion began on a Wednesday, i.e., the day when He was arrested [and crucified]**" (Lietzmann, *A History of the Early Church*, p. 69).

demned to death, and have crucified him. But we trusted that it had been he which should have redeemed Israel: and beside all this, today is the third day since these things were done" (Luke 24:13-21, *KJV*).

Because this statement was made on the first day of the week, many have incorrectly assumed that Jesus rose from the dead early Sunday morning. However, the Gospel accounts clearly show that Jesus had already risen from the dead before the women came to the tomb at sunrise. There is no question that Jesus was in the tomb for "three days and three nights"—beginning at sunset on Wednesday, Nisan 14, and ending at sunset on the weekly Sabbath, Nisan 17. Jesus rose at the end of three full days and three full nights, exactly as He had declared.

The problem with Luke 24:21, according to A. T. Robertson, is that the phrase "today is the third day" is an idiomatic expression—and is most difficult to translate into English (*Word Pictures in the New Testament*, on Luke 24:21). Because the phrase is idiomatic, its actual meaning cannot be understood by a literal translation—which only serves to cloud the true meaning.

With this in mind, scholars and translators have studied how such idiomatic expressions were used by various writers of that era—such as the historian Josephus and others who used classical Greek. What they have discovered is that the idiom is an expression of *completed* time. In other words, "today is the third day" actually indicates "as of today, three days have already passed."

Berkley's translation, for example, renders the phrase as "three days have already passed"; Moffat translates the phrase as "three days ago." Both of these translations properly convey the idiom to show a period of time which has been completed. Based on this information, a precise translation of Luke 24:21 would be: "But besides all these things, as of today, the third day has already passed since these things took place." Thus, Luke 24:21 in no way supports the teaching that Jesus was raised from the dead on the first day of the week at sunrise.

Just as He foretold, Jesus was entombed for *exactly* three days and three nights. This was "the appointed time" the Messiah was to be in the grave—which was followed immediately by "the appointed time" of His resurrection on the evening ending the weekly Sabbath.

CHAPTER SIX

The Appointed Time of The Father's Acceptance of the Risen Jesus

How the Wave Sheaf Offering Pictures Jesus' Acceptance as the First of the Firstfruits

The scriptural records and the computations of the Calculated Hebrew Calendar (CHC) prove conclusively that "the appointed time" of Jesus' resurrection occurred as the sun was *setting* toward the end of the weekly Sabbath. Although the Gospel accounts do not give specific details, we can piece together what Jesus must have done from the time He was resurrected until He ascended into heaven the following morning to be *accepted* by God the Father as the true, premier "wave sheaf offering." As we will see, Jesus' ascension to heaven was for the specific purpose of being *accepted* by the Father as the "first of the firstfruits"—a crucial "appointed time" in the role of the Messiah.

The account in the Gospel of John gives us an understanding of what Jesus did first when He came back to life in the tomb: "Then Simon Peter came following him, and he went into the tomb and **saw the linen cloths lying, and the napkin that had been on His head, not lying with the linen cloths but folded up in a place by itself**" (John 20:6-7). This shows that when Jesus came back to life, He rose straight out of the burial wrappings without disturbing them. When Peter entered the tomb, he saw Jesus' burial wrappings still in the form of His body. This was absolute proof that Jesus had risen from the dead, and that no one had taken His body (if someone had taken away His body, it would still have been wrapped with the linen burial cloths).

After rising out of the burial wrappings, Jesus took off the napkin that covered His head and neatly folded it and placed it close by, separate from the other burial cloths. This was another proof that He had been resurrected. If anyone had taken His body, the napkin would have either remained on His head or fallen to the ground. It would not have been folded and placed neatly by itself. The apostle John, who was with Peter, saw these things and believed (verse 8).

Upon folding the napkin, Jesus undoubtedly offered a prayer of thanksgiving to God the Father for raising Him back to life. Perhaps Jesus thought of the prophecy of His resurrection in Psalm 16: "The LORD is the portion of My inheritance and of My cup; You shall uphold My lot. The lines have fallen to Me in pleasant places; yea, I have a beautiful inheritance.... Therefore My heart is glad, and My glory rejoices; **My flesh also**

shall rest in hope, for You will not abandon My soul to the grave; neither will You allow Your Holy One to see corruption. You will make known to Me the path of life; in Your presence is fullness of joy. At Your right hand are pleasures forevermore" (verses 5-6, 9-11).

After offering His prayer of thanksgiving, Jesus left the tomb. In fact, it is certain that He left almost immediately after He was resurrected. Remember, Jesus had said that "the Son of man shall be in the heart of the earth three days and three nights." If He had remained in the tomb for any length of time after His resurrection, He would have been in the heart of the earth for more than three days and three nights.

When Jesus was resurrected from the dead, He was once again a Spirit Being and had the ability to pass through matter. Therefore, He did not need to have the stone removed from the entrance of the tomb in order to leave. He simply walked through the stone and left. Luke records that approximately twenty-four hours after His resurrection, Jesus suddenly appeared in a *closed* room where the disciples were assembled. This took place late on the first day of the week, after He had walked with two of the disciples to the village of Emmaus: "And they [the two disciples] rose up that very hour *and* returned to Jerusalem; and they found the eleven and those with them assembled together, saying, 'In truth, the Lord has risen! And He has appeared to Simon.' Then they related the things that had happened *to them* on the road, and how He was known to them in the breaking of the bread. Now as they were telling these things, **Jesus Himself stood in their midst** and said to them, 'Peace *be* to you' "(Luke 24:33-36).

The apostle John also wrote of Jesus' sudden appearance: "Afterwards, as evening was drawing near that day, the first *day* of the weeks, and **the doors were shut where the disciples had assembled for fear of the Jews, Jesus came and stood in the midst**, and said to them, 'Peace *be* to you.' And after saying this, He showed them His hands and His side. Then the disciples rejoiced, *because* they had seen the Lord" (John 20:19-20).

Where did Jesus go after He left the tomb? The Scriptures do not specify. However, it is probable that He went to a place on the Mount of Olives. Luke records that Jesus was accustomed to going there—where He had a special place of prayer. On the Passover night, after Jesus instituted the New Covenant ceremony, He and the disciples had gone to the Mount of Olives: **"Then He left *the house and* went, as He was accustomed, to the Mount of Olives**; and His disciples also followed Him. And when He arrived at the place, He said to them, 'Pray *that you* do not enter into temptation.' **And He withdrew from them about a stone's throw; and falling to *His* knees, He prayed**" (Luke 22:39-41).

In his account, Matthew identifies the place of prayer as Gethsemane: "Then Jesus came with them to a place called Gethsemane; and He said to His disciples, 'Sit here, while I go onward and pray' " (Matt. 26:36). This is the place where Jesus prayed for nearly three hours before He was arrested (verses 37-44).

Since Jesus did not ascend to the Father until the morning after His resurrection, it is likely He went to the Mount of Olives to His special place of prayer in the Garden of Gethsemane. Once there, Jesus would have offered up prayers of praise and thanksgiving to God the Father during the entire night for having raised Him from the dead. We are able get a glimpse of what Jesus might have prayed from the prophecies in the book of Psalms that foretold Jesus' death and resurrection.

Jesus Christ had unwavering faith that God the Father would raise Him from the dead. Psalm 108 verifies Jesus' faith for that deliverance: "O God, My heart is fixed; I will sing and I will give praise, even with My glory. Awake, harp and lyre; I will awake early. **I will praise You, O LORD, among the people; and I will sing praises to You among the nations**, for Your mercy is great above the heavens; and Your truth reaches unto the clouds.

"**Be exalted, O God, above the heavens, and Your glory above all the earth, so that Your beloved** [Jesus Christ, the Father's beloved Son] **may be delivered** [from the power of death]; **save with Your right hand**, and answer Me. God has spoken in His holiness [to raise Jesus from the dead]: "I will rejoice…" (Psa. 108:1-7).

Paul's epistle to the Hebrews testifies that while Jesus was still in the flesh He cried out to the Father to save Him from death: "Who, in the days of His flesh, **offered up both prayers and supplications with strong crying and tears to Him Who was able to save Him from death, and was heard because *He* feared *God***. Although He was a Son, *yet* He learned obedience from the things that He suffered; and having been perfected, He became *the* Author of eternal salvation to all those who obey Him…" (Heb. 5:7-9). During His life in the flesh, Jesus prayed fervently to the Father for strength to resist temptation. Because He prayed so fervently before He died, He must have been equally fervent in thanking and praising the Father for having raised Him from the dead.

We know that the words of Psalm 22 were uttered by Jesus as He was dying on the cross. The following psalm, Psalm 23, has far more meaning when viewed in the context of His crucifixion and resurrection. Could He not also have uttered these words in His prayers to God the Father after He was resurrected?

> "The LORD is My Shepherd; I shall not want [lack any thing]. He makes Me to lie down in green pastures; He leads Me beside the still waters. He restores My soul [by the resurrection]; He leads Me in the paths of righteousness for His name's sake. Yea, though I walk through the valley of the shadow of death [the crucifixion], I will fear no evil, for You are with Me; Your rod and Your staff, they comfort Me. You prepare a table for Me in the presence of My enemies. You anoint My head with oil; My cup runs over. Surely goodness

> and mercy shall follow Me all the days of My life, and I shall dwell in the house of the LORD forever [into the ages of eternity]."

The Morning After Jesus' Resurrection

The Gospel accounts show that as the sun was rising, early in the morning on the first day of the week, the women came bringing spices to anoint Jesus' body. Although Mary Magdalene left home while it was still dark, by the time she arrived at the tomb it was light enough for her to see that the stone had been removed (John 20:1). Apparently, just before she and the other women arrived, an angel had opened the tomb. If it had been opened for any length of time before the women arrived, the soldiers would not have been standing guard. "And *in the morning* suddenly there was a great earthquake; for an angel of *the* Lord descended from heaven, and came and rolled away the stone from the door, and sat upon it. Now his appearance was as lightning, and his raiment white as snow. And for fear of him, those who were keeping guard trembled, and became as dead *men*" (Matt. 28:2-4).

As the women were approaching the tomb, they were wondering who would roll away the huge stone from the entrance of the tomb in order for them to anoint Jesus' body with the spices. But when they arrived, they saw that the stone had already been removed and the tomb was open. Mark gives this account: "And very early on the first *day* of the weeks, at the rising of the sun, they were coming to the tomb; and they were asking themselves, 'Who will roll away the stone for us from the entrance to the tomb?' For it was a massive *stone*. **But when they looked up, they saw that the stone had been rolled away**. And after entering the tomb, they saw a young man [the angel who had rolled away the stone] sitting on the right, clothed in a white robe; and they were very frightened. But he said to them, **'Do not be afraid. You are seeking Jesus the Nazarene, Who was crucified. He has risen; He is not here. Look, *there is* the place where they laid Him**. But go, tell His disciples and Peter that He goes before you into Galilee; there you shall see Him, as He said to you.' And they went out quickly and fled from the tomb, for trembling and astonishment had seized them; and they did not say anything to anyone because they were afraid" (Mark 16:2-8).

The Gospel account is emphatic! The angel told the women, "**He is risen. He is not here**." **Jesus was not in the tomb**! Jesus was not there because He had been resurrected from the dead as the weekly Sabbath ended over twelve hours earlier. He did not need the stone to be rolled away to leave the tomb, because He had the power to pass through matter. However, it was obligatory for the stone to be removed in order for the women to see He was not there. They found the tomb empty except for the grave cloths that had been wound around His body.

When the other women left to tell the disciples, Mary Magdalene ran to tell Peter and John:

> "Then she ran and came to Simon Peter and to the other disciple whom Jesus loved, and said to them, 'They have taken away the Lord from the tomb, and we do not know where they have laid Him.' As a result, Peter and the other disciple went out and came to the tomb. Now the two ran together, but the other disciple ran faster than Peter and came to the tomb first; and he stooped down *and* saw the linen cloths lying *there*, but he did not enter.
>
> "Then Simon Peter came following him, and he went into the tomb and saw the linen cloths lying, and the napkin that had been on His head, not lying with the linen cloths but folded up in a place by itself. Then the other disciple, who had come to the tomb first, also went in and saw *these things*; and he believed. For they did not yet understand the scripture *which decreed* that He must rise from *the* dead. Then the disciples went away again to their *home*" (John 20:2-10).

When Peter and John left, Mary Magdalene remained at the tomb because she thought that "they had taken away the Lord," and she did not know where He was. "But Mary stood outside the tomb weeping; and as she wept, she stooped down *and looked* into the tomb. And she saw two angels in white who were sitting, one at the head and the other at the feet, where the body of Jesus had been laid. And they said to her, 'Woman, why are you weeping?' She said to them, 'Because they have taken away my Lord, and I do not know where they have laid Him' " (John 20:11-13).

Aware of Mary's dedication and unfailing love, Jesus returned to the tomb and appeared to her:

> "And after saying these things, she turned around and saw Jesus standing, but did not know that it was Jesus. Jesus said to her, 'Woman, why are you weeping? Whom are you seeking?' Thinking that He was the gardener, she said to Him, 'Sir, if you have carried Him off, tell me where you have laid Him, and I will take Him away.' Jesus said to her, 'Mary.' Turning around, she said to Him, 'Rabboni'; that is to say, 'Teacher.' Jesus said to her, **'Do not touch Me, because I have not yet ascended to My Father.** But go to My brethren and tell them that I am ascending to My Father and your Father, and My God and your God.' Mary Magdalene came to the disciples, bringing word that she had seen the Lord, and that He had said these things to her" (verses 14-18).

Correcting the Misinterpretation of Mark 16:9

In the *King James Version*, Mark 16:9 reads as follows: "**Now when *Jesus* was risen early the first day of the week,** He appeared first to Mary Magdalene…." This translation incorrectly makes it appear that Jesus was resurrected early in the morning on the first day of the week. However, the Gospel accounts unquestionably show that Jesus was raised at the *close* of the weekly Sabbath, approximately 12 hours before the women came to the tomb. The erroneous impression that the *KJV* translation gives can be corrected simply by the addition of a comma in the proper place: "**Now when *Jesus* was risen,** early *the* first *day* of the week He appeared…." A more accurate translation, *with the comma*, clears up any misunderstanding: "**Now after Jesus had risen**, early *the* first *day* of the week He appeared first to Mary Magdalene…." With the proper placement of the comma, this verse harmonizes with the rest of the scriptural facts as found in the other Gospel accounts.

Jesus Fulfilled the Wave Sheaf Offering

In John's Gospel we find this post-resurrection account: "Jesus said to her [Mary Magdalene], '**Do not touch Me, because I have not yet ascended to My Father**. But go to My brethren and **tell them that I am ascending to My Father and your Father, and My God and your God**' " (John 20:17).

When Jesus appeared to Mary Magdalene, He did not allow her to touch Him because He had not yet ascended to God the Father. The words that He spoke to her show that He was about to ascend. We can conclude that He ascended to the Father soon after she left to tell the disciples. When Jesus ascended, **He fulfilled a very special Temple ceremony that God had commanded for this day**. This ceremony was the presentation of the wave sheaf offering of the *first of the firstfruits* of the grain harvest, which was performed at approximately 9 AM in the morning, after the morning burnt offering had been made. It was at this "appointed time" that Jesus, the resurrected Messiah, ascended to God the Father.

The wave sheaf was offered each year on the first day of the week during the Feast of Unleavened Bread. As the sacrifice of the Passover lamb was a fore-type of the crucifixion and death of Jesus Christ, so the offering of **the wave sheaf was a fore-type of Jesus' ascension to the Father**. This day was a special day, but not a holy day. At the Temple, on the first day of the week during the Feast of Unleavened Bread, the priest would perform the wave sheaf ritual. We find God's command for the wave sheaf offering in the book of Leviticus: "And the LORD spoke to Moses, saying, 'Speak to the children of Israel and say to them, "When you have come into the land which I give to you, and shall reap the harvest of it, then you shall bring *the premier* sheaf of the firstfruits of your harvest to the priest. And he shall wave the sheaf before the LORD to be accepted for you. On the next day after the [weekly] Sabbath [the first day of the week during the Feast of Unleavened Bread] the priest shall wave it" ' " (Lev. 23:9-11).

Messianic Rabbi Alfred Edersheim records the details of the harvesting of the wave sheaf in his book *The Life and Times of Jesus the Messiah:*

> "This Passover-sheaf was reaped in public the evening before it was offered, and it was to witness this ceremony that the crowd had gathered around the elders. Already on the 14th [of] Nisan the spot whence the first sheaf was to be reaped had been marked out, by tying together in bundles, while still standing, the barley that was to be cut down, according to custom, in the sheltered Ashes-Valley across Kidron. When the time for cutting the sheaf had arrived—that is, on the evening of the 15th [of] Nisan [by Pharisaic reckoning], even though it were a Sabbath [the journey to harvest was undertaken before the end of the Sabbath, but was within the prescribed traditional "Sabbath day's journey"], just as the sun went down, three men, each with a sickle and basket, set to work.
>
> "Clearly to bring out what was distinctive in the ceremony, they first asked of the bystanders three times each of these questions: 'HAS THE SUN GONE DOWN?' 'With this sickle?' 'Into this basket?' 'On this Sabbath? (or first Passover-day)'—and lastly, 'Shall I reap?' Having each time been answered in the affirmative, they cut down barley to the amount of one *ephah*, or about three pecks and three pints of our English measure" (*The Life and Times of Jesus the Messiah,* p. 619).

There was a dispute between the Pharisees and the Sadducees as to *which Sabbath* this verse is describing. The Pharisees applied this command to the first holy day of the Feast of Unleavened Bread, which was the 15th day of the first month. In their view, the "morrow after the Sabbath"—the day for harvesting the wave sheaf—was always the 16th of Nisan. On the other hand, the Sadducees, who were in charge of the Temple during the days of Christ, understood that God's command in Leviticus 23:11 was referring to the *weekly* Sabbath which occurred in conjunction with the Feast of Unleavened Bread. In years when the first day of the Feast of Unleavened Bread fell on the weekly Sabbath, both the Sadducees and the Pharisees would observe the 16th of Nisan as the day for the wave sheaf offering. Although the Sadducees and the Pharisees generally disagreed over the correct *day* for the wave sheaf offering, there was never any question about the correct *time* of the day for harvesting it.

After it was cut, the bundled sheaf was brought to the Temple and placed alongside the altar of burnt offering. Then, in the *morning*, after the daily burnt offering of a lamb, the priest would "wave" or elevate the sheaf to be accepted of the Lord. This was a special ceremonial sheaf. In *The Shocken Bible*, Volume I, The Five Books of Moses, Everett Fox translates Leviticus 23:10-11 in this manner: "Speak to the children of Israel and say to them; When you enter the land that I am giving you, and you harvest its harvest, you are to bring **the premier sheaf** of your harvest to the priest. He is to elevate the sheaf before the presence of YHWH for acceptance for you; on the morrow of the Sabbath the priest shall elevate it."

Especially note the key words in God's instructions for the wave sheaf offering: "for acceptance for you," meaning "on your behalf." When Jesus Christ ascended to the Father on the wave sheaf day, *as the first of the firstfruits*, His sacrifice for our sins was accepted by the Father on our behalf. Jesus, as the Lamb of God, was *accepted* as the sin offering not only for our sins but for the sins of all mankind—as "the lamb of God, Who takes away the sin of the world" (John 1:29).

Jesus fulfilled the wave sheaf offering as the *first* of the firstfruits to be *resurrected* from the dead. The premier sheaf symbolized the risen Christ. When the priest elevated the sheaf to be accepted by the Lord, it represented Jesus Christ *ascending* to the Father to be accepted as the first of the firstfruits. The apostle Paul makes it clear that this premier sheaf of the firstfruits was a type of Jesus Christ after He rose from the dead and ascended into heaven to present Himself to God the Father: "But now Christ has been raised from *the* dead; **He has become the firstfruit of those who have fallen asleep**. For since by man *came* death, by man also *came the* resurrection of *the* dead. For as in Adam all die, so also in Christ shall all be made alive. But each one in his own order: **Christ *the* firstfruit;** then, those who are Christ's at His coming" (I Cor. 15:20-23).

Because Jesus is the first of the many who will be resurrected from the dead as immortal children of God, He is also called "the firstborn from among the dead," as Paul writes to the Colossians: "Because by Him were all things created, the things in heaven and the things on earth, the visible and the invisible, whether *they be* thrones, or lordships, or principalities, or powers: all things were created by Him and for Him. And He is before all, and by Him all things subsist. **And He is the Head of the body, the church; Who is *the* beginning, *the* firstborn from among the dead, so that in all things He Himself might hold the preeminence**" (Col. 1:16-18).

In his epistle to the Romans, Paul makes it clear that *many* will be resurrected from the grave and be added to the Family of God as immortal, spirit-born brethren of Christ: "Because those whom He did foreknow, He also predestinated *to be* conformed to the image of His own Son, **that He might be *the* firstborn among many brethren**" (Rom. 8:29). Paul also tells the Corinthians that those who die in the faith will be resurrected at His coming. The resurrection of the saints of God to immortality and glory will mark the *end of the firstfruits harvest*, just as the resurrection of Jesus signaled its beginning. As He ascended to heaven in the clouds, so He will return, and all the transformed saints will rise into the air to meet Him. The entrance of the saints into the Family of God has been made possible through the sacrifice of Jesus Christ, which was accepted by God the Father on the wave sheaf day.

Jesus Christ Accepted by God the Father

The ascension of Jesus to God the Father was an awesome event. Christ had finished the work that the Father had given Him to do. As God manifest in the flesh, He had lived a perfect, sinless life and had died by crucifixion to become the perfect sacrifice for the sins of all mankind. At the *appointed time*, God the Father had raised Jesus back to life, and on the wave sheaf day He was ready to ascend to the throne of God the Father to be accepted as the first of the firstfruits, the firstborn among many brethren, and the perfect sacrifice to propitiate the sins of the world—all in fulfillment of the "appointed times" of the Messiah.

As He was ascending to the Father, Jesus must have been filled with great joy and anticipation. He would see the Father face-to-face for the first time since He had become a pinpoint of life when He divested Himself of His power and glory as God to be born of the virgin Mary. Again, the Psalms help us comprehend some of the thoughts and feelings that Jesus might have experienced as He looked forward to being reunited with the Father: "**O God, You are My God**, early I will seek You! My soul thirsts for You. My flesh longs for You, as in a dry and thirsty land where no water is, **to see Your power and Your glory—as I have seen You in the sanctuary**. Because Your loving-kindness is better than life, My lips shall praise You" (Psa. 63:1-3).

As previously noted, Psalm 23 foreshadowed the prayers of Jesus *after* He was resurrected from the dead. The psalm to follow, Psalm 24, is in prophetic sequence and depicts Jesus' ascension to be received of God the Father. When He arrived in heaven, the angels sang and shouted for joy. Perhaps this psalm was sung by the angels as they opened the everlasting doors and announced that the King of glory was entering into the presence of God the Father:

> "The earth is the LORD'S, and the fullness of it, the world, and those who dwell in it, for He has founded it upon the seas and established it upon the waters. **Who shall ascend into the hill of the LORD? Or who shall stand in His holy place? He who has clean hands and a pure heart, who has not lifted up his soul to vanity and has not sworn deceitfully** [the perfect life of Jesus Christ]. **He shall receive the blessing from the LORD and righteousness from the God of his salvation**.
>
> "**Lift up your heads, O you gates; and be lifted up, O you everlasting doors; that the King of glory may come in.**

> **Who is this King of glory? The LORD strong and mighty, the LORD mighty in battle** [He was victorious over human nature, sin, Satan the devil and death]. **Lift up your heads, O you gates; lift them up, you everlasting doors; that the King of glory may come in. Who is this King of glory? The LORD of hosts, He is the King of glory**" (Psa. 24:1-5, 7-10).

What a magnificent scene of splendor and glory Jesus would have seen when He entered through the everlasting gates of heaven! Standing on the sea of glass, He would have seen the resplendent glory and awesome majesty of God the Father seated on His throne with the heavenly host round about. The apostle John, the one whom Jesus loved, saw a vision of God's throne and recorded it in the book of Revelation. What John recorded is what Jesus would have seen when He ascended to the Father.

> "After these things I looked, and behold, **a door opened in heaven**, and the first voice that I heard *was* as if a trumpet were speaking with me, saying, 'Come up here, and I will show you *the* things that must take place after these things.' And immediately I was in *the* Spirit; and **behold, a throne was set in heaven, and *one was* sitting on the throne**. And He Who *was* sitting was in appearance like a jasper stone and a sardius stone: and a rainbow *was* around the throne, like an emerald in its appearance.
>
> "And around the throne *were* twenty-four thrones, and on the thrones I saw twenty-four elders sitting, clothed in white garments; and they had on their heads golden crowns. **And proceeding from the throne were lightnings and thunders and voices**; and seven lamps of fire, which are the seven Spirits of God, *were* burning before the throne. **And before the throne *was* a sea of glass, like crystal. And around the throne and over the throne *were* four living creatures, full of eyes before and behind**; and the first living creature *was* like a lion, and the second living creature *was* like a calf, and the third living creature had the face of a man, and the fourth living creature *was* like a flying eagle. And each of *the* four living creatures had six wings respectively; *and* around and within *they were* full of eyes; **and day and night they ceased not saying, 'Holy, holy, holy, Lord God Almighty, Who was, and Who is, and Who *is* to come.'**
>
> "And when the living creatures give glory and honor and thanksgiving to Him Who sits on the throne, Who lives into the ages of eternity, the twenty-four elders fall down

> before Him Who sits on the throne; and they worship Him Who lives into the ages of eternity, and cast their crowns before the throne, saying, '**Worthy are You, O Lord, to receive glory and honor and power because You did create all things, and for Your will they were created and exist**' " (Rev. 4:1-11).

This was the splendorous scene that Jesus would have seen as He walked forward in triumph to present Himself to His Father as the perfect sacrifice for sin. He was rightfully the first of the firstfruits and the firstborn from the dead. As He walked on the sea of glass toward the Father sitting on His throne, the angels, the twenty-four elders, and God the Father would see on His body the wounds of the lashes that He had received when He was beaten with the cat-of-nine-tails which tore open His flesh. They would see the wounds in His hands and feet where the soldiers had brutally nailed Him to the cross. When the Father's beloved Son reached Him, They must have opened their arms and embraced each other in profound love and shed tears of great joy. Thus Jesus, the Lamb of God, was *accepted* by God the Father on the wave sheaf day—an "appointed time" of the Messiah.

After He was accepted of the Father, Jesus was selected to open the seven seals. He and He alone was qualified, because He had overcome all. The apostle John saw this tremendous scene in the vision and recorded it:

> "And in the right hand of Him Who sits on the throne I saw a book, written within and on *the* back, which had been sealed with seven seals. And I saw a strong angel proclaiming with a loud voice, '**Who is worthy to open the book and to loose its seals**?' But no one in heaven, or on the earth, or under the earth was able to open the book, or to look inside it. And I [John] was weeping greatly because no one was found worthy to open and to read the book, or to look into it.
>
> "Then one of the elders said to me, 'Do not weep. Behold, the Lion Who is of the tribe of Judah, the Root of David, has overcome to open the book, and to loose its seven seals.' **Then I saw, and behold, before the throne and the four living creatures, and before the elders, *was* standing a Lamb as having been slain**, having seven horns and seven eyes, which are the seven Spirits of God that are sent into all the earth; and **He came and took the book out of the right hand of Him Who sits on the throne**.
>
> "And when He took the book, the four living creatures and the twenty-four elders fell down before the Lamb, each having harps and golden bowls full of incense, which are the prayers of the saints. And they sang a new song, saying,

> **'Worthy are You to take the book, and to open its seals because You were slain, and did redeem us to God by Your own blood, out of every tribe and language and people and nation,** and did make us unto our God kings and priests; and we shall reign on the earth.'
>
> **"And I saw, and I heard *the* voices of many angels around the throne, and *the voices* of the living creatures and the elders, and thousands of thousands, saying with a loud voice, 'Worthy is the Lamb Who was slain to receive power, and riches, and wisdom, and strength, and honor, and glory and blessing.' And every creature that is in heaven, and on the earth, and under the earth, and those that are on the sea, and all the things in them, I heard saying, 'To Him Who sits on the throne, and to the Lamb, *be* blessing, and honor, and glory, and sovereignty into the ages of eternity.' And the four living creatures said, 'Amen.'** And the twenty-four elders fell down and worshiped *Him Who* lives into the ages of eternity" (Rev. 5:1-12).

This is the glory and majesty that Jesus Christ received when He was accepted by God the Father as the Savior and Redeemer of mankind on the wave sheaf day. Jesus had overcome sin in the flesh and gained complete victory over death and Satan the devil, opening the way for the redemption and salvation of all mankind through faith in Him. Now He lives in eternal glory, as the first of many sons of God who will be resurrected at His second coming to share His eternal glory and immortality. Those who are Jesus Christ's are now being perfected through the love, grace and power of God the Father. They will be granted the spiritual existence that the Father and the Son have. They will be the sons and daughters of God the Father, and the brethren of Jesus Christ. Jesus shared human existence with mankind in order to become the sin offering for the world so that all who believe in Him may ultimately share His eternal existence and glory in the Family of God throughout the ages of eternity.

The Feast of the "Firstfruits" is Key

The agricultural cycle of ancient Israel revolved around two harvests, one in the spring and the other in the fall. As we have seen, the wave sheaf offering was a ceremony tied to the spring harvest. The children of Israel were forbidden to begin harvesting the spring grain crop of barley and wheat until this special offering had taken place (Lev. 23:10-11, 14). In a sense, this unusual ceremony served to *inaugurate* the spring harvest season. Once the offering of the premier sheaf was "accepted" by God, the grain harvest would immediately begin.

Count from Christ's Resurrection To His Final Ascension and Pentecost

30 AD

Nisan - 1st month (Calculated Hebrew Calendar)

March - April (Julian Calendar)

Day One	Day Two	Day Three	Day Four	Day Five	Day Six	Sabbath
				1 **23**	*2* **24**	*3 SAB* **25**
4 **26**	*5* **27**	*6* **28**	*7* **29**	*8* Six Days before Passover **30**	*9* Five Days before Passover **31**	*10 SAB* Four Days before Passover Jesus Selected as Passover Lamb Jn. 12:27-33 **1**
11 Three Days before Passover **2**	*12* Two Days before Passover **3**	*13* One Day before Passover **4**	*14 Passover* Christ Crucified Christ placed in grave just before sunset. **5**	*15 Holy Day* First Day of Unleavened Bread **6**	*16* **7**	*17 SAB* Christ resurrected just before sunset. **8**
18 Christ accepted by the Father. [1] Jn 20:14-19 Wave Sheaf **9**	*19* [2] **10**	*20* [3] **11**	*21 Holy Day* [4] Last Day of Unleavened Bread **12**	*22* [5] **13**	*23* [6] **14**	*24 SAB* [7] **15**
25 [8] **16**	*26* [9] **17**	*27* [10] **18**	*28* [11] **19**	*29* [12] **20**	*30* [13] **21**	

Hebrew Dates—in small bold italics

Roman Dates—in bold

40 Days to Ascension in Boxes ☐

50 Days Count to Pentecost—Large Bold

30 AD

Iyar - 2nd month (Calculated Hebrew Calendar)
April - May (Julian Calendar)

Day One	Day Two	Day Three	Day Four	Day Five	Day Six	Sabbath
						1 SAB 14 22
2 15 23	*3* 16 24	*4* 17 25	*5* 18 26	*6* 19 27	*7* 20 28	*8 SAB* 21 29
9 22 30	*10* 23 1	*11* 24 2	*12* 25 3	*13* 26 4	*14* 27 5	*15 SAB* 28 6
16 29 7	*17* 30 8	*18* 31 9	*19* 32 10	*20* 33 11	*21* 34 12	*22 SAB* 35 13
23 36 14	*24* 37 15	*25* 38 16	*26* 39 17	*27* Christ ascended into heaven Acts 1:9 40 18	*28* 41 19	*29 SAB* 42 20

Sivan - 3rd month (Calculated Hebrew Calendar)
May - June (Julian Calendar)

1 43 21	*2* 44 22	*3* 45 23	*4* 46 24	*5* 47 25	*6* 48 26	*7 SAB* 49 27
8 Pentecost 50 Church receives Holy Spirit Acts 2 28	*9* 29	*10* 30	*11* 31	*12* 1	*13* 2	*14 SAB* 3

The timing of this offering was also important, as it initiated a 50-day count to the next annual high day, the feast of firstfruits (Pentecost). As noted earlier, the offering is always "waved" on the first day of the week—"the morrow after the [weekly] Sabbath" (*KJV*). Thus commenced a count of *seven complete weeks*—Sunday through the Sabbath—for a total of 49 days. The next day, the 50th day, was then celebrated as an annual feast or high day—known today as Pentecost.

Continuing in Leviticus 23: "And you shall count to you beginning with the next day after the [weekly] Sabbath [a Sunday], beginning with the day that you brought the sheaf of the wave offering; seven Sabbaths shall be complete [49 days]. Even unto the day after the seventh Sabbath you shall number fifty days…" (verses 15-16).

The significance of the wave sheaf offering—along with its connection to Pentecost—is of primary importance for Christians today. Jesus' acceptance by the Father as the "first of the firstfruits" opened the way for the firstfruits—the Church—to receive salvation. Moreover, a *second harvest*—which was concluded and celebrated in the fall of the year—pictures the saving work of Christ on behalf of the remainder of mankind, ultimately bringing billions into the family of God.

After "Firstfruits"—the Greater Fall "Harvest"

The apostle Paul writes that many of the physical events occurring in the history of Israel were designed to be *types* of the spiritual (I Cor. 10:11; the Greek *tupos* means type or pattern). Accordingly, the spring and fall harvests of ancient Israel were *types* of the spiritual "harvesting" of humans, wherein they are granted eternal life. Contrary to the Protestant idea that God is *now* trying to "save" all of mankind, the Scriptures actually teach that **God's plan of salvation occurs in stages** which distinctly follow the pattern of the biblical holy days. Thus, the holy days are, in effect, God's *prophetic* "appointed times."

The spring harvest, followed by the fall harvest, completed the annual harvest cycle. Notice Exodus 23:16: "Also [observe] the [spring] Feast of the **Harvest of the Firstfruits** of your labors, which you have sown in the field. And [later, in the fall, observe] the **Feast of Ingathering** [Tabernacles], in the end of the year, when you have gathered in your labors out of the field." Anciently, this "Feast of Firstfruits" (later known as Pentecost, meaning to "count fifty") was held in celebration of the spring harvest. But notice that the spring harvest was only the *firstfruits*—that which is harvested *first* in sequence. If there are *first* fruits, then there must be *additional* fruit to be harvested. This is where the second harvest festival comes into play—the Feast of Ingathering, also called the Feast of Tabernacles. This feast was held in celebration of the completion of the *fall* harvest—when all *remaining fruit* had been gathered in.

Again, God is not now trying to "save" all of mankind. He has a *plan*, which involves offering salvation only to a select few *first*, ahead of the masses of humanity. This is what James was referring to in the following passage: "According to His own will, He begat us by *the* Word of truth, that **we might be a kind of firstfruits of all His created beings**" (James 1:18). The harvest of the firstfuits—which takes place in the first resurrection—includes all the faithful patriarchs from Abel until Jesus' first coming, as well as all who are called, converted and faithful to the end of their lives up to His second coming. Those saints who are alive "unto the coming of the Lord" will be changed from flesh to spirit in a moment, in the twinkling of an eye (I Cor. 15:51-55; I Thess. 4:15-17). Finally, the firstfruits harvest includes those who are saved out of the Great Tribulation—the 144,000 and "innumerable multitude" of Revelation seven.

The Festival of Firstfruits, or Pentecost, pictures this key part of God's plan—the calling of the elect, the Church of God, the bride of Christ to salvation—*ahead of* the remainder of mankind. The same feast was observed in the New Testament—then called Pentecost. It was most fitting that the Holy Spirit was given on Pentecost, as it is through God's Spirit that the firstfruits are given the power to become deeply converted, to grow and overcome—all in preparation for their collective marriage to Christ at His second coming.

Again, it is through the wave sheaf offering that the "count" to Pentecost begins—and Pentecost ultimately pictures the salvation of the firstfruits, the Church. Anciently, the *premier* sheaf of grain had to be *accepted* by God before *any other grain* could be harvested. All of this points to Jesus Christ as the *first*—the forerunner—*of the firstfruits*. Only when Jesus had been *raised to life* and subsequently **presented before God the Father in heaven for His acceptance** could salvation even *begin* to be offered to man. As Paul brings out, "now Christ has been raised from *the* dead; **He has become the firstfruit** of those who have fallen asleep." Others will be likewise raised, "but each in his own order: Christ *the* firstfruit; **then, those who are Christ's at His coming**" (I Cor. 15:20, 23).

But the granting of salvation to the firstfruits is only the *beginning*. God has promised to Abraham that his seed would become *innumerable* (Gen. 13:16; 15:5: 16:10)—pointing to the time when the entire human family will become heirs of the promises of the New Covenant—when the Kingdom of God will have grown until it fills the earth (Matt. 13:33; Rev. 21:3). Those of the firstfruits harvest will be the kings, priests, leaders and teachers used under Christ to bring salvation to the masses in the age to come (Rev. 5:10; 20:6).

The fall Feast of Ingathering (Feast of Tabernacles), pictures this time of the harvesting of *all mankind* into the Kingdom of God—all of which is *initiated* and made possible by the saving work of the Messiah, the *premier* Wave Sheaf Offering of God the Father, offered at the "appointed time."

CHAPTER SEVEN

The Appointed Time of Jesus' Return—Part I

How Jesus Christ's Second Coming is Pictured by The Annual Feasts of Pentecost and Trumpets

There are numerous prophecies in both the Old and New Testaments that discuss the second coming of Jesus the Messiah. During His three and one-half year ministry, Jesus taught the disciples that He was going to establish the Kingdom of God on earth, and that they would rule with Him. Consequently, some disciples thought that after Jesus was raised from the dead He would establish the kingdom immediately. However, it was not until after the resurrected Christ had appeared to the disciples over a forty-day period that they first began to realize He would ascend to heaven and then come *again*—at "the appointed time" in the future—to establish the Kingdom of God on the earth.

Yet, Jesus' followers did not know *when* or *how* He would return. In fact, Jesus had already informed them that no one would know the "day or hour" of His coming (Matt. 24:36; 25:13). This is why, just before His final ascension into heaven, they asked Him, "**Lord, will You restore the kingdom to Israel at this time?**" Jesus answered: "**It is not for you to know *the* times or *the* seasons, which the Father has placed in His own authority**; but you yourselves shall receive power when the Holy Spirit has come upon you, and you shall be My witnesses, both in Jerusalem and in all Judea and Samaria, and unto *the* ends of the earth" (Acts 1:6-8).

Being witnesses of Jesus' teachings and resurrection "unto the ends of the earth" would obviously take time; thus, the disciples began to realize that it would be some period of time before Christ would return to establish the kingdom. Later, the apostles came to understand that Jesus was not going to return until God's own *set* or "appointed time" in the future, as shown by what Peter preached after he and John had performed a miraculous healing of a crippled man: "Therefore, repent and be converted in order that your sins may be blotted out, so that *the* times of refreshing may come from *the* presence of the Lord; and *that* He may send Him Who was before proclaimed to you, Jesus Christ, **Whom *the* heaven must indeed receive until *the* [appointed] times of restoration of all things, of which God has spoken by *the* mouth of all His holy prophets since the world began**" (Acts 3:19-21).

While the apostles did not know "the times or the seasons" in 30 AD, they learned more and more of God's plan as time went on. By 51 AD, when the apostle Paul wrote to the Thessalonians, the apostles understood considerably more about the timing of the end, primarily based on the framework of God's annual feasts and holy days. "Now then, **concerning the times and the seasons**, brethren, there is no need that I write to you; for you yourselves understand perfectly that the day of *the* Lord will come exactly as a thief *comes* by night. For when they say, 'Peace and security,' then sudden destruction will come upon them, as travail *comes* upon a woman who is with child; and they shall by no means escape" (I Thess. 5:1-3). From this passage it is apparent the apostles were growing in their understanding of end-time events. Yet, it was still quite incomplete. The disciples did not know *how* or *when* the end would come. Ultimately, no one can fully understand "the time and the seasons," which are under the authority of God the Father.

After decades of preaching, teaching and watching events lead up to the destruction of Jerusalem and the Temple, the apostles started to understand that Jesus was not going to return in their lifetimes, but in the *distant* future. This is why God led them to compile their inspired writings into what became the New Testament, which was first finalized by the apostles Paul, Peter and John. (Later, John, assisted by Andrew, Philip and Mark, canonized the New Testament in 98 AD into its present form).

When John received the vision as recorded in the book of Revelation in about 95 AD, a sequence of prophetic events was unveiled to show *how* and approximately *when* Jesus was to return. However, the revelation was given to John in such a manner that it was nearly impossible to fathom the book at the time he wrote it. Even today, after 1900 years have passed, the majority of people cannot understand the Bible, let alone the book of Revelation. Indeed, many scholars and learned theologians have, down through the centuries, tried and failed. Subsequently, this mysterious last book of the Bible has been regarded as nothing more than religious myth.

On the other hand, astute Bible students and scholars generally recognize that many of the prophecies in the Old Testament book of Daniel provide the *first part* of the prophecies concerning the end time, while the book of Revelation provides the *second part*. Although God gave Daniel these prophecies, it was impossible for him to understand them. When Daniel wanted to know their meaning, God told him that it was not for *him* to know:

> " '**But you, O Daniel, shut up the words and seal the book, even to the time of the end.** Many shall run to and fro, and knowledge shall be increased.' Then I, Daniel, looked; and behold, there stood two others, the one on this side, and the one on that side of the bank of the river. And one said to the man clothed in linen who was above the waters of the river: 'How long shall it be to the end of these wonders?' And I heard the man clothed in linen, who was above the waters of the river, when he held up his right and

> his left hand to heaven, and swore by Him who lives forever, *saying*, 'It shall be for a time, times, and a half *a time*. And when they have accomplished to scatter the power of the holy people, all these things shall be finished.'
>
> "And I heard, but I did not understand. Then I said, 'O my lord, what shall be the end of these things?' And he said, '**Go your way, Daniel, for the words *are* closed up and sealed until the time of the end**. Many shall be purified, and made white, and refined. But the wicked shall do wickedly; and none of the wicked shall understand, but the wise shall understand' " (Dan. 12:4-10).

Down through the centuries, many have *tried* and *failed* to understand these prophecies. However, God informed Daniel that such prophecies were to be understood ***only* at the "time of the end**." Until then, they would be closed and sealed. Moreover, in the end times, the understanding of these prophecies would be given only to those who truly *love* and *obey* God the Father and Jesus Christ, and are *led by* the Holy Spirit. Thus, the world—in the grip of spiritual blindness—would never understand, even to the end.

As we have seen throughout this book, God has precisely designed the role of Jesus the Messiah in accordance with the "appointed times" of His holy days and festivals. Indeed, every key event in the life and ministry of Jesus Christ has been correlated to the various aspects of the Passover and holy day framework. Would the time of Jesus' return be any different? Christ's birth as a human occurred at "the appointed time"—most likely, as the evidence shows, on the Feast of Trumpets. Is it not likely, then, that God the Father would plan Jesus' *second* coming so that it paralleled His first coming—and culminated on the same high day, the Feast of Trumpets? Again, we cannot know the "day or hour." Clearly, the Feast of Trumpets **pictures Jesus' second coming**—even if not the exact day of His return. As the books of Isaiah, Haggai and Revelation show, by the time the *last* Feast of Trumpets occurs, the sun, the earth, the moon and the stars will have been shaken out of their present orbits. This disruption of the heavens will cause tremendous confusion and chaos, making it *impossible* for any man to know the exact "day or hour" of Jesus' return. Even though that time is pictured by specific biblical holy days, time itself will be in such disarray that only God the Father will know.

Daniel's 70th Week: Setting the Stage for Jesus' Return

Before we can properly outline key events surrounding "the appointed time" of Christ's second coming, we must first revisit Daniel's 70-week prophecy—for there is one, final "week" that *belongs to the end time*. This "week" is actually a period of seven years, and sets the stage for the coming of the prophesied Antichrist, the Great Tribulation, and the final events surrounding Jesus' dramatic, visible, powerful, awesome return.

The crucifixion of Christ in 30 AD fulfilled the portion of the prophecy which declares, in Daniel 9:26, that **the Messiah would be cut off** ***after*** **the completion of the sixty-two weeks**. Following this statement in verse 26 is an indeterminate period of time—for the remainder of the prophecy through verse 27 projects forward into the "last days." Verse 27 speaks of "one week"—the *third* and *final* division of the 70-week prophecy. The *seventieth* week, which represents a period of seven years, is thus separated from the second division of the prophecy by approximately 2000 years.

> "And after sixty-two weeks Messiah shall be cut off, but not for Himself. And the people of **the prince who shall come** [at the time of the end] shall destroy the city and the sanctuary. But his end shall be with a flood, and **unto the end of the war** desolations are determined. And he [the prince who invades Judea] **shall confirm a covenant with many for one week** [seven years]. And **in the midst** [the halfway point] **of the week** he shall cause the sacrifice and the offering to cease, and upon the wing of abominations shall come one who makes desolate even until the consummation. And the fully determined end which is decreed shall be poured out upon the desolator" (verses 26-27).

This passage describes a time of war and conflict leading *up to* the establishment of a particular covenant or treaty between a powerful "prince" and the Jews concerning what is called the State of Israel today. This treaty is "confirmed" for "one week"—that is, it actually *ushers in* Daniel's seventieth week, or the final seven years. Midway through this seven-year period (after three and one-half years) the "covenant" will be *broken* by this "prince"—evidenced by his abolishment of the daily sacrifices and his defilement of the restored Temple (apparently the daily sacrifices and other Temple functions will be reinstituted some time after the beginning of the seven years as part of the "treaty"). The defilement of the Temple by this "prince"—*the Antichrist*—corresponds to the setting up of the "abomination of desolation" in the Temple, a key event referred to by both Daniel and Jesus.

The Coming European Beast System

Bible prophecy does not indicate a specific time frame for these events to develop leading up to the seventieth week. Rather, Scripture gives us a *sequence of events* as a framework. Only at the very end—the last seven years—do we find a specific time sequence laid out for us, showing that it is divided into two segments of three and one-half years (or 42 months). The "prince" of Daniel 9:26-27, the evil king of Daniel 11:36-45, and the final Beast of Revelation 13 are one in the same. Paul refers to him as the "man of sin," the "son of perdition" who comes into the end-time Temple in Jerusalem and proclaims himself to be the manifestation of God in the flesh (II Thess. 2:3-12).

Notice John's vision in Revelation 13, which foretells of the rise and development of a satanic world government depicted as a "beast with seven heads and ten horns":

> "And I stood on the sand of the sea; and I saw a beast rising up out of the sea, having seven heads and ten horns, and on his horns ten crowns, and upon his heads the name of blasphemy. And the beast that I saw was like a leopard, and his feet like the feet of a bear, and his mouth like the mouth of a lion [depicting the great Gentile empires of Daniel 7]; **and the dragon [Satan the devil] gave him his power, and his throne and great authority**. And I saw one of his heads as if it were slain to death, but his deadly wound was healed; and **the whole earth was amazed and followed the beast**.
>
> "**And they worshiped the dragon, who gave his authority to the beast. And they worshiped the beast, saying, 'Who is like the beast? Who has the power to make war against him?'** And a mouth speaking great things and blasphemies was given to him; and authority was given to him to continue for forty-two months [after the deadly wound is healed]. And he opened his mouth in blasphemy against God, to blaspheme His name, and His tabernacle, and those who dwell in heaven. And **he was given power to make war against the saints**, and to overcome them; **and he was given authority over every tribe and language and nation** [thus, a world government].
>
> "And **all who dwell on the earth will worship him** [as the manifestation of God in the flesh], whose names have not been written in the book of life of the Lamb slain from the foundation of the world. If anyone has an ear, let him hear" (Rev. 13:1-9).

The "Beast" has three aspects to it. First, it will be a **world *system* of government**. Second, it is clear from other prophecies that there must be a complete revival of Europe as the center of world power. Third, Revelation 13 transitions into its **final leader**—also called the "Beast"—who is given **total rule over all the world** for the last seven years. The first three and one-half years will probably be a time of unprecedented peace and prosperity (I Thess. 5:2-3). However, at the conclusion of the first three and one-half years its great leader will suffer a deadly wound—but his wound will be healed.

The Coming False Prophet

Working with him will be *another beast*—depicted as a lamb with two horns but speaking like a dragon (Satan the devil). This second beast is the end-time great *false prophet* who will perform miraculous signs and wonders, even calling fire down from heaven. In partnership with the Beast, he will be the leader of a *new world religion*. The signs and wonders he performs will convince all people, and hence all religions, to come together and worship the Beast—the Antichrist—as God manifested in the flesh:

> "And I saw another beast rising out of the earth; and he had **two horns like a lamb, but spoke like a dragon**; and he exercises all the [worldwide] authority of the first beast before him; and **he causes the earth and those who dwell therein to worship the first beast**, whose deadly wound was healed. And he performs great wonders, so that he even causes fire to come down to the earth from heaven in the sight of men.
>
> "And **he deceives those who dwell on the earth** by means of the wonders that were given to him to perform in the sight of the beast, saying to those who dwell on the earth that they should make an image for the beast, which had the wound by the sword, yet was alive. And he was given power to give life to the image of the beast, so that the image of the beast also could speak; and **he causes everyone who will not worship the image of the beast to be killed**" (Rev. 13:11-15).

After the Beast's deadly wound is healed, the "false prophet" will pronounce him to be "the manifestation of God on earth." The whole world will then worship the Beast and Satan the devil. Moreover, after his deadly wound is healed, the Beast, also called the Antichrist, continues for 42 months, ruling with absolute power as "God on earth"—even killing the saints.

Prior to the final seven years of Daniel 9:27, the Bible does not tell us *how long* this world government will be functioning—and it could be a number of years. It will undoubtedly take a number of years to reach its full power; moreover, the Bible does not indicate how many leaders this European system will have prior to the establishment of its final leader, the king of the north (Dan. 11:40), as the great leader of the new world government, the final Beast. Ultimately, he and the "false prophet" will be cast alive into the lake of fire when Christ and the resurrected saints take over the world and institute God's rule of the Kingdom of God (Rev. 19:11-21).

Three Major Events that Signal the Return of Christ

Many of the signs Jesus said would precede His return have reoccurred over and over again from the first century AD—such as false prophets, wars, rumors of wars, famine, pestilence, earthquakes, persecutions and martyrdom. But there are *three major events*—yet to develop—which will signal the beginning of the end, the Great Tribulation, and the return of Jesus Christ. Other *preparatory* events arise in conjunction with these major events, serving as key end-time benchmarks.

Event Number One—the rebuilding of the Temple in Jerusalem and the work of the Two Witnesses. *The Temple*: When the "prince" of Daniel 9:26-27 and the Jews agree to the prophesied end-time "covenant," there is little question that the agreement will thrust open the door for the Jews to rebuild the Temple and reinstitute animal sacrifices. In as much as Jesus made known to His disciples that the "abomination of desolation" spoken of by Daniel would *stand in* the "holy place" (Matt. 24:15; etc.), we can conclude that the Temple must, in the end time, be restored and functioning.

This is detailed in Revelation 11, where the apostle John sees a vision of a yet future Temple: "Then *the angel* gave me a measuring rod like a staff, saying, 'Arise and measure the temple of God, and the altar, and those who worship in it. But leave out the court that *is* within the temple *area*, and do not measure it because it has been given *up* to the Gentiles; and they shall trample upon the holy city Jerusalem *for* forty-two months' " (verses 1-2).

It is a well-known fact that the *Temple Institute* in Jerusalem has already prepared many of the instruments needed for the Temple rituals—including the rules covering animal sacrifices, washings, etc. Animals are being bred specifically for this purpose, priests are being trained, priestly and Levitical garments have been fashioned—even the "lots" used by the High Priest to select the Day of Atonement sacrifice are ready. Though we are not told, it is feasible that much of the Temple itself may *already* be prepared in prefabricated form. The *key*, however, is that only this "covenant" with the Antichrist will pave the way for the Jews to actually proceed with their plans for a new, functioning Temple, as he will guarantee them protection and peace with the Islamic nations.

***The Two Witnesses*:** Immediately following the vision of the Temple, God tells John that He will raise up His "Two Witnesses" in Jerusalem and give them extraordinary powers. Their mission will be to powerfully witness to the *whole world* that Jesus Christ—the *true* Messiah—is about to return! "**And I will give *power* to My two witnesses, and they shall prophesy a thousand two hundred *and* sixty days, clothed in sackcloth. These are the two olive trees, and *the* two lampstands that stand before the God of the earth**" (Rev. 11:3-4).

The Two Witnesses will be personally selected and chosen by God the Father and Jesus Christ. Who are these two men and *where* will they come from? When we carefully examine the prophecies of Zechariah chapters 3-4, we discover that one of the Two Witnesses will be the *high priest* of this end-time Temple, and the other will be the *governor* of Judea. John's vision in Revelation 11 refers to them as "two olive trees." Notice the similarity in Zechariah's prophecy: "And I answered and said to him, 'What *are* these **two olive trees** on the right side of the lampstand and on its left side?' And I answered again and said to him, 'What *are* the two olive branches beside the two golden pipes, emptying the golden *oil* out of themselves?' And he answered me and said, 'Do you not know what these *are*?' And I said, 'No, my lord.' And he said, '**These *are* the two anointed ones who stand by the LORD of the whole earth**' " (Zech. 4:11-14). This description can be nothing other than the Two Witnesses of Revelation 11.

The Two Witnesses will not be self-proclaimed or appointed by any man. They will have such awesome power that no one will be able to harm them throughout the 1260 days of their testimony. Notice: "And if anyone attempts to harm them, fire will go out of their mouths and devour their enemies. For if anyone attempts to harm them, he must be killed in this manner. **These [Two Witnesses] have authority to shut heaven so that no rain may fall in *the* days of their prophecy; and they have authority over the waters, to turn them into blood, and to smite the earth with every plague, as often as they will**" (Rev. 11:5-6).

When the Two Witnesses have completed their testimony, God will permit the prince of the people, the Beast who made the covenant with the Jews, to finally kill them. The Two Witnesses will die as the last two martyrs for Jesus Christ—and the world will rejoice!

> "And when they have completed their testimony, the beast who ascends out of the abyss will make war against them, and will overcome them, and will kill them. And their bodies *will lie* in the street of the great city, which spiritually is called Sodom and Egypt, where also our Lord was crucified. Then those of the peoples and tribes and languages and nations [the *whole* world] shall see their bodies three and a half days, for they will not allow their bodies to be put into tombs. And those who dwell on the earth will rejoice over them, and will make merry, and will send gifts to one another, because these two prophets had tormented those who dwell on the earth" (verses 7-10).

However, immediately *prior* to the blowing of the seventh trumpet—which signals the first resurrection—God will raise them back to life. Thus, the Two Witnesses—the last two martyrs—will be the *first* ones to rise from the dead, precisely fulfilling Jesus' saying that "the last shall be first." As they are ascending into heaven, the seventh trumpet will sound and the resurrection of the saints will take place.

"Then after the three and a half days, *the* spirit of life from God entered into them and they stood on their feet; and great fear fell upon those who were watching them. And they heard a great voice from heaven, say, 'Come up here!' And they ascended into heaven in a cloud; and their enemies saw them *rise*. And in that hour there was a great earthquake, and a tenth of the city fell; and seven thousand men were killed in the earthquake. And the rest were filled with fear, and gave glory to the God of heaven. The second woe is past. Behold, the third woe is coming immediately.

"**Then the seventh angel sounded *his* trumpet**; and *there* were great voices in heaven, saying, 'The kingdoms of this world have become *the kingdoms* of our Lord and His Christ, and He shall reign into the ages of eternity.' And the twenty-four elders, who sit before God on their thrones, fell on their faces and worshiped God, saying, 'We give You thanks, O Lord God Almighty, Who is, and Who was, and Who *is* to come; for You have taken *to Yourself* Your great power, and have reigned. For the nations were angry, and Your wrath has come, and the time for the dead to be judged, and to give reward to Your servants the prophets, and to the saints, and to *all* those who fear Your name, the small and the great; and to destroy those who destroy the earth' " (verses 11-18).

Recall that the Beast/Antichrist will have made a covenant with the Jews for "one week"—seven years. At precisely the midpoint of the seven years—in the "midst of the week"—the Antichrist will stop the Temple sacrifices and establish himself in the Temple "as God" (II Thess. 2:4). **This event is the "abomination that makes desolate" of which both Daniel and Jesus warned**. The Two Witness will have come on the scene *just prior to* the middle of that seven-year period—just prior to the setting up of the "abomination." Thus, these two powerful prophets will warn the world of what the Beast is about to do—proclaim himself to be "God"!

Event Number Two—the "abomination that makes desolate" and the Great Tribulation. Jesus was very specific in describing the "abomination that makes desolate" standing in the "holy place" because the Great Tribulation of the end cannot begin until the Temple in Jerusalem has been *rebuilt*—and is fully functioning again—and the "abomination of desolation" stands in the holy place. Notice what Jesus warned: "Therefore, **when you see the abomination of desolation**, which was spoken of by Daniel the prophet, standing in the holy place (the one who reads, let him understand).... **For then shall there be great tribulation, such as has not been from *the* beginning of *the* world until this time, nor ever shall be *again***" (Matt. 24:15, 21).

The parenthetical phrase "the one who reads, let him understand" was not actually spoken by Jesus. Rather, the apostle John—who oversaw the final canonization of the New Testament—was inspired to *add* the phrase as a late edit. In 95 AD, when John wrote the book of Revelation, the Temple had already been destroyed—twenty-five years earlier in 70 AD. Yet, at the time it was destroyed, John knew there had been no "abomination of desolation" that stood in the holy place, and the Great Tribulation did not begin. Also, in the prophecy of the Two Witnesses in Revelation 11, John was given a vision of a Temple in Jerusalem. So he knew that *before the end would come* the Temple had to be rebuilt. **This is why God inspired him to add this phrase in Matthew 24:15 and Mark 13:14**—"the one who reads, let him understand"—**to let future generations know that the end cannot come until the Jews rebuild the Temple, and that it would be desecrated by the "abomination of desolation**."

John also understood from Paul's second epistle to the Thessalonians that the "abomination of desolation" would be in the person of the *Antichrist*, boasting that he himself was God:

> "Now we beseech you, brethren, concerning the coming of our Lord Jesus Christ and our gathering together to Him, that you not be quickly shaken in mind, nor be troubled—neither by spirit, nor by word, nor by epistle, as if from us, *saying* that the day of Christ is present. **Do not let anyone deceive you by any means because *that day will not* come unless the apostasy shall come first, and the man of sin shall be revealed—the son of perdition, the one who opposes and exalts himself above all that is called God, or that is an object of worship; so that HE COMES INTO THE TEMPLE OF GOD AND SITS DOWN AS GOD, PROCLAIMING THAT HE HIMSELF IS GOD!**
>
> "Do you not remember that when I was still with you, I told you these things? And now you understand what is holding *him* back in order for him to be revealed in his own set time. For the mystery of lawlessness is already working; only *there is* one Who is restraining at the present *time* until it arises out of *the* midst. **And then the lawless one will be revealed (whom the Lord will consume with the breath of His mouth, and will destroy with the brightness of His coming); *even* the one whose coming is according to *the* inner working of Satan, with all power and signs and lying wonders**, and with all deceivableness of unrighteousness in those who are perishing because they did not receive the love of the truth, so that they might be saved. And for this cause, God will send upon them a powerful deception that will cause them to believe *the* lie, so that all may be judged who

> did not believe the truth, but who took pleasure in unrighteousness" (II Thess. 2:1-12).

Paul's phrase concerning the man of sin—"whom the Lord will consume with the breath of His mouth, and will destroy with the brightness **of His coming**"—clearly defines the time setting as near Christ's return, linking the man of sin to the end-time "abomination" that makes desolate. These Scriptures also tell us that, in addition to the Temple being rebuilt, the Antichrist—the "Beast" of Revelation 13—must appear before the return of Christ. **This key event, in addition to all the others, must occur first!**

In fact, the Antichrist sitting in the Temple of God proclaiming himself to *be* God is the *key event* that triggers the Great Tribulation. As Jesus explained, it cannot begin until then: "Therefore, WHEN you see the abomination of desolation, which was spoken of by Daniel the prophet, standing in the holy place (the one who reads, let him understand).... For THEN shall there be great tribulation, such as has not been from *the* beginning of *the* world until this time, nor ever shall be *again*" (Matt. 24:15, 21).

In Daniel chapter 11, this key event is prophesied in detail. Keep in mind that this lengthy prophecy has already been fulfilled *in type* by the Syrian dictator Antiochus IV Epiphanes (175-164 BC). Many of the details of the passage (verses 21-35) apply *only* to the time of Antiochus' desecration of the Temple in 168 BC, and thus serve as a *foreshadowing* of the coming Antichrist and the "abomination of desolation" (see Appendix C). However, the latter portion of the passage—verses 36-45 and parts of chapter 12—brings the prophecy into the modern era at the end time dealing specifically with the coming *Antichrist*.

> "And the king [the "prince" of Daniel 9:26-27—the *Antichrist*] shall do according to his will. And **he shall exalt and magnify himself above every god** [just as Paul warned, he will *sit* in the Temple proclaiming himself to *be* God], and **shall speak astonishing things against the God of gods** [showing that he is the *Antichrist*], and shall prosper until the indignation be accomplished [until the end of the seven-year period], for that which is decreed [prophesied] shall be done. He will not regard the gods of his fathers, nor the desire of women, nor regard any god, for **he shall magnify himself above all**. But in his place he shall honor the god of forces [the strongest fortresses]; and a god whom his fathers did not know shall he honor with gold and silver, and with precious stones and costly things. So he shall deal against the fortresses of the strongest with a strange [foreign] god, whom he shall acknowledge; and shall increase with glory. He shall cause them to rule over many and shall divide the land for a price.

> "And **at the time of the end**, the king of the south [a confederacy of Arab nations] shall push [strike] at him. And the king of the north [the *Antichrist*, the "beast" of Revelation 13] shall come against him [in war] like a whirlwind with chariots and with horsemen and with many ships; and he shall enter into the countries and shall overflow and sweep through [the entire Middle East]. He shall also enter into the glorious land [the land of Israel], and many countries shall be overthrown. But these shall escape out of his hand: Edom and Moab, and the chief of the children of Ammon [Jordan]. And he shall stretch out his hand also upon the countries. And the land of Egypt shall not escape. But he shall have power over the treasures of gold and silver, and over all the precious things of Egypt. And the Libyans and the Ethiopians shall be at his steps. But tidings [of opposition] out of the east and out of the north [from the northeast—a massive Asian alliance led by Russia and China] shall alarm him. Then he will go forth with great fury to destroy and to utterly annihilate many [nuclear war]. And he shall plant his royal tents between the seas in the glorious holy mountain [in Jerusalem]. Yet **he shall come to his end** [Christ will return to fight and defeat him], and none shall help him" (Dan. 11:36-45).

Again, Jesus Himself points us to this vital prophecy recorded by Daniel. He said to His followers: "Therefore, **when you see the abomination of desolation, which was spoken of by Daniel the prophet, standing in the holy place** (the one who reads, let him understand), then let those who are in Judea flee into the mountains.... **For then shall there be great tribulation, such as has not been from the beginning of the world until this time**, nor ever shall be again. And if those days were not limited, there would no flesh be saved; but for the elect's sake those days shall be limited" (Matt. 24:15-16, 21-22). Daniel chapter 12 confirms this amazing prophecy: "And **there shall be a time of trouble** [the Great Tribulation], **such as never was since there was a nation even until that time**" (Dan. 12:1).

Thus, the ***second event*** pointing to "the appointed time" of Jesus' return is the setting up by the Antichrist of the "abomination of desolation"—which includes the abolishment of the Jews' "daily sacrifice" ritual at the Temple. This event signals that the Antichrist has *violated* the treaty he had deviously made with the Jews—at the end of the *first* three and one-half years—and that the Great Tribulation has begun.

This time of *unprecedented trouble* will continue throughout the remaining three and one-half years, and will be brought to an end *only* by Christ's direct intervention during the "Day of the Lord" and by His final return at "the appointed time."

In a prophecy of the Great Tribulation in the Old Testament, we find that God instructs the prophet Jeremiah to take a cup from the Lord's hand and make all the nations of the world "drink" from it—depicting that **the Great Tribulation will involve all the nations of the world**. Of course, Jeremiah could not have gone to all the nations of the world at that time, as this is a prophecy of the coming Great Tribulation in the last days:

> "[Go to] **all the kingdoms of the world, which *are* on the face of the earth**; and the king of Sheshach [the coming Antichrist] shall drink after them. Therefore you shall say to them, 'Thus says the LORD of hosts, the God of Israel, "Drink and be drunk, and vomit, and fall, and rise no more because of the sword which I will send among you." ' And it shall come to pass if they refuse to take the cup at your hand to drink, then you shall say to them, 'Thus says the LORD of hosts, "You shall certainly drink. For, lo, I begin to bring evil on the city which is called by My name; and shall you go unpunished? You shall not go unpunished. For I will call for a sword on all the inhabitants of the earth," says the LORD of hosts.'
>
> "And prophesy against them all these words, and say to them, 'The LORD shall roar from on high, and utter His voice from His holy habitation. He shall mightily roar over His dwelling place. **He shall give a shout, like those who tread out *grapes*, against all the people of the earth. A noise shall come to the ends of the earth; for the LORD has a controversy with the nations; He will plead with all flesh**. He will give those *who are* wicked to the sword,' says the LORD.
>
> "Thus says the LORD of hosts, '**Behold, evil shall go forth from nation to nation, and a great whirlwind shall be stirred up from the farthest corners of the earth. And the slain of the LORD shall be at that day from *one* end of the earth even to the *other* end of the earth**; they shall not be mourned, nor gathered, nor buried. They shall be *as* dung on the ground' " (Jer. 25:26-33).

Jeremiah's prophecy verifies Jesus' description of the Great Tribulation, that it would be an *unprecedented* time of trouble in the world: "For then shall there be **great tribulation, such as has not been from *the* beginning of *the* world until this time**, nor ever shall be *again*" (Matt. 24:21).

Prior to the *third key event* signaling Christ's return are two important preparatory events—the "message of the three angels" and the enforcement of the "mark of the beast." The messages of the three angels are powerfully given to the whole world prior to the start of the Great Tribulation. God will send these three mighty angels to warn the world:

> "And I saw **another angel** [the first angel] flying in the midst of heaven, having the everlasting gospel to proclaim to those who dwell on the earth, and to every nation and tribe and language and people; saying with a loud voice, 'Fear God, and give glory to Him, because the hour of His judgment has come; and worship Him Who made the heaven, and the earth, and the sea, and the fountains of waters.' Then **another angel followed** [the second angel], saying, 'The great city Babylon is fallen, is fallen, because of the wine of the wrath of her fornication, which she has given all nations to drink.'
>
> "And **a third angel followed them**, saying with a loud voice, 'If anyone worships the beast and his image, and receives the mark in his forehead or in his hand, he shall also drink of the wine of the wrath of God, which is mixed undiluted in the cup of His wrath; and he shall be tormented in fire and brimstone in the sight of the holy angels, and of the Lamb. And the smoke of their torment ascends into the ages of eternity; and those who worship the beast and his image, and all who receive the mark of his name, have no rest day and night' " (Rev. 14:6-11).

To summarize: The **first angel** proclaims the gospel message to the whole world, warning all mankind to "fear God and give Him glory"—for His judgment is at hand. The **second angel** foretells of the imminent fall of "Babylon"—the entire political, economic and religious system formed by the nations led by the Beast and the false prophet. **The third angel warns all of mankind to *not* worship the Beast or his image, and to *not* receive the "mark" of the Beast**.

From the context of Revelation 13 and 14, the three angels must give their warnings *before* the worship of the Beast and his image begins, and before the enforcement of the mark. **God always gives a warning before something takes place, not after it has already happened—that is clearly evident throughout the Bible.**

Revelation 13 shows that the Beast will enforce a global monetary solution called the "mark of the Beast." Without this mark, no one will be able to buy or sell. "And he [the beast whose deadly wound was healed] causes all, the small and the great, and the rich and the poor, and the free and the bond, to receive a mark in their right hands, or in their foreheads; so that no one may have the ability to buy and sell unless he has the mark, or the name of the beast, or the number of his name" (Rev. 13:16-17).

By the time the Beast system fully develops, a new *world banking system* will have already been instituted—with digital and paper currency for a number of years. This will pave the way for the "mark of the Beast." Never before in the history of the world has it been possible for such a monetary control system to be instituted. However, the technology now exists to bring about a global financial system in which literally everyone's participation can be monitored and regulated. Interestingly, there have been recent reports that scientists are developing an invisible tattoo that can be applied on a person's hand or forehead. Could this be a forerunner of the coming "mark"?

At the beginning of the Beast's rule, the "mark" will not be immediately enforced. As we read Revelation 13, it is evident that the "mark" will not be enforced until *after* the Beast has recovered from his "deadly wound" and the final three and one-half years are ready to begin with the Great Tribulation. At that time, everyone on earth will be commanded by the "false prophet" to make an "image" for the Beast—probably to celebrate his return to life. Anyone refusing to do so will be killed (verses 14-15). Then the "mark of the Beast" will be fully forced upon everyone. The saints, however, will refuse to make the "image" for the Beast, or to worship it; and they will refuse to allow the "mark" to be put on their right hands or foreheads. As a result, the saints will be martyred for Christ.

The Third Event Signaling Jesus' Appointed Return

The *third event* pointing to Christ's return involves "the sign of the Son of Man in heaven" (Matt. 24:30). As we will see in the next chapter, this dramatic event *begins* at a set or "appointed time" and continues over an extended period of time. In order to properly understand this key event, we must examine its unique place in the framework of the holy days—particularly the Feasts of Pentecost and Trumpets.

CHAPTER EIGHT

The Appointed Time of Jesus' Return—Part II

How Jesus Christ's Second Coming is Pictured by The Annual Feasts of Pentecost and Trumpets

While the apostles did not completely understand "the times or the seasons" in 30 AD, it is apparent that they learned more of God's plan as time advanced. Likewise, over time God's servants in the latter days have increased in knowledge concerning the timing of Jesus' return. Clearly, as Christ said, no one can know the exact day or hour of His return. But we can know the approximate time (I Thess. 5:1-2). The ultimate key to pinpointing the "appointed times" of Jesus the Messiah is to understand the prophetic significance of God's holy days and festivals.

God's holy days form a framework or substructure upon which prophecy, as it is fulfilled, is ordered or arranged. God has precisely designed the role of Jesus the Messiah in accordance with the "appointed times" of His holy days. Indeed, each key event in the life and ministry of Jesus Christ has been correlated to the various aspects of the Passover and holy day framework. As this chapter will demonstrate, **the Feasts of Pentecost and Trumpets clearly picture Jesus' second coming**.

Scripture gives us *three key events* that signal the beginning of the end, the Great Tribulation, and the return of Jesus Christ. Other *preparatory events* occur in conjunction with these major events, and serve as end-time benchmarks. Chapter Seven outlined the first two of these key events—**1) the rebuilding of the Temple in Jerusalem**, and **2) the setting up of the "abomination of desolation"** by the Antichrist. Other *preparatory events* include the work of the Two Witnesses, the three angels' messages, and the enforcement of the "mark of the beast." These events set the stage for **the third and final event announcing the awesome return of Jesus Christ, which everyone on earth shall see**.

The Third Event Signaling Jesus' Appointed Return

Jesus Christ Himself foretold of this *third major event* signaling His return—**the *sign* of the Son of Man in heaven**. As we will see from the Scriptures, this colossal event transpires over a period of time. While it *begins* at a set or "appointed time," it is not a single day's event—neither is it a "secret rapture." In order to better understand this key development, we must look at its place in the framework of the holy days—particularly

Pentecost and Trumpets—as they unfold in the book of Revelation.

This event is the *sixth seal* of Revelation six—*the heavenly signs*. When Jesus opens the sixth seal, He dramatically reveals Himself by an awesome display of divine power. The whole world will know it and see it—but they won't believe it.

> "And when He opened the sixth seal, I looked, and behold, there was a great earthquake; and the sun became black as *the* hair *of* sackcloth, and the moon became as blood; and the stars of heaven fell to the earth, as a fig tree casts its untimely figs when it is shaken by a mighty wind. **Then *the* heaven departed like a scroll that is being rolled up, and every mountain and island was moved out of its place**. And the kings of the earth, and the great men, and the rich men, and the chief captains, and the powerful men, and every bondman, and every free *man* hid themselves in the caves and in the rocks of the mountains; and they said to the mountains and to the rocks, 'Fall on us, and hide us from *the* face of Him Who sits on the throne, and from the wrath of the Lamb, because **the great day of His wrath has come**, and who has the power to stand?' " (Rev. 6:12-17).

As Lord God of the Old Testament, Jesus Christ prophesied that He is going to shake the heavens and the earth at His second coming: "For thus says the LORD of hosts, 'Once *again*—it *is* yet a little while—**I will shake the heavens, and the earth, and the sea, and the dry land. And I will shake all the nations**; and the desire of all nations [Jesus Christ, the true Messiah] shall come' " (Haggai 2:6-7).

Isaiah also wrote of this event. Notice how similar this is to Revelation six: "And they shall go into the holes of the rocks, and into the caves of the earth for fear of the LORD and for the glory of His majesty, **when He arises to shake *terribly* the earth**. In that day a man shall cast his idols of silver, and his idols of gold, which they made *each one* for himself to worship, to the moles and to the bats; to go into the clefts of the rocks, and into the tops of the ragged rocks, for fear of the LORD and for the glory of His majesty, **when He arises to shake *terribly* the earth**" (Isa. 2:19-21).

What happens when the heavens are rolled back like a scroll? Instantly, the heavens all around the world will be changed. The heavens, our entire solar system, the earth, the oceans, and all nations will be shaken! Such an event has never happened in the history of mankind. Everyone will witness and experience awesome, all-encompassing terror! Jesus Himself described to His disciples how these occurrences would unfold, beginning with the start of the Great Tribulation:

> "For then shall there be great tribulation [it begins when the "abomination of desolation" is set up in the holy place], such

> as has not been from *the* beginning of *the* world until this time, nor ever shall be *again*. And if those days were not limited [to three and one-half years], there would no flesh be saved; but for the elect's sake those days shall be limited. Then if anyone says to you, 'Behold, here *is* the Christ,' or, '*He is* there,' do not believe *it*. For there shall arise false Christs and false prophets, and they shall present great signs and wonders, in order to deceive, if possible, even the elect. Behold, I have foretold *it* to you. **Therefore, if they say to you, '*Come and* see! He is in the wilderness'; do not go forth. '*Come and* see! *He is* in the secret chambers'; do not believe *it*"** (Matt. 24:21-26).

Clearly, Jesus is not coming as an ordinary man. Rather, He is coming in *power* and *glory* as God and King to *rule* the world! (Zech. 14:9).

When we combine Revelation 6:12-17—picturing the heavens rolling back as a scroll—with the following passages of Matthew 24, we can begin to visualize the overwhelming and fearful power of the sixth seal.

> **"For as the light of day** [the sun], **which comes forth from *the* east and shines as far as *the* west, so also shall the coming of the Son of man be**.... But immediately after the tribulation [of two years of punishment on the twelve tribes of Israel] of those days, **the sun shall be darkened, and the moon shall not give her light, and the stars shall fall from heaven, and the powers of the heavens shall be shaken. And then shall appear the SIGN OF THE SON OF MAN in heaven**; and then shall all the tribes of the earth mourn, and they shall see the Son of man coming upon the clouds of heaven with power and great glory" (Matt. 24:27-30).

Luke records some additional details: "And there shall be signs in *the* sun and moon and stars, and on the earth distress and anxiety among *the* nations, *the* seas roaring with rolling surges; men dying of heart attacks from fear and dread of the things that are coming on the whole world; **for the powers of heaven shall be shaken**" (Luke 21:25-26).

When the heavens roll back as a scroll, the entire world will suddenly see the *sign* of the Son of Man. But what will people see? Jesus said that the sign of the Son of Man will shine from east to west, as does the sun. Therefore, we can conclude that all the people of the world will see what appears to be a *new* sun—a *second* sun—never before observed in the heavens. Undoubtedly, it will appear to have suddenly originated from somewhere beyond our solar system. This will be an alarming event, indeed! As a result, with two suns shining in the heavens, there will be *confusion* as to which day is which. This is why no man will be able to know the day or hour of the return of Christ. Moreover, from these passages we can determine that the return of Jesus Christ does not take place in a single day. When we put together the rest of the scriptures from the book of Revelation, it is evident that the whole world will *continue to see the sign* of the Son of Man—**this new "sun" shining in the heavens**—*for more than a year.*

As we will see later, it is significant that the sign of the Son of Man appears in the heavens just before the next-to-the-last Pentecost during the three and one-half year Tribulation. This mind-boggling action by Jesus Christ occurs after the first two years of the Great Tribulation have been completed (Rev. 6:12-17).

As foretold by the prophet Hosea, the first two years of the Great Tribulation is the time of God's punishment on the modern-day, end-time descendants of the twelve tribes of Israel for their sins. Concerning the start of the Great Tribulation, when God *begins* to punish Israel, He says, "I will go; I will return to My place until they confess their guilt and seek My face; in their affliction they will seek Me earnestly" (Hosea 5:15).

While in captivity for grievously departing from the Lord, the twelve tribes of Israel will repent when they witness the events of the sixth seal—the heavenly signs, when the heavens are rolled back as a scroll. **They will know that this is the hand of God!** Notice, as the prophecy of Hosea continues, that there is a time period defined in terms of "days." However, as we see in Numbers 14:3 and Ezekiel 4:4-6, a "day" in prophecy typically equals a *year* in fulfillment. Notice what the children of Israel will say as they repent: "Come and let us return to the LORD, for He has torn, and He will heal us; He has smitten, and He will bind us up. **After two days** [two years in fulfillment] **He will revive us; in the third day** [after the beginning of the third year] **He will** [begin to] **raise us up, and we shall live in His sight**" (Hosea 6:1-2).

From these Scriptures we can conclude that God's correction on the modern nations of the twelve tribes of Israel for their sins will last for *two* years. Then, just after the *beginning* of the third year, He will end their time of punishment and begin to deliver them, starting with the 144,000 of Revelation seven.

The Sealing of the 144,000 in Revelation Seven And the Great Innumerable Multitude

From Revelation six, the sequence of events continues in chapter seven. There, the sealing of the 144,000 from the tribes of the children of Israel signals that God has begun to liberate them from captivity in the third year, after two years of punishment for forsaking the Lord.

Immediately after the heavens are rolled back as a scroll—when the heavens and earth are shaken and the sign of the Son of Man appears as a *new sun* in the heavens—there is suddenly a great calm. John writes:

"And after these things I saw four angels standing on the four corners of the earth, holding back the four winds of the earth, so that the wind might not blow on the earth, or on the sea, or on any tree. Then I saw another angel ascending from *the* rising of *the* sun, having *the* seal of *the* living God; and he cried out with a loud voice to the four angels, to whom it was given to damage the earth and the sea, saying, 'Do not damage the earth, or the sea, or the trees until we have sealed the servants of our God in their foreheads.'

"And I heard the number of those who were sealed: **one hundred forty-four thousand, sealed out of every tribe of *the* children of Israel**. From *the* tribe of Judah, twelve thousand *were* sealed; from *the* tribe of Reuben, twelve thousand *were* sealed; from *the* tribe of Gad, twelve thousand *were* sealed; from *the* tribe of Asher, twelve thousand *were* sealed; from *the* tribe of Naphtali, twelve thousand *were* sealed; from *the* tribe of Manasseh, twelve thousand *were* sealed; from *the* tribe of Simeon, twelve thousand *were* sealed; from *the* tribe of Levi, twelve thousand *were* sealed; from *the* tribe of Issachar, twelve thousand *were* sealed; from *the* tribe of Zebulon, twelve thousand *were* sealed; from *the* tribe of Joseph, twelve thousand *were* sealed; from *the* tribe of Benjamin, twelve thousand *were* sealed" (Rev. 7:1-8).

Combining the prophecies of Hosea and Revelation shows us that God *begins* to raise up or deliver the children of Israel by sealing the 144,000. Since this is after the beginning of the *third year* of the three and one-half year Great Tribulation, there is approximately one and one-half years of the Tribulation left, which comes against the rest of the world.

Furthermore, not only are the 144,000 of the twelve tribes of Israel sealed—that is, they are given the Holy Spirit for salvation—a great, innumerable multitude is also sealed. Notice:

"After these things I looked, and behold, **a great multitude, which no one was able to number, out of every nation and tribe and people and language**, was standing before the throne and before the Lamb, clothed with white robes and *holding* palms in their hands; and they were calling out with a loud voice to Him Who sits on the throne and to the Lamb, saying, 'The salvation of our God *has come*' [showing that they will also receive the Holy Spirit and salvation].

"Then all the angels stood around the throne, and the elders and the four living creatures, and fell on their faces before the throne and worshiped God, saying, 'Amen. Blessing, and

> glory, and wisdom, and thanksgiving, and honor, and power and strength *be* to our God into the ages of eternity. Amen.'
>
> "And one of the elders answered *and* said to me, 'These who are clothed with white robes, who are they, and where did they come from?' Then I said to him, 'Sir, you know.' And he said to me, "**They are the ones who have come out of the great tribulation; and they have washed their robes, and have made their robes white in the blood of the Lamb**' " (Rev. 7:9-14).

Based on the framework of the holy days for the time of the end, this sealing takes place at "the appointed time" on the next-to-the-last Pentecost during the three and one-half year Great Tribulation. This is God's own personal harvest. Just as the apostles and others were sealed with the Holy Spirit on the day of Pentecost in 30 AD, as recorded in Acts two, the 144,000 and the great innumerable multitude are likewise sealed on *this* Pentecost—which is one year before the first resurrection that will take place at the *next* Pentecost. In the parable of the vineyard master and laborers, the workers hired at the eleventh hour are a type of those who are sealed as shown in Revelation seven on this next-to-the-last Pentecost (Matt. 20:1-16).

Approximately three and one-half months after rescuing and sealing the 144,000 and the great multitude, the final year of the Great Tribulation starts on the next-to-last Feast of Trumpets. The Tribulation will continue with greater intensity upon the rest of the nations of the world for one year until the *next* Feast of Trumpets. This last year is called the "Day of the Lord" (Rev. 8:1-6).

The Seven Trumpet Plagues

Each of the seven angels sound a great trumpet in succession to announce the seven trumpet plagues.

> "*[T]here* was silence in heaven *for* about a half hour. Then I saw the **seven angels** who stand before God, and **seven trumpets** were given to them. And another angel, who had a golden censer, came and stood at the altar; and much incense was given to him, so that he might offer *it* with the prayers of all the saints on the golden altar that *was* before the throne. And the smoke of the incense went up before God from *the* hand of the angel, ascending with the prayers of the saints. And the angel took the censer, and filled it with fire from the altar, and cast *it* into the earth; and there were voices, and thunders, and lightnings, and an earthquake" (Rev. 8:1-5).

These "trumpet plagues" begin a more *intense* phase of the Great Tribulation, pitting the angels of God against Satan, his demons and wicked men. The first four trumpet plagues occur in rapid succession (Rev. 8:6-12); the last three plagues escalate in such intensity and power that they are called the three "woes." In Revelation nine, when the fifth angel sounds his trumpet, which is the first woe, demons like "locusts" are loosed out of the Abyss (a prison for demons) to join with men in inflicting pain for five months upon the armies of the East and North (Dan. 11:44). Their torment is caused by some satanic "secret weapon" that causes grievous pain as if one is stung by powerful scorpions (Rev. 9:1-12).

When the sixth angel sounds his trumpet, which is the second woe, it is even more horrific. Using powerful futuristic weapons, the armies of 200 million men and demons launch a counter attack against the Beast and the False Prophet and their armies in the holy land. Four demons bound in the great Euphrates River are loosed and the river dries up, opening the way for the hoards from Asia (Rev. 9:13-19).

While these great battles are being waged, the sign of the Son of Man—the new "sun"—will continue to shine every day from the east to the west. By this time, "day and night" and time in general will be in great disarray. Indeed, with *two suns* in the sky it will be impossible to determine the beginning and ending of a day. This is why we cannot know "the day or the hour" of Jesus' actual return to resurrect and gather the saints. Only God the Father and Jesus Christ will know *exactly* when the day of the *last* Pentecost for the first resurrection will be—for that is under the Father's authority.

After this new "sun" has been in the sky for a nearly a year and a half, people will have become used to its presence, taking it for granted. They will shrug it off, dismiss it as an astronomic anomaly. But at the *set time*—just before the first resurrection—this shining new "sun" will suddenly streak toward the earth. The whole world will be *terrified* that it will collide with the earth. But as it comes into the clouds, this "sun" will suddenly be changed into a great "Sea of Glass." Indeed, that is when "every eye" will see Jesus Christ coming in the clouds with great power and glory—as the Sea of Glass descends into the clouds at a point right over Jerusalem. Rather then repenting, however, the nations will interpret this as a vast "alien" invasion and gather to fight against Christ.

Once the Sea of Glass is positioned over Jerusalem, the *seventh* angel will sound his trumpet—on the *final* Pentecost—and the dead in Christ Jesus will be raised to immortality and carried to the Sea of Glass. Next, those who are alive will be changed and caught up in the air by angels and brought to the Sea of Glass. Notice: "And He shall send His angels with a **great sound of a trumpet** [the *seventh* trumpet]; and they shall **gather together His elect** [to the Sea of Glass] from the four winds, from one end of heaven to the other" (Matt. 24:30-31; also see Rev. 11:15-19; I Thess. 4:13-17; Rev. 14:14-16; Rev. 15:2-4). No doubt the people of the world will witness the resurrection of the saints to immortal glory—and assume that it is part of this "alien" invasion! This is how all those in the resurrection of the saints will meet Christ in the air, in the clouds—from righteous Abel to the Two Witnesses.

***The Seven Last Plagues—the Wrath of God*:** From the time of the first resurrection—on the *final* Pentecost during the last three and one-half years—until the next Feast of Trumpets is a period of three and one-half months. During this time the seven angels will pour out the seven last plagues—which are the wrath of God—upon the armies of the nations that continue to fight against Christ and the resurrected saints on the Sea of Glass in the clouds over Jerusalem. After the first resurrection has been completed and the saints are all standing on the Sea of Glass, John writes:

> "Then I saw another sign in heaven, great and awesome: seven angels having **the seven last plagues, for in them the wrath of God is filled up**.... And the seven angels who had the seven *last* plagues came out of the temple; they were clothed in linen, pure and bright, and girded about the chest with golden breastplates. And one of the four living creatures gave to the seven angels seven golden vials, **full of the wrath of God**, Who lives into the ages of eternity. And the temple was filled with smoke from the glory of God, and from His power; and no one was able to enter inside the temple until the seven plagues of the seven angels were fulfilled" (Rev. 15:1, 6-8).
>
> "Then I heard a loud voice from the temple say to the seven angels, 'Go and pour out the vials of the wrath of God onto the earth.' And **the first *angel* went and poured out his vial onto the earth**; and an evil and grievous sore fell upon the men who had the mark of the beast, and upon those who were worshiping his image. **And the second angel *went and* poured out his vial into the sea**; and it became blood, like *that* of a dead *man*; and every living soul in the sea died. **And the third angel poured out his vial upon the rivers**, and into the fountains of waters; and they became blood.
>
> "Then I heard the angel of the waters say, 'You are righteous, O Lord, Who are, and Who was, even the Holy One, in that You have executed this judgment. For they have poured out *the* blood of saints and of prophets, and You have given them blood to drink; for they are worthy.' And I heard another *voice* from the altar say, '**Yes, Lord God Almighty, true and righteous *are* Your judgments**.'
>
> "**And the fourth angel poured out his vial upon the sun**; and *power* was given to it to scorch men with fire. Then men

> were scorched with great heat; and they blasphemed the name of God, Who has authority over these plagues, and did not repent to give Him glory. **And the fifth angel poured out his vial upon the throne of the beast; and his kingdom** became full of darkness; and they gnawed their tongues because of the pain, and blasphemed the God of heaven because of their pains and their sores; yet they did not repent of their works" (Rev. 16:1-11).

When the sixth angel pours out his plague, the Euphrates is again dried up "so that the way of the kings from the rising of *the* sun might be prepared" (Rev. 16:12). In a last desperate attempt to defeat Jesus Christ and the saints, Satan, the Beast and the False Prophet will send out demonic spirits to persuade the nations and their armies to come and fight against Jesus Christ and the resurrected saints—they are convinced it is an alien invasion from outer space:

> "Then I saw three unclean spirits like frogs *come* out of the mouth of the dragon, and out of the mouth of the beast, and out of the mouth of the false prophet; for they are spirits of demons working miracles, going forth to the kings of the earth, even of the whole world, to gather them together to *the* battle of that great day of the Almighty God.... **And he gathered them together to the place that in Hebrew is called Armageddon**" (verses 13-14, 16).

The prophet Joel describes God's preparation for this battle against all nations:

> "I will also gather all nations and will bring them down into the valley of Jehoshaphat. And I will fight with them there for My people and for My inheritance Israel, whom they have scattered among the nations, and divided My land.... Proclaim this among the nations, 'Prepare for war!' Wake up the mighty men, let all the men of war draw near; let them come up. Beat your plowshares into swords, and your pruning hooks into spears. Let the weak say, 'I *am* strong.'
>
> "**Gather yourselves and come, all you nations**, and gather yourselves together all around; cause Your mighty ones to come down there, O LORD. Let the nations be awakened and come up to the valley of Jehoshaphat; for there I will sit to judge all the nations all around. Put in the sickle, for the harvest is ripe. Come, come down; for the press is full; the vats overflow—for their wickedness is great [see Rev. 14:18-20].

> "**Multitudes, multitudes in the valley of decision; for the day of the LORD *is* near in the valley of decision!** The sun and the moon shall be darkened, and the stars shall withdraw their shining. The LORD shall also roar out of Zion and utter His voice from Jerusalem. And the heavens and the earth shall shake. But the LORD *will be* the hope of His people and the strength of the children of Israel" (Joel 3:2, 9-16).

Thus, the nations gather at Armageddon for the final, end-time battle—where they are utterly destroyed:

> "**Then the seventh angel poured out his vial into the air**; and a loud voice came out of the temple of heaven, from the throne, saying, 'IT IS FINISHED.' And there were voices and thunders and lightnings; and there was a great earthquake, such as was not since men were on the earth, so mighty an earthquake, *and* so great. And the great city was divided into three parts; and the cities of the nations fell; and Babylon the Great was remembered before God to give her the cup of the wine of the fury of His wrath. And every island disappeared, and no mountains were found; and great hail, *each stone* the weight of a talent, fell down from heaven upon men; and men blasphemed God because of the plague of the hail, for the plague was exceedingly great" (Rev. 16:17-21).

Then, on the final Feast of Trumpets ending the Great Tribulation, after God's judgment against Babylon the Great (Revelation 17-18), Jesus Christ and the saints prepare for the final battle against the Beast, False Prophet, Satan the devil and His demons, and the remnant of their armies. As Revelation 19 depicts:

> "And after these things I heard *the* loud voice of a great multitude in heaven [all those of the first resurrection standing on the "sea of glass"], saying, 'Hallelujah! The salvation and the glory and the honor and the power *belong* to the Lord our God. **For true and righteous *are* His judgments; for He has judged the great whore, who corrupted the earth with her fornication, and He has avenged the blood of His servants at her hand**.' And they said a second time, 'Hallelujah! And her smoke shall ascend upward into the ages of eternity.' And the twenty-four elders and the four living creatures fell down and worshiped God, Who sits on the throne, saying, 'Amen. Hallelujah!'
>
> "And a voice came forth from the throne, saying, 'Praise our God, all His servants, and all who fear Him, both small and

great.' And I heard a voice like that of a great multitude, and like *the* sound of many waters, and *the* sound of mighty thunderings, saying, 'Hallelujah! For *the* Lord God Almighty has reigned. Let us be glad and shout with joy; and let us give glory to Him; for the marriage of the Lamb has come, and His wife has made herself ready.'

"And it was granted to her that she should be clothed in fine linen, pure and bright; for the fine linen is the righteousness of the saints. And he said to me, 'Write: Blessed *are* those who are called to the marriage supper of the Lamb.' And he said to me, '**These are the true words of God**.' And I fell at his feet to worship him. And he said to me, 'See *that you do* not *do this*! I am a fellow servant of yours, and of your brethren, who have the testimony of Jesus. Worship God. For the testimony of Jesus is the spirit of prophecy.'

"Then I saw heaven open; and behold, a white horse; and **He Who sat on it *is* called Faithful and True, and in righteousness He does judge and make war**. And His eyes *were* like a flame of fire, and on His head *were* many crowns; *and* He had a name written that no one knows except Him. And *He was* clothed with a garment dipped in blood; and His name is The Word of God. **And the armies in heaven were following Him on white horses**; *and* they were clothed in fine linen, white and pure.

"And out of His mouth goes a sharp sword, that with it He might smite the nations; and He shall shepherd them with an iron rod; and He treads the winepress of the fury and the wrath of the Almighty God. And on *His* garment and on His thigh He has a name written: **King of kings and Lord of lords**.

"Then I saw an angel standing in the sun; and he cried out with a loud voice, saying to all the birds that fly in *the* midst of heaven, 'Come and gather yourselves together to the supper of the great God so that you may eat *the* flesh of kings, and *the* flesh of chief captains, and *the* flesh of mighty *men*, and *the* flesh of horses, and of those who sit on them, and *the* flesh of all, free and bond, and small and great.'

"**And I saw the beast and the kings of the earth and their armies, gathered together to make war with Him Who sits on the horse, and with His army**. And the beast was taken, and with him the false prophet who worked miracles

> in his presence, by which he had deceived those who received the mark of the beast and those who worshiped his image. **Those two were cast alive into the lake of fire, which burns with brimstone**; and the rest were killed by the sword of Him Who sits on the horse, *even the sword* that goes out of His mouth; and all the birds were filled with their flesh" (Rev. 19:1-21).

The prophet Zechariah also foretold of Jesus Christ's powerful return to the earth with the resurrected saints:

> "Behold, the day of the LORD comes, and your spoil shall be divided in your midst, 'For I will gather all nations to battle against Jerusalem; and the city shall be taken, and the houses plundered, and the women raped. And half of the city shall go into exile, and the rest of the people shall not be cut off from the city.' **And the LORD shall go out and fight against those nations, as when He fought in the day of battle. And His feet shall stand in that day upon the Mount of Olives, which *is* before Jerusalem on the east, and the Mount of Olives shall split in two, from the east and to the west, and make a very great valley. And half of the mountain shall move toward the north, and half of it toward the south**....
>
> "And it shall come to pass in that day, that the light shall not be clear, nor dark. And it will be one day which shall be known to the LORD, neither day nor night; but it shall come to pass that at evening time it shall be light.... **And the LORD shall be King over all the earth; in that day there shall be one LORD, and His name shall be one**.... And this shall be the plague with which the LORD will smite all the people who have fought against Jerusalem. Their flesh shall consume away while they stand on their feet, and their eyes shall consume away in their sockets. And their tongue shall consume away in their mouth. And it shall be in that day *that* a great panic from the LORD shall be among them. And they shall each one lay hold of his neighbor, and his hand shall rise up against the hand of his neighbor. And Judah also shall fight at Jerusalem; and the wealth of all the nations all around shall be gathered—gold, and silver, and clothing in great abundance. And likewise shall be the plague of the horse, the mule, the camel, and the donkey, and of all the beasts which shall be in these camps—*it shall be* as this plague" (Zech. 14:1-4, 6-7, 9, 12-15).

Immediately following Jesus' return with the resurrected immortal saints, He will dispatch an angel to *bind* Satan the devil and his demons in a great abyss for the entire 1,000-year period during which Christ and the saints rule. This is "the appointed time" Satan will be bound and imprisoned in the abyss: "Then I saw an angel descending from heaven, having the key of the abyss, and a great chain in his hand. **And he took hold of the dragon, the ancient serpent, who is *the* Devil and Satan, and bound him *for* a thousand years. Then he cast him into the abyss, and locked him *up*, and sealed *the abyss* over him**, so that he would not deceive the nations any longer until the thousand years were fulfilled; and after that it is ordained that he be loosed *for* a short time" (Rev. 20:1-3).

Every year on the Day of Atonement this "appointed time" was depicted by a ritual at the Temple. The high priest was commanded to select two goats—one for the Lord, a type of the Lord—and one for "Azazel," which is another name for Satan the devil. The goat for the Lord was sacrificed and its blood sprinkled upon the Ark of the Covenant in the holy of holies, signifying "the appointed time" when God makes the sacrifice of Jesus Christ available for the people of the whole world. The goat for Azazel was not sacrificed; rather, it was left alive as it represented Satan the devil who is composed of spirit and does not die. The priest confessed all the sins and transgressions of the children of Israel upon the head of the Azazel goat, thus showing that all human sin originated with Satan the devil. Ultimately, a "strong man"—a type of the angel of Revelation 20—led the Azazel goat into the wilderness where it was "let loose," signifying Satan's imprisonment in the abyss (Lev. 16:8-10, 20-22).

After Satan has been bound, the world is then poised for a *new beginning* at "the appointed time"—the restoration of all things (Acts 3:21)! Indeed, the resurrected immortal children of God will help Jesus Christ rescue this world from sin, corruption and vanity:

> "Now if *we are* children, *we are* also heirs—truly, heirs of God and joint heirs with Christ—if indeed we suffer together with Him, so that we may also be glorified together with Him. For I reckon that the sufferings of the present time *are* not worthy *to be compared* with the glory that shall be revealed in us. **For the earnest expectation of the creation itself is awaiting the manifestation of the sons of God; because the creation was subjected to vanity, not willingly, but by reason of Him who subjected *it* in hope, in order that the creation itself might be delivered from the bondage of corruption into the freedom of the glory of the children of God**" (Rom. 8:17-21).

Thus, the prophecies concerning *the appointed times* of the return of Jesus the Messiah, the resurrection of the saints, and the establishment of the

Kingdom of God are fulfilled—and the glorious millennial reign of God begins at "the appointed time" as pictured by the Feast of Tabernacles. Revelation 20 describes this glorious event: "And I saw thrones; and they that sat upon them, and judgment was given to them; and *I saw* the souls of those who had been beheaded for the testimony of Jesus, and for the Word of God, and those who did not worship the beast, or his image, and did not receive the mark in their foreheads or in their hands; and they lived and reigned with Christ a thousand years.... This *is* the first resurrection. Blessed and holy is the one who has part in the first resurrection; over these the second death has no power. But they shall be priests of God and of Christ, and shall reign with Him a thousand years" (Rev. 20:4-6).

The Final "Appointed Time"—The Last Great Day

There remains to be examined one, *final* "appointed time" in the work of Jesus the Messiah. Mentioned only three times in the Bible, it is the least understood of all the "appointed feasts" of God. This *final* holy day, commanded in Leviticus 23:36, is called the "eighth day" because it follows the seven days of the Feast of Tabernacles. This "appointed" festival is a holy convocation, a high day.

As pictured by the Feast of Tabernacles, the 1000-year rule of Jesus Christ with the saints is the time of the "restoring of all things" (Acts 3:21). The Millennium, however, is only preparatory to this final "appointed time" pictured by the "eighth day"—the Last Great Day. As heir to David's throne, Jesus the Messiah has been promised an *eternal* dominion (Isa. 9:7; Luke 1:33). Thus, "the appointed time" of Jesus' reign is not limited to the millennial age—but extends into the ages of eternity!

This is why this particular feast falls on the "eighth" day. The number eight points to *abundance*. The Hebrew root word for eight means "to be fat"—as in plentiful. Based on its use in the Old Testament, the number eight is primarily associated with *new beginnings*. For example, circumcision was on the eighth day, signifying a *new beginning* under the sign of the Abrahamic covenant; a sacrificial animal had to be at least eight days old to be sacrificed; and, various cleansings were for a full seven days, allowing the person to re-enter the camp on the eighth day. Noah was called the "eighth person" (II Pet. 2:5) as mankind embarked upon a new beginning after the Flood.

The apostle John writes what Jesus said *on this very day* during His ministry: "Now in the last day, the great *day* of the feast [of Tabernacles], Jesus stood and called out, saying, 'If anyone thirsts, let him come to Me and drink' " (John 7:37). Verses 38-39 show that Jesus was referring to the living waters of the Holy Spirit—which makes eternal life possible.

Thus, this feast is called the Last Great Day—but *why*? For the answer, we need to look again at the 70-week prophecy, as this decree is *all encompassing*—reaching from Daniel's time to the beginning of the New Heavens and New Earth (Rev. 21-22). Notice what Daniel was commanded to write: "Seventy weeks are decreed upon your people and upon your holy city **to finish the transgression** and **to make an end of sin,** and to make reconciliation for iniquity, **and to bring in everlasting righteousness**, and to seal up the vision and prophecy, and to anoint the Most Holy" (Dan. 9:24). According to this decree, there are *three* aspects of the work of the Messiah which He must yet accomplish to completely fulfill the prophecy. They are: **1) finish the transgression**; **2) make an end of sin**; and **3) bring in everlasting righteousness**.

Throughout the 1000-year reign of Jesus and the saints of the first resurrection, Satan and his evil spirits will be bound in the abyss (Rev. 20:2-3). At the end of the Millennium they are released for a very short period of time (verse 7), during which they mastermind a brief but destructive rebellion against God (verses 8-9). Once this rebellion is put down, Satan and the demons face their final judgment (verse 10)—to be cast into the lake of fire and then banished forever into *eternal* "blackness of darkness" where they can never again exert their evil influence (Jude 13).

After God executes His judgment against Satan and the demons, the final "appointed time" of the 70-week prophecy begins. It is known as the "Great White Throne Judgment" (Rev. 20:11-13), wherein all who have ever lived and died without having received an opportunity for salvation are resurrected to a *second* physical life for a "first opportunity" for salvation (Ezek. 37:1-14). In Revelation 20:5, they are referred to as *the rest of the dead*: "But the rest of the dead did not live again until the thousand years were completed." This resurrection is known as the *second resurrection.* Based on Isaiah 65:20, a period of 100 years is allotted for those of this resurrection to learn God's way of life and qualify for His gift of eternal life (Rev. 20:11-13). In spite of His offer of mercy and forgiveness, an incorrigible *few* will reject God and His way. They will be cast into the lake of fire and suffer eternal destruction (verse 15). Ultimately, *the grave and death itself* are destroyed (verse 14). When this 100-year period has been completed, Jesus will deliver the kingdom up to God the Father (I Cor. 15:24). Now the stage is set for the New Heavens, the New Earth, the New Jerusalem, and the eternal presence of God the Father.

> "Then I saw a **new heaven** and a **new earth**; for the first heaven and the first earth were passed away, and there was no more sea. And I, John, **saw the holy city, *the* new Jerusalem**, coming down from God out of heaven, prepared as a bride adorned for her husband. And I heard a great voice from heaven say, 'Behold, t**he tabernacle of God *is* with men; and He shall dwell with them, and they shall be His people; and God Himself shall be with them *and be* their God**. And God shall wipe away every tear from their eyes; and *there* shall not be any more death, or sorrow, or crying; neither shall *there* be any more pain, because the former things have passed away' " (Rev 21:1-4).

Thus, Jesus the Messiah will entirely fulfill the 70-week prophecy of Daniel nine: **1) The transgression of Satan and the demons has been finished**; **2) He has made an end of all human sin**; and **3) He brings in everlasting righteousness**—into the ages of eternity.

The entire spiritual Family of God—now composed of billions and billions of immortal spirit beings who were once human—will live forever as the spirit-composed sons and daughters of God the Father. Jesus will proclaim, "**Behold, I make all things new!**" It will truly be a *new beginning* in a perfect world, in a perfect universe—an "open door" to all eternity (Rev. 21-22).

Finally, Jesus the Messiah will triumphantly announce, "**It is done!**" The entire plan of God has been fulfilled, leading to a completely *new eternal, spiritual beginning*—"I am Alpha and Omega, the Beginning and the End. To the one who thirsts, I will give freely of the fountain of the water of [eternal] life" (Rev. 21:6).

What, then, will be the new "appointed times" of God the Father and Jesus Christ for "the ages of eternity?"

Conclusion

When it comes to the salvation of mankind through Jesus Christ, the prophet Amos instructs us that God will do nothing except He first reveal His plans through His servants the prophets (Amos 3:7). Of all the prophets of old, Moses was the most renowned. As this book thoroughly authenticates, God used Moses to reveal—albeit in a veiled form—His Master Plan for human salvation in a *series* of "appointed times."

God's "appointed times" take the unique form of *annual festivals* based, for the most part, on the agricultural cycle. To scholars and religionists, these festivals (which include the weekly Sabbath and the annual high days or holy days) look like nothing more than rituals tied to the harvest seasons—unimportant relics of ancient peoples, obscured by time, and having no significance to "New Testament" Christians. But they could not be more mistaken!

Israel's "harvest festivals" were carefully crafted by God to teach powerful lessons and to provide awesome spiritual realities. The apostle Paul wrote that Israel served as an *archetype* for the Church, stating that certain things "happened to them *as* examples," which were "written for our admonition, on whom the ends of the ages are coming" (I Cor. 10:11). The word "examples" is translated from the Greek *tupos*, from which we get the English word *type*. Thus, numerous benchmarks in the history of Israel would serve as *prototypes* for the Church (which is *spiritual* Israel), and foremost among them are the *annual festivals* and *holy days* God gave to that nation. These festivals were also faithfully observed by both Jews and Gentiles of the apostolic New Testament Church.

What more appropriate parallel could be found—using the *physical*, agrarian harvest cycle to portray the *spiritual* harvesting of mankind into the Kingdom of God (Matt. 13). Properly understood, these "appointed" festivals are arranged in *three* seasons (Ex. 23:14; Deut. 16:16), and encompass *seven* annual holy days. Briefly, by way of review, the spring festival season includes Passover and the seven days of Unleavened Bread (of which the first and last days are high days); the late spring festival is the Feast of Firstfruits, more widely known as Pentecost (a single high day). The fall festival season begins with the Day of Trumpets, a high day, followed nine days later by the Day of Atonement, also a high day. Later, on the 15th day of the month, comes the seven-day Feast of Tabernacles, of which the first day is a high day. That leaves one final high day—the Last Great Day—which comes as an "eighth day" after Tabernacles ends. (For a complete, detailed study on the meaning of God's annual festivals, please request our book *God's Plan for Mankind Revealed by His Sabbath and Holy Days.* This first-of-its-kind, 598-page work provides a comprehensive look at God's amazing Master Plan for the human family, precisely as it is outlined by the biblical seventh-day Sabbath and annual holy days. Each chapter is a transcript of an in-depth sermon or Bible study revealing God's purpose from Genesis to Revelation. All the sermons are included on an accompanying set of four CDs.)

God's festivals and high days are actually "appointed times"—that is, they are to be observed 1) in their appropriate season, and 2) they are to be kept on their duly *appointed days*. For example, in Exodus 13:10 we are instructed to keep the Feast of Unleavened Bread "in its season" or "appointed time" (the Hebrew term used is *moed*, literally meaning an "appointed time"). In Leviticus 23, where all of God's holy days are listed together, they are called "the appointed feasts [*moadim*, plural—*appointed times*] of the LORD, holy convocations which you shall proclaim in their appointed seasons [*moadim*]" (verses 2, 4). In a sense, God's "appointed times" are appointments *with Him*—and must be kept!

The focal point of this book has been Jesus, the Messiah of God. Indeed, at the heart and core of God's plan of salvation is the Christ, Who is the central figure in each of these "appointed festivals." As this book has demonstrated, Jesus' entire life, ministry, as well as His future role in the age to come, are ordered according to these same "appointed times." As messianic prophecies have been fulfilled across the centuries, they have done so in a *highly organized* manner—according to God's specific "appointed times" in conjunction with the 70-week prophecy in Daniel nine. Thus, God's holy days weave a kind of framework or substructure upon which all prophecy is ordered, arranged and fulfilled.

The first "appointed time" of Jesus the Messiah relates to His *birth* as the Savior of mankind. As Paul wrote, "when **the [appointed] time** for the fulfillment [of the promise to Abraham of a "Seed" (Gal. 3:16)] came, God sent forth His own Son, born of a woman…" (Gal. 4:4). Thus, Jesus' birth occurred according to a carefully planned *timetable*. Using both Scripture and secular history, we have shown that Jesus' birth corresponded to "the appointed time" of the fall festival season—specifically the Day of Trumpets. Trumpets is also widely acknowledged for its association with the return of Christ; thus, it is only fitting that God would choose the same holy day to have His Son enter the world the first time!

There has been great debate as to exactly *when* Jesus began His ministry—as well as how long it lasted. The answer, again, is made clear by carefully examining the "appointed times" and the 70-week prophecy as they relate to the Messiah. As brought out in Chapter Two, our historical and biblical analysis of Daniel's 70-week prophecy places the beginning of Jesus' ministry in the fall of 26 AD—and specifically at the beginning of a Jubilee year, the 50th year in the continuous land Sabbath cycle (Lev. 25:1-13). The fact that Jubilee years are announced and begin on the high day of Atonement means that Jesus began His ministry with the 40-day temptation by Satan the devil on "the appointed time" of Atonement.

However, Jesus did not publicly announce the fact that He was the "Anointed One" until the following Pentecost—the 50th day, a mini-jubilee.

One of the focal points of Jesus' ministry was the building of His Church (Matt. 16:18)—those who would become the firstfruits of God's salvation. Since "the appointed time" of Pentecost points to the resurrection of the saints—those who make up the true Church—Pentecost was the most appropriate high day on which to emphasize the fact that Jesus was indeed the Messiah of God, the one Who would bring salvation to mankind, beginning with the firstfruits.

The next "appointed time" of the Messiah relates to His sacrificial death for mankind. Paul tells us that "at **the appointed time** Christ died for the ungodly" (Rom. 5:6). Thus, Jesus' death also occurred according to a carefully planned *timetable*. In fact, long before the creation of the world, *this momentous event* had been planned: A member of the very God Family would divest Himself of His glory and manifest Himself as a human being; then, at "the appointed time," He would *give Himself* in death—*lay down His life* as the ultimate sacrifice for the sins of man. Indeed, Jesus was as good as "slain from *the* foundation of *the* world" (Rev. 13:8). In time, Jesus would come and *pay with His own blood* in order to release man from the power of Satan and the bondage of sin, and to reconcile mankind to God the Father. Paul would later write that "Christ our Passover"—at "the appointed time" of Nisan 14th—"was sacrificed for us" (I Cor. 5:7). All true Christians, then, have been bought with a great price and now belong to Jesus the Messiah.

The time Jesus spent entombed in the grave directly corresponds to one of God's holy days—the first day of the Feast of Unleavened Bread—and ends with the weekly Sabbath during this particular feast. Jesus Himself pronounced "the appointed time" that He would be in the grave. By referring to Jonah's "entombment" in the belly of a great fish (Jonah 1:17), Christ foretold that He would be in the grave for *exactly* three days and three nights. This was the only sign He gave as proof that He was the Messiah. Thus, the fulfillment of this prophecy was a testimony not only to that generation, but to all future generations that Jesus was, and is, the "Anointed One" of God. Jesus' "appointed time" in the grave was followed immediately by "the appointed time" of His resurrection on the weekly Sabbath, just before sunset as that Sabbath was ending. Misinterpreting the scriptural record, Christians today typically believe that Jesus was crucified and laid in a tomb on a Friday, and that He was resurrected on Sunday morning. Thus, according to their reasoning, He was not actually in the tomb for three days and three nights, as He had prophesied, but for only two nights and one full day—which, if true, would discredit Him as our Savior.

During the Feast of Unleavened Bread, the high priest at the Tabernacle/Temple was instructed to take a premier sheaf of the first-ripe barley and "wave" it before God (Lev. 23:9-11). The instructions for this unusual ceremony are found along with the listing of the annual holy days; however, the "wave sheaf offering" (as it came to be known) is not itself a high day. As shown in Chapter Six, this unique ceremony points to a crucial "appointed time" of the Messiah. As the sacrifice of the Passover lamb was a type of the crucifixion and death of Christ, so the offering of the wave sheaf was a type of Jesus' ascension to God the Father in heaven to be accepted as the *first of the firstfruits—as the firstborn from among the dead!*

On this day, Jesus—as the Lamb of God, having been beaten and slain as "appointed"—ascended to the throne of God the Father and was *accepted* as the sin offering for the sins of all mankind. Anciently, the *premier* sheaf of grain had to be *accepted* by God before *any other grain* could be harvested. Likewise, only when Jesus had been *raised to life* and subsequently presented before God the Father in heaven for His acceptance could salvation even *begin* to be offered to man. Interestingly, it is through the wave sheaf offering that the "count" to Pentecost begins—and Pentecost ultimately pictures the salvation of the firstfruits, the Church, culminating in the first resurrection.

As previously noted, God's holy days form an intricate framework or substructure upon which prophecy is arrayed, ordered and fulfilled. Prophecies dealing with the latter days will also be fulfilled according to God's "appointed times." Our careful exegesis of the Scriptures dealing with the timelines presented by the books of Daniel and Revelation has proven that Jesus' return will occur only *after* specific signs and events. In fact, Scripture gives *three key events* in this regard: 1) the rebuilding of the Temple in Jerusalem, which signals the beginning of the end; 2) the setting up of the "abomination of desolation," which marks the beginning of the Great Tribulation; and 3) the *sign* of the Son of Man in heaven, which heralds the return of Christ. An accurate understanding of these events demonstrates that Jesus' return corresponds to the "appointed times" of Pentecost and Trumpets. While we cannot know the "day or hour" of Jesus' return, it is apparent that the Feast of Trumpets pictures Christ's second coming—and undoubtedly it is the *very day* of His literal return to the earth to usher in the Kingdom of God. The Day of Atonement, of course, pictures the removal of Satan the devil, while the Feast of Tabernacles and Last Great Day portray the age to come under the peaceful reign of Christ and His bride, when universal salvation will be offered to all mankind.

As you have seen throughout this book, God has divinely designed the salvation-centered role of Jesus the Messiah in accordance with the 70-week prophecy of Daniel nine and the "appointed times" of His holy days. *Each key event* in the life and ministry of Jesus Christ—from His birth to His second coming to establish the millennial age—has been correlated to various aspects of the three festival seasons. Indeed, it is only within this unique framework of God's "appointed times" that the pivotal role of Jesus as the Messiah can be rightly understood.

Appendices

Appendix A

A Synchronized Chart of Historical and Scriptural Records That Establish The Year of Christ's Birth

Few Bible students realize that a vast amount of evidence is available with which to *prove* the year of Jesus' birth. In keeping with the biblical principle that a matter should be established by the testimony of two or three witnesses (Deut. 17:6; Matt. 18:16; etc.), we find that there are indeed *three* witnesses—history, Scripture and astronomy—which corroborate the year of Christ's birth. These three witnesses combined build a valid case, proving conclusively that Jesus was born in the fall of 5 BC.

The primary scriptural records are those provided by Matthew and Luke. The astronomical evidence includes the full lunar eclipse of September 15, 5 BC, used to pinpoint the time of Herod's death.

The primary historical references that enable us to determine when Christ was born are those of Roman historians and of the Jewish historian Josephus, who lived from about 37 AD to 100 AD. These secular records can be used to establish the reign of Herod the Great, who attempted to kill the infant Jesus. Josephus records the names of the consuls who ruled in Rome at the time that Herod began his reign. Lists of all the consuls who ruled during the years from 509 BC to 337 AD have been preserved by Roman historians, giving us an exact time frame for dating the reign of Herod, which is essential to identifying the year of Christ's birth.

Josephus records that Herod received the kingdom in Rome in the 184th Olympiad (*Antiquities*, 14:14:5). Each Olympiad was four years in length, with the years being reckoned from July 1 through June 30. The 184th Olympiad was from July 1, 44 BC, to June 30, 40 BC. Josephus also records that Herod began his reign when Calvinus and Pollio were consuls of Rome. Calvinus and Pollio were consuls from January 1, 40 BC, to December 31, 40 BC. Since the 184th Olympiad ended on June 30, 40 BC, it is evident that the reign of Herod as king in Rome began sometime between January 1, 40 BC, and June 30, 40 BC.

According to Josephus, Herod reigned thirty-seven years from the time of his coronation in Rome (*Antiquities of the Jews*, 17:8:1; *Wars of the Jews*, 1:33:8). Consequently, the end of his reign occurred sometime between January 1, 4 BC, and June 30, 4 BC. Since Jesus was born during the final months of Herod's reign, the historical facts limit the time of His birth to the period from June 30, 5 BC, to June 30, 4 BC. Because the Gospels place His birth during the fall festival season, the time is further limited to the year 5 BC.

The historical and scriptural records are presented in chart form on the following pages.

Synchronized Chart Establishing the Year of Christ's Birth

Greek Olympiad		Year of Rome	Year BC - AD	Hasmonian Rule	Reign of Herod	
					Roman Count	Jewish Count
179	1	691	63*	100		
	2	692	62	101		
	3	693	61	102		
	4	694	60	103		
180	1	695	59	104		
	2	696	58	105		
	3	697	57	106		
	4	698	56	107		
181	1	699	55	108		
	2	700	54	109		
	3	701	53	110		
	4	702	52	111		
182	1	703	51	112		
	2	704	50	113		
	3	705	49	114		
	4	706	48	115		
183	1	707	47	116		
	2	708	46	117		
	3	709	45	118		
	4	710	44	119		
184	1	711	43	120		
	2	712	42	121		
	3	713	41	122		
	4	714	40•	123	1	
185	1	715	39	124	2	
	2	716	38	125	3	
	3	717	37†	126	4	1
	4	718	36		5	2
186	1	719	35		6	3
	2	720	34		7	4
	3	721	33		8	5
	4	722	32		9	6

* 63 BC Jerusalem captured by Roman general Pompey during 179th olympiad. Antonius and Cicero are Roman consuls (Josephus, *Ant.*, 14:4:3).

• 40 BC Herod receives kingdom in Rome during 184th olympiad. Calvinus and Pollio are Roman consuls (Josephus, *Ant.*, 14:14:5).

† 37 BC Hasmoneans' 126-year rule of Jerusalem ends during 185th olympiad. Herod receives kingdom in Jerusalem. Agrippa and Gallus are Roman consuls (Josephus, *Ant.*, 14:16:4).

Greek Olympiad		Year of Rome	Year BC - AD	Life of Christ	Reign of Augustus	Reign of Herod		Temple Rebuilt
						Roman Count	Jewish Count	
187	1	723	31*		1	10	7	
	2	724	30		2	11	8	
	3	725	29		3	12	9	
	4	726	28		4	13	10	
188	1	727	27		5	14	11	
	2	728	26		6	15	12	
	3	729	25•		7	16	13	
	4	730	24		8	17	14	
189	1	731	23		9	18	15	
	2	732	22		10	19	16	
	3	733	21†		11	20	17	
	4	734	20§		12	21	18	1
190	1	735	19		13	22	19	2
	2	736	18		14	23	20	3
	3	737	17		15	24	21	4
	4	738	16		16	25	22	5
191	1	739	15		17	26	23	6
	2	740	14		18	27	24	7
	3	741	13		19	28	25	8
	4	742	12		20	29	26	9
192	1	743	11		21	30	27	10
	2	744	10		22	31	28	11
	3	745	9		23	32	29	12
	4	746	8		24	33	30	13
193	1	747	7		25	34	31	14
	2	748	6		26	35	32	15
Jesus Born	3	749	5★	0	27	36	33	16
	4	750	4Ω	1	28	37	34	17

* 31 BC Battle of Actium, seventh year of Herod's reign, 187th olympiad (Josephus, *Ant.*, 15:5:1; 15:5:2).

• 25 BC Two-year famine begins in Herod's thirteenth year (Josephus, *Ant.*, 15:9:1).

† 21 BC Augustus visits Syria during seventeenth year of Herod's reign; Apuleius and Silvius are Roman consuls (*Dio's Roman History*, LIV:7:4-6; Josephus, *Ant.*, 15:10:3).

§ 20 BC Construction of Herod's temple begins in Herod's eighteenth year (Josephus, *Ant.*, 15:11:1).

★ 5 BC Jesus born during fall festival season—most likely on the Feast of Trumpets.

Ω 4 BC Herod dies in thirty-seventh year of having received kingdom in Rome and thirty-fourth year of having received kingdom in Jerusalem (Josephus, *Ant.*, 17:8:1; *Wars*, 1:33:8).

Synchronized Chart Establishing the Year of Christ's Birth

Greek Olympiad		Year of Rome	Year BC - AD	Life of Christ	Reign of Augustus	Reign of Tiberius	Pilate Governs Judea	Temple Rebuilt
194	1	751	3	2	29			18
	2	752	2	3	30			19
	3	753	1 BC	4	31			20
	There is no year zero	There is no year zero		There is no year zero		There is no year zero	There is no year zero	
	4	754	1 AD	5	32			21
195	1	755	2	6	33			22
	2	756	3	7	34			23
	3	757	4	8	35			24
	4	758	5	9	36			25
196	1	759	6	10	37			26
	2	760	7	11	38			27
	3	761	8	12	39			28
	4	762	9	13	40			29
197	1	763	10	14	41			30
	2	764	11	15	42			31
	3	765	12	16	43	1		32
	4	766	13	17	44	2		33
198	1	767	14	18	45	3		344
	2	768	15	19		4		35
	3	769	16	20		5		36
	4	770	17	21		6		37
199	1	771	18	22		7		38
	2	772	19	23		8		39
	3	773	20	24		9		40
	4	774	21	25		10		41
200	1	775	22	26		11		42
	2	776	23	27		12		43
	3	777	24	28		13		44
	4	778	25	29		14		45
201	1	779	26*	30		15	1	46
	2	780	27	31		16	2	
	3	781	28	32		17	3	
	4	782	29	33	Crucified	18	4	
202	1	783	30★	33½	Nisan 14	19	5	
	2	784	31			20	6	
	3	785	32			21	7	
	4	786	33			22	8	

* 26 AD Pontius Pilate assumes governance of Judea (Luke 3:1). Jesus begins ministry at about age thirty (Lk. 3:23). Herod's temple 46 years in building (John 2:20).

★ 30 AD Jesus crucified, Wednesday, April 5, 30 AD – The Passover Day, Nisan 14.

Appendix A

Greek Olympiad		Year of Rome	Year AD	Reign of Tiberius	Pilate Governs Judea
203	1	787	34	23	9
	2	788	35	24	10
	3	789	36	25	
	4	790	37	26	
204	1	791	38		
	2	792	39		
	3	793	40		
	4	794	41		
205	1	795	42		
	2	796	43		
	3	797	44		
	4	798	45		
206	1	799	46*		
	2	800	47		
	3	801	48		
	4	802	49		
207	1	803	50		
	2	804	51		
	3	805	52		
	4	806	53		
208	1	807	54		
	2	808	55		
	3	809	56		
	4	810	57		
209	1	811	58		
	2	812	59		
	3	813	60		
	4	814	61		
210	1	815	62		
	2	816	63		
	3	817	64		
	4	818	65		
211	1	819	66•		
	2	820	67		
	3	821	68		
	4	822	69		
212	1	823	70†		

* 46 AD The apostle Paul begins his missionary journeys.
• 66 AD Jewish wars begin.
† 70 AD Destruction of Temple occurs.

Appendix B

Twenty-Eight Prophecies Fulfilled On the Crucifixion Day

On the Passover day, the day of the crucifixion, all the words of the prophets concerning the suffering of the Christ, or the Anointed One, were fulfilled. Their fulfillment in every detail stands today as a lasting testimony to the Messiahship of Jesus Christ.

The first prophecy, the oldest of all, had been given by the Lord Himself at the time of Adam and Eve's first sin:

1) The serpent would bruise the seed of the woman.
Prophesied: "And I will put enmity between you and the woman, and between your seed and her Seed; He will bruise your head, and you shall bruise His heel" (Gen. 3:15).
Fulfilled: " 'Now is *the* judgment of this world. Now shall the prince of this world be cast out. And if I be lifted up from the earth, I will draw all to Myself.' But He said this to signify by what death He was about to die" (John 12:31-33).

2) The Messiah would be cut off, but not for Himself, as prophesied by Daniel.
Prophesied: "And after sixty-two weeks Messiah shall be cut off, but not for Himself…" (Dan. 9:26).
Fulfilled: " 'Nor consider that it is better for us that one man die for the people, than that the whole nation should perish.' Now he did not say this of himself, but being high priest that year, prophesied that Jesus would die for the nation; and not for the nation only, but also that He might gather together into one the children of God who were scattered abroad" (John 11:50-52).

3) The betrayal of Jesus by Judas was foretold by David.
Prophesied: "Even a man, My friend in whom I trusted, who ate of My bread, has lifted up his heel against Me" (Psa. 41:9).
Fulfilled: "Then Judas Iscariot, one of the twelve, went to the chief priests in order that he might deliver Him up to them. And after hearing *this*, they were delighted and promised to give him money. And he sought how he might conveniently betray Him" (Mark 14:10-11).

4) Jesus Christ would be forsaken by His disciples, as prophesied by Zechariah.
Prophesied: " 'Awake, O sword, against My Shepherd, and against the Man who is My companion,' says the LORD of hosts. 'Strike the Shepherd [Jesus], and the sheep shall be scattered…' " (Zech. 13:7).
Fulfilled: "Then they all forsook Him and fled" (Mark 14:50).

5) The price of His betrayal was also foretold by Zechariah.
Prophesied: "And I said to them, 'If *it is* good, give me my price; and if not, let it go.' So they weighed my price—thirty *pieces* of silver" (Zech. 11:12).
Fulfilled: "*And* said, 'What are you willing to give me, and I will deliver Him up to you?' And they offered him thirty pieces of silver" (Matt. 26:15).

6) Zechariah also foretold what would be done with the betrayal money.
Prophesied: "And the LORD said to me, 'Throw it to the potter'—the princely price at which I was valued by them. And I took the thirty *pieces* of silver and threw them to the potter in the house of the LORD" (Zech. 11:13).
Fulfilled: "Now when Judas, who had betrayed Him, saw that He was condemned, he changed his mind *and* returned the thirty pieces of silver to the chief priests and the elders, saying, 'I have sinned and have betrayed innocent blood.' But they said, 'What *is that* to us? You see *to it* yourself.' And after throwing down the pieces of silver in the temple, he went out and hanged himself. But the chief priests took the pieces of silver *and* said, 'It is not lawful to put them into the treasury, since it is *the* price of blood.' And after taking counsel, they bought a potter's field with the *pieces of silver*, for a burial ground for strangers" (Matt. 27:3-7).

7) Isaiah prophesied that Jesus Christ would be sacrificed as the Passover Lamb of God.
Prophesied: "He is brought as a lamb to the slaughter…" (Isa. 53:7).
Fulfilled: "For Christ our Passover was sacrificed for us" (I Cor. 5:7). "Knowing that you were not redeemed by corruptible things … but by *the* precious blood of Christ, as of a lamb without blemish and without spot; Who truly was foreknown before *the* foundation of *the* world, but was manifested in *these* last times for your sakes" (I Pet. 1:18-20).

8) Isaiah also prophesied the scourging and mocking that He would suffer.
Prophesied: "I gave My back to the smiters [scourgers], and My cheeks to them that plucked off the hair; I did not hide My face from shame and spitting" (Isa. 50:6).
Fulfilled: "Then he released Barabbas to them; but after scourging Jesus, he delivered *Him* up so that He might be crucified. Then the governor's soldiers, after taking Jesus with *them* into the Praetorium, gathered the entire band against Him; and they stripped Him *and* put a scarlet cloak around Him. And after platting a crown of thorns, they put *it* on His head; and a rod in His right hand; and bowing *on* their knees before Him, they mocked Him, and *kept on* saying, 'Hail, king of the Jews!' Then, after spitting on Him, they took the rod and struck *Him* on the head" (Matt. 27:26-30).

9) Both Isaiah and David prophesied that Jesus' body would be mutilated.
Prophesied: "Many were astonished at Him—for *His body was* so disfigured—even His form beyond that of the sons of men" (Isa. 52:14). "I can count all My bones; they look and gloat over Me" (Psa. 22:17).

Fulfilled: "But after scourging Jesus, he delivered *Him* up so that He might be crucified" (Matt. 27:26). "Then Pilate therefore took Jesus and scourged *Him*" (John 19:1).

10) David prophesied of the shame and dishonor Jesus would suffer, being condemned as a common criminal.
Prophesied: "[T]he reproaches of those who reproached You have fallen upon Me…. You have known My reproach, and My shame, and My dishonor; My enemies are all before You. Reproach has broken My heart, and I am full of heaviness; and I looked for some to take pity, but there was none; and for comforters, but I found none" (Psa. 69:9, 19-20).
Fulfilled: "At that point Jesus said to the crowd, 'Have you come out to take Me with swords and clubs, as against a robber?' " (Matt. 26:55). "They answered *and* said, 'He is deserving of death!' " (Matt. 26:66).

11) David also foretold that false witnesses would testify against Christ.
Prophesied: "Cruel witnesses rose up; they asked Me of things that I knew nothing about" (Psa. 35:11).
Fulfilled: "And the chief priests and the whole Sanhedrin were trying to find testimony against Jesus, to put Him to death; but they did not find *any*. For many bore false witness against Him, but their testimonies did not agree. And some rose up and bore false witness against Him…" (Mark 14:55-57).

12) Isaiah prophesied that Jesus would not make an effort to defend Himself at the trial.
Prophesied: "He was oppressed, and He was afflicted; yet He opened not His mouth. He is brought as a lamb to the slaughter; and as a sheep before its shearers is dumb, so He opened not His mouth" (Isa. 53:7).
Fulfilled: "Then Pilate said to Him, 'Don't You hear how many things they testify against You?' And He did not answer even one word to him, so that the governor was greatly amazed" (Matt. 27:13-14).

13) Isaiah also foretold Jesus Christ's crucifixion as the sin offering for the world.
Prophesied: "Surely He has borne our infirmities, and carried our sorrows; yet we esteemed Him stricken, smitten of God, and afflicted. But He *was* wounded for our transgressions; *He was* crushed for our iniquities; the chastisement of our peace *was* upon Him; and with His stripes we ourselves are healed. All we like sheep have gone astray; we have turned each one to his own way; and the LORD has laid on Him the iniquity of us all…. Yet the LORD willed to crush Him and He has put Him to grief: You shall make His life an offering for sin. He shall see His seed; He shall prolong His days, and that the purpose of the LORD might prosper in His hand. He shall see of the travail of His soul. He shall be fully satisfied. By His knowledge shall My righteous Servant justify many; and He shall bear their iniquities" (Isa. 53:4-6, 10-11).

Fulfilled: "Therefore, he then delivered Him up to them so that He might be crucified. Now they took Jesus and led *Him* away; and He went out bearing His own cross to the place called 'A Skull,' which is called in Hebrew 'Golgotha,' where they crucified Him, and with Him two others, one on this side and *one* on the other side, and Jesus in the middle. Now Pilate also wrote a title and put it on the cross. And it was written, 'Jesus the Nazarean, the King of the Jews' " (John 19:16-19).

14) As Isaiah had prophesied, He was numbered among lawbreakers.
Prophesied: "He was counted among the transgressors…" (Isa. 53:12).
Fulfilled: "And also two other malefactors were led away with Him to be put to death. And when they came to the place called 'Skull,' there they crucified Him and the malefactors, one on *the* right and one on *the* left" (Luke 23:32-33).

15) David prophesied that His hands and feet would be pierced.
Prophesied: "Dogs have surrounded Me; a band of evildoers have encircled Me; they have pierced My hands and My feet" (Psa. 22:16).
Fulfilled: "And they crucified Him" (Mark 15:25). "Then the other disciples said to him, 'We have seen the Lord!' But he said to them, 'If I do not see the nail marks in His hands, and put my finger into the nail marks, and put my hand into His side, I will not believe at all!' Now after eight days, His disciples were within, and Thomas with them. After the doors were shut, Jesus came and stood in the midst, and said, 'Peace to you.' Then He said to Thomas, 'Bring forth your finger, and see My hands; and bring *forth* your hand, and put *it* into My side; and be not unbelieving, but believing' " (John 20:25-27).

16) The parting of His garments was also prophesied by David.
Prophesied: "They divide My garments among them and cast lots upon My vesture" (Psa. 22:18).
Fulfilled: "Then they said to one another, 'Let us not tear it, but let us cast lots for it *to determine* whose it shall be,' that the Scripture might be fulfilled, which says, 'They divided My garments among them, and they cast lots for My vesture.' Therefore the soldiers did these things" (John 19:24).

17) In another psalm, David prophesied that they would give Him vinegar to drink.
Prophesied: "They also gave Me gall for My food; and in My thirst they gave Me vinegar to drink" (Psa. 69:21).
Fulfilled: "They gave Him vinegar mingled with gall to drink; but after tasting *it*, He would not drink" (Matt. 27:34).

18) David also prophesied that many would be watching Jesus during the crucifixion.
Prophesied: "[T]hey look and gloat over Me" (Psa. 22:17).

Fulfilled: "And the guards sat down there to guard Him" (Matt. 27:36). "And all the people who were gathered together to this sight, after seeing the things that took place, beat their breasts *and* returned" (Luke 23:48).

19) Among those watching would be Jesus' family and friends, who would stand at a distance.
Prophesied: "My loved ones and my friends stand apart from my plague [wounds]; and My neighbors stand far off" (Psa. 38:11).
Fulfilled: "Now all those who knew Him stood afar off observing these things, *the* women also who followed Him from Galilee" (Luke 23:49).

20) Some of His observers would shake their heads at Him.
Prophesied: "And I also became a reproach to them when they looked upon Me; they shook their heads" (Psa. 109:25).
Fulfilled: "But those who were passing by railed at Him, shaking their heads and saying, "You who *would* destroy the temple and build *it* in three days, save Yourself! If You are the Son of God, come down from the cross!" (Matt. 27:39-40).

21) Even the words of His reproachers were prophesied by David.
Prophesied: "He trusted on the LORD; let Him deliver Him; let Him rescue Him, since He delights in Him" (Psa. 22:8).
Fulfilled: " 'He trusted in God; let Him deliver Him now, if He will *have* Him; for He said, "I am the Son of God." ' And the two robbers who were also crucified with Him reproached Him with the same *words*" (Matt. 27:43-44).

22) Isaiah prophesied that Jesus would make intercession for sinners; this intercession began even during His crucifixion.
Prophesied: "He bore the sin of many, and made intercession for transgressors" (Isa. 53:12).
Fulfilled: "Then Jesus said, 'Father, forgive them, for they do not understand what they are doing.' And they divided His garments, and cast lots" (Luke 23:34).

23) David prophesied of Jesus' thoughts at the height of His suffering.
Prophesied: "My God, My God, why have You forsaken Me, and *why are You so* far from helping Me, and from the words of My groaning?" (Psa. 22:1).
Fulfilled: "And about the ninth hour, Jesus cried out with a loud voice, saying, 'Eli, Eli, lama sabachthani?' That is, 'My God, My God, why have You forsaken Me?' " (Matt. 27:46).

24) Zechariah prophesied that His body would be pierced with a spear.
Prophesied: "And they shall look upon Me whom they have pierced…" (Zech. 12:10).

Fulfilled: "But one of the soldiers had pierced His side with a spear, and immediately water and blood had come out.... And again, another scripture says, 'They shall look upon Him Whom they pierced' " (John 19:34, 37).

25) David prophesied that Jesus would commit His spirit to God.
Prophesied: "Into Your hand I commit My spirit..." (Psa. 31:5).
Fulfilled: "And after crying out with a loud voice, Jesus said, 'Father, into Your hands I commit My spirit.' And when He had said these things, He expired" (Luke 23:46).

26) David also prophesied of Jesus' last words.
Prophesied: "They shall come and shall declare His righteousness unto a people that shall yet be born, that He has done this" (Psa. 22:31). In Hebrew, the phrase "that He has done this" literally reads, "for it is finished."
Fulfilled: "Therefore, when Jesus had received the vinegar, He said, 'It is finished.' And after bowing His head, He yielded up *His* spirit" (John 19:30).

27) As no bone of the Passover lamb was to be broken (Ex. 12:46), not a bone of His would be broken.
Prophesied: "He keeps all His bones; not one of them is broken" (Psa. 34:20).
Fulfilled: "Then the soldiers came and broke the legs of the first *one*, and *the legs* of the other who was crucified with Him. But when they came to Jesus *and* saw that He was already dead, they did not break His legs.... For these things took place so that the Scripture might be fulfilled, 'Not a bone of Him shall be broken' " (John 19:32-33, 36).

28) His burial in the tomb of a rich man was foretold by Isaiah.
Prophesied: "By oppression and judgment He was taken away; and with His generation who did consider that He was cut off out of the land of the living; for the transgression of My people He *was* stricken?... His grave [was appointed] with the wicked [criminals], [but He was, instead, buried] with the rich in His death; although He had done no violence, nor *was any* deceit in His mouth " (Isa. 53:8-9).
Fulfilled: "And when evening was coming on, a rich man of Arimathea came, named Joseph, who was himself a disciple of Jesus. After going to Pilate, he begged *to have* the body of Jesus. [Jesus would otherwise have been buried among criminals.] Then Pilate commanded the body to be given over *to him.* And after taking the body, Joseph wrapped it in clean linen cloth, and placed it in his new tomb which he had hewn in the rock; and after rolling a great stone to the door of the tomb, he went away" (Matt. 27:57-60).

All these prophecies were fulfilled by the suffering, death and burial of Jesus Christ on the Passover day.

Appendix C

The Historical Fulfillment of the Seventy-Week Prophecy of Daniel Nine

Research and Composition by Carl D. Franklin

Introduction

The seventy-week prophecy in the book of Daniel has intrigued scholars and sages down through the centuries. A succession of differing views and interpretations of this prophecy can be found in historical writings dating back to antiquity.

Dr. Gerhard F. Hasel, professor in Old Testament studies, has very aptly described the difficulties involved in attempting to interpret the true meaning of Daniel's prophetic vision. Dr. Hasel's survey of literature covering the various interpretations of the prophecy, entitled *The Seventy Weeks of Daniel 9:24-27*, was published in 1976 by the Biblical Research Institute of Washington, D.C. In this publication, Dr. Hasel points out that biblical scholars rank this section of Daniel nine among the most complicated passages in Scripture. Hundreds of years of debate have failed to produce a consensus of opinion on the dates for the fulfillment of the prophecy. The only point on which scholars agree is the total number of years designated by the wording in the Hebrew text.

> "The passage of Daniel 9:24-27 is a *crux interpretum* in OT studies. One recent writer summed up his assessment of this passage by pointing out that 'there is no more intricate problem in Old Testament study than the interpretation of Daniel 9:24-27.'... In the trackless wilderness of interpretations there is nevertheless one common denominator. There is virtually unanimous agreement among interpreters of all schools of thought that the phrase 'seventy weeks' or literally 'sevens seventy' (*shabu im shib im*) means 490 years" (*The Seventy Weeks of Daniel 9:24-27*, p. 5).

There is great variation in the dates that are proposed for the historical fulfillment of the prophecy. Some scholars place the beginning of the fulfillment in 564 BC and some as late as 398 BC. Most scholars favor a beginning date of 457 BC, which falls between the two extremes.

Many churches support the year 457 BC as the beginning of the prophecy because this date agrees with the teaching that the crucifixion of Christ took place in 31 AD. This teaching may appear to fit the Gospel accounts, but it actually conflicts with the scriptural and historical evidence, which establishes 30 AD as the year of the crucifixion. According to the intercalary cycle of the Hebrew Calendar, Passover in 31 AD fell on Monday, which does not fit the chronology in the Gospel accounts. In 30 AD, however, the Passover fell on Wednesday, and an abundance of historical evidence confirms that the crucifixion took place in that year.

One factor that contributed to the erroneous dating of the year of the crucifixion was the application of an alternate intercalary cycle to the Hebrew Calendar, which made it appear that Passover fell on Wednesday in 31 AD. This alternate cycle was at first applied only to the time of Christ and the apostles. Over the years, calculations using this variant cycle were extended to 104 AD, 142 AD, 161 AD and finally 256 AD. In recent decades, however, historical records that previously were not accessible have been translated and published, making it possible to completely disprove the existence of a variant intercalary cycle during the life of Jesus or any period of years after His crucifixion. (See *The Calendar of Christ and the Apostles* at www.cbcg.org.)

In view of the historical facts, it is evident that the crucifixion could not have occurred in 31 AD. For those who uphold a messianic fulfillment of Daniel 9:24-27, this knowledge is a key element in the chronology of the seventy weeks. The date of the crucifixion serves as a historical marker for determining the beginning of Christ's ministry, which signified the completion of the sixty-ninth week of the prophecy. Counting backward three and one-half years from the spring of 30 AD leads to a ministry beginning in the fall of 26 AD. This historical date provides a fixed standard for evaluating the accuracy of the various chronologies that have been proposed by scholars in their endeavor to interpret the seventy-week prophecy.

No interpretation of the seventy-week prophecy can be valid unless it gives full consideration to the chronological records that are preserved in the Scriptures. These scriptural facts cannot be ignored or glossed over by explaining them in a way that circumvents their true meaning. They must be accepted and acknowledged as the inspired words of God.

With this perspective, we will examine the evidence that is found in the books of the Old Testament. We will then explain the historical fulfillment of the seventy weeks of Daniel's prophecy by using the internal evidence in the Hebrew text and the chronology of the kings who reigned in the days of Daniel, Ezra and Nehemiah.

Part One

Understanding the Fulfillment Of the Seventy-Week Prophecy

Major events in the unfolding of the seventy-week prophecy are recorded by a number of Old Testament writers. Jeremiah prophesied a period of seventy years of desolation in the land of Judah while the people were held captive in Babylon. The prophet Isaiah foretold the reign of a king named Cyrus who would release the captives and allow them to return to their own land to rebuild the city of Jerusalem.

The fulfillment of these prophesied events is described in the books of Ezra and Nehemiah. Ezra records the decree of Cyrus and the return of more than 40,000 exiles with Zerubbabel, who laid the foundation of the Temple. After construction of the Temple was interrupted for a period of time by persecution from enemies in the surrounding lands, the prophets Haggai and Zephaniah were inspired by God to stir up the people of Judah and Jerusalem to resume work on the Temple. The book of Haggai describes this time and contains a vital message from God to the remnant who were dwelling in the city of Jerusalem. The people responded to the urging of God's prophets and, under the leadership of Zerubbabel, set to work rebuilding the Temple. A number of years after the completion of the Temple, Nehemiah returned to Jerusalem as governor of Judah and led the people in rebuilding the walls of the city. Nehemiah records that his governorship began in the twentieth year of Artaxerxes (Neh. 5:14).

In his writings, Ezra declares that he journeyed from Babylon to Jerusalem in the seventh year of Artaxerxes (Ezra 7:1, 8). Scholars have used this date as a chronological marker for establishing the beginning of the seventy weeks of Daniel's prophecy. However, dating the fulfillment of the prophecy by the reign of Artaxerxes is complicated by the fact that this title was used by more than one king of Persia.

Over the decades, the three kings who used this title as a throne name—Artaxerxes I, Artaxerxes II and Artaxerxes III—have each found support among scholars as the Artaxerxes of Ezra seven. The general opinion of scholars today is that Ezra's reference applies to the reign of Artaxerxes I. Some scholars dispute this opinion and identify this king as Darius I, who bore the title Artaxerxes in the century before the three kings who used it as a throne name. It was during the reign of Darius I that the Temple was completed.

Is the Artaxerxes in Ezra seven the same king as the Artaxerxes in Nehemiah's account? By examining the chronological records in the scriptural accounts, it is possible to identify the Persian kings in the books of Ezra and Nehemiah. The scriptural and historical facts, like the pieces of a puzzle, provide a complete picture that enables us to understand the true chronology of the events that took place in the historical fulfillment of the prophecy in Daniel nine.

The Historical Setting of the Seventy-Week Prophecy

The book of Daniel records that the seventy-week prophecy was delivered "in the first year of Darius, the son of Ahasuerus, of the seed of the Medes" (Dan. 9:1). The title *Darius* was used by a number of Persia kings, but Daniel enables us to identify this king by recording that he began to reign at the time God's judgment was executed upon Belshazzar, king of Babylon (Dan. 5:22-31).

Historical writings describe this event, which was accomplished by Cyrus the Great. His army invaded Babylon and slew Belshazzar on October 12, 539 BC. Cyrus gave Belshazzar's throne to his father's brother, Darius the Mede, while Cyrus himself reigned at Shushan.

The defeat of Babylon marked the end of the seventy years of desolation in Jerusalem and the land of Judah, which Jeremiah had prophesied (Jer. 25:11-12; 29:10). The seventy years of desolation extended from 609 BC to 539 BC. Daniel records that he "understood by books" that the seventy years of desolation had come to an end. He had been reading the books of the prophets and was attempting to understand how their inspired writings applied to the events of his day. He knew of Isaiah's prophecy that a king named Cyrus would "dry up" rivers and conquer a city by entering through "two leaved gates" that would be opened by the hand of God (Isa. 44:27; 45:1). This prophecy was fulfilled when Cyrus and his army diverted the waters of the Euphrates, which flowed through the city of Babylon, and walked down the empty riverbed into the city. As Isaiah had prophesied, the gates that had been built to bar entry by this route were unlocked and wide open.

Knowing that Isaiah's writings included a prophecy that the *same* king who conquered Babylon in this manner would also issue a command to rebuild Jerusalem and the Temple, Daniel began to supplicate God to fulfill this part of the prophecy (Dan. 9:4-19). While he was praying, the angel Gabriel arrived with a commission from God to inform Daniel of the events that would come to pass in Jerusalem from that time to the rule of the Messiah.

Let us examine the prophecy as recorded in Daniel nine, beginning with Daniel's supplication to God to show favor to His people and the city of Jerusalem. Verses 17-23:

> " 'And now therefore, O our God, hear the prayer of Your servant, and his supplications, and cause Your face to shine upon Your sanctuary that is desolate for the LORD'S sake. O my God, incline Your ear and hear. Open Your eyes and behold our desolations, and the city which is called by Your name. For we do not present our supplications before You on account of our righteousness, but because of Your great mercies. O LORD, hear; O LORD, forgive; O LORD, hearken and

> do. Do not delay, for Your own sake, O my God; for Your city and Your people are called by Your name.'
>
> "And while I was speaking, and praying, and confessing my sin, and the sin of my people Israel, and presenting my supplication before the LORD my God for the holy mountain of my God; yea, while I was speaking in prayer, even the man Gabriel, whom I had seen in the vision at the beginning, being caused to fly swiftly, came to me, about the time of the evening sacrifice. And he made me to understand, and talked with me, and said, 'O Daniel, I have now come forth to give you insight and understanding. At the beginning of your supplications the word went forth, and I have come to declare it, for you are greatly beloved; therefore consider the word, and understand the vision.' "

These words of Gabriel show that the seventy-week prophecy was given to impart understanding to Daniel. This was not a prophecy to remain sealed until the end of the age (Dan. 12:9-10). Its fulfillment would begin to take place in that very year. The following verses in Daniel nine describe the sequence of events that would come to pass during its fulfillment. Note that these events are all centered at Jerusalem and the Temple.

> "**Seventy weeks** are decreed upon your people and upon your holy city to finish the transgression and to make an end of sin, and to make reconciliation for iniquity, and to bring in everlasting righteousness, and to seal up the vision and prophecy, and to anoint the Most Holy. Know therefore and understand that from the going forth of the commandment to restore and to build Jerusalem, to Messiah the Prince, shall be **seven weeks**, and **sixty-two weeks**. It shall be built again with streets and the wall, even in troublous times. And after sixty-two weeks Messiah shall be cut off, but not for Himself. And the people of the prince who shall come shall destroy the city and the sanctuary. But his end shall be with a flood, and unto the end of the war desolations are determined. And he shall confirm a covenant with many for **one week**. And in the midst of the week he shall cause the sacrifice and the offering to cease, and upon the wing of abominations shall come one who makes desolate even until the consummation. And the fully determined end which is decreed shall be poured out upon the desolator" (verses 24-27).

In verse 24, the seventy-week prophecy is summed up as a whole. The following verses describe the division of the seventy weeks into three distinct periods: seven weeks, sixty-two weeks and one week. The words "weeks" and "week" in these verses are translated from the Hebrew *shabua*, which is a unit of time composed of seven years. These units of time, known today as *heptads*, were used by ancient Israel to calculate the sabbatical years. The use of *shabua* in the Hebrew text signifies that the seventy weeks are not literal weeks of seven days' duration, but are each composed of seven years. Thus the three divisions of weeks in the prophecy add up to a total of 490 years.

Verse 24 states that these 490 years are "determined" for specific events to take place in the city of Jerusalem in preparation for the coming of the Messiah. The Hebrew verb that is translated "determined" may also be translated "divided" and includes the definition of "cut" or "cut off." In modern terminology, this verb might be translated "marked out." The basic meaning is that these prophetic "weeks" are time periods of years "cut out" by God in the course of history. The prophecy does not state whether these three periods are separated from each other by intervening years, but the Hebrew verbs *do* convey that potential; moreover, the historical fulfillment of the first two periods of weeks establishes that idea as factual.

The first period of seven weeks, or 49 years, was prophesied to begin with "the going forth of the commandment to restore and to build Jerusalem." That proclamation was issued by Cyrus the Great in 539 BC, which was the same year that Daniel received the vision. The vision of the seventy weeks announced the intervention of God to bring the remnant of Judah back to their land to rebuild Jerusalem and the Temple and to again dwell in the land. All these events were necessary in order for the birth of the Messiah to take place in Bethlehem as foretold by the prophets (Micah 5:2; Isa. 9:6-7).

Even before the decree was issued, the hand of God had begun to guide the course of history in the powerful kingdoms that surrounded the land of Judah. This divine intervention is recorded in the book of Esther.

How Events in the Book of Esther Relate to the Seventy-Week Prophecy

Most scholars place the events in the book of Esther many years after the conquest of Babylon by Cyrus II (the Great). According to scholars, the events that are recorded in the book of Esther did not take place until the reign of Xerxes I (485-464 BC), who was engaged in war against Greece.

To the contrary, the scriptural account of these events portrays a period of peace in the Persian Empire when it was favorable to hold an extended feast and celebrate for several months (Esther 1:1-9). Furthermore, the book of Esther records that Esther's cousin, Mordecai, who had taken Esther into his care after the death of her parents, was among the captives who were taken to Babylon when Nebuchadnezzar defeated Jeconiah, king of Judah (Esther 2:5-7). This captivity took place in 597 BC, which was the eighth year of Nebuchadnezzar (II Kings 24:11-16).

Since Mordecai was born before 597 BC, he would have been well over 100 years old when the reign of Xerxes I began. This chronology is not within the realm of possibility, considering that Esther, the daughter of Mordecai's uncle, was a young virgin in the third year of the king (Esther 1:3; 2:3, 8). As her cousin, Mordecai could not have been more than 40-45 years old. Thus the chronological records limit the dating of the events in the book of Esther to a period from the 590s BC to the 550s BC. These were the years that led to the rise of the Medo-Persian Empire under Cyrus II (the Great).

Scholars object to placing the time of Esther before Cyrus the Great as they believe that he was the first Persian king to reign in Shushan, which was the center of rule of the Ahasuerus of the book of Esther. "Now it came to pass in the days of Ahasuerus (this is the Ahasuerus who reigned from India even to Ethiopia, over a hundred and twenty-seven provinces), in those days, when **King Ahasuerus sat upon the throne of his kingdom in Shushan** the palace..." (Esther 1:1-2).

Contrary to the opinion of scholars, historical records of the wars of the kings of the Medes reveal that Shushan came under the dominion of the kingdom of Media during the reigns of the ancestors of Cyrus the Great. These records of Median history date to the 580s BC, more than forty years before Cyrus II conquered Babylon. At that time, the Median king, Cyaxares, was engaged in war against the kingdom of Lydia. These events are described in Olmstead's *History of the Persian Empire* (page 33).

> "**Since the road to the south was closed by the alliance with the Chaldean, who also held Susa** [Shushan], **Cyaxares followed the Zagros** as it bends westward into the cold uplands of Armenia, where other Iranian bands had destroyed the kingdom of Haldia and introduced their own Indo-European speech. The fertile valleys of Armenia led down through the Anti-Taurus into the broad plains of Cappadocia and **to the river Halys, frontier of Lydia. Five years of warfare ended in a drawn battle at the time of a solar eclipse (May 28, 585)** and a peace by which the Halys remained the boundary."

Olmstead declares that when Cyaxares attacked Lydia in the 580s BC, Susa (Shushan) was held by the Chaldean ruler of Babylon. Cyaxares had made an alliance with Babylon and had given his daughter in marriage to the Chaldean ruler. Cyaxares therefore bypassed Susa (Shushan) and set out to make war against Lydia. When the truce with Lydia was reached in 585 BC, Susa (Shushan) was apparently still ruled by Babylon.

How and when did Shushan become the palace of the Medo-Persian kings?

The works of Dr. Hugo Winckler help to shed light on this question. Dr. Winckler was able to translate the cuneiform and Parsee inscriptions of the ancient Middle East and was recognized as a leading authority of his day. His writings give much insight into the relationship between Media and Chaldea in that period of history. He reveals that when Cyaxares advanced toward Lydia through the Elamite province of Susiana, there was a strong alliance between the Medes and the Chaldeans. Cyaxares, king of Media, and Nabopolassar, king of Babylon, had together battled the Assyrians and conquered the city of Nineveh. In addition, Cyaxares had given his daughter in marriage to Nebuchadnezzar, son of Nabopolassar.

When the truce with Lydia was established in 585 BC, the alliance became threefold—with Media the leading power and Lydia and Babylon in secondary roles. As agreed in the truce, the boundary of Lydia remained intact. However, all the area of Susiana through which Cyaxares had traveled to reach Lydia came under his rule. As Susa (Shushan) was the capital of Susiana, it came under the dominion of the Medes at this time.

According to Olmstead, the date of the solar eclipse that led to the truce between Media and Lydia was May 28, 585 BC. In searching for astronomical verification of a solar eclipse visible from the Halys River region of Lydia/Cappadocia on that date, I found a NASA publication describing this eclipse in great detail. The event was a total solar eclipse that undoubtedly brought an instantaneous halt to all action on the battlefield. NASA records that the eclipse lasted 6 minutes and 4 seconds. It began around 5:45 PM, covered a total width of 271 kilometers, and was best seen at latitude 38.2N and longitude 45.0W—a grid stretching for many miles on all sides of the armies engaged in combat along the Halys River. Jupiter could be clearly seen to the immediate northwest of the eclipsed sun. By 6:45 the sun had set.

The record of this eclipse confirms May 28, 585 BC, as the date of the truce that ended five years of war between the kingdoms of Media and Lydia. This date, which falls during the period of time that has been established for the events in the book of Esther (590s to 550s BC), can be used to determine the identity of the king in the scriptural account. The three kings who ruled during this period were Cyaxares, Astyages and Cyrus II (the Great). Archaeological records of the genealogy of Cyrus the Great and Darius I enable the exact years of the reigns of these kings to be determined.

In the Cylinder of Cyrus II, found at Babylon, Cyrus the Great declares his genealogy:

> "**I am Cyrus**, king of the world, the great king, the powerful king, king of Babylon, king of Sumer and Akkad, king of the four quarters of the world, **son of Cambyses**, the great king, king of the city of Anshan, **grandson of Cyrus**, the great king, king of the city of Anshan; **great-grandson of Teispes**, the great king, king of the city of Anshan."

This record of Cyrus's ancestry includes his great-grandfather **Teispes**, his grandfather **Cyrus (I)** and his father **Cambyses (I)**. By comparing the genealogy of Cyrus II with the genealogy of Darius I, it is possible to link these Persian kingly names with the names used by Herodotus.

In the Behistun inscription, Darius Hystaspes (Darius I) declares his genealogy as follows: "I am Darius, the great king, king of kings, the king of Persia, the king of countries, the son of Hystaspes, the grandson of Arsames, the Achaeminid."

In three additional statements, King Darius says: "My father is **Hystaspes**; the father of Hystaspes was **Arsames**; the father of Arsames was **Ariaramnes**; the father of Ariaramnes was **Teispes**; the father of Teispes was **Achaemenes**." "That is why we are called Achaemenids; from antiquity we have been noble; from antiquity has our dynasty been royal." "**Eight of my dynasty were kings before me; I am the ninth**. Nine in succession we have been kings."

The ancestry of Darius I listed from the earliest down to his father are his great-great-great grandfather **Achaemenes**, his great-great-grandfather **Teispes**, his great-grandfather **Ariaramnes**, his grandfather **Arsames**, and his father **Hystaspes**.

According to the records of Cyrus II and Darius I, **Teispes** was a common ancestor. Below is a chart showing the synchronized genealogies of Cyrus II and Darius I. Note Herodotus' record of the nine generations in Darius' lineage, beginning with Sosarmus of the House of Arbacus.

Herodotus		**Cylinder of Cyrus**	**Behistun Inscription**
House of Arbacus		**House of Achaemenid Persian Kings**	**House of Achaemenid Persian Kings**
Sosarmus	**768-738 (1)**		
Artycas	**738-708 (2)**		
House of Deioces Following Revolt of 700-699 BC			
Phraortes I	**700-699 (3)**		
Deioces	699-646	Achaemenes	**Achaemenes (4)**
Phraortes II	646-624	Teispes	**Teispes (5)**
Cyaxares I	624-584	Cyrus I	**Ariaramnes (6)**
Astyages	584-549	Cambyses I	**Arsames (7)**
Cyrus II	558-539 (joint reign)		
		Medo-Persian Empire	
		Cyrus II (the Great) 539-530	
		Cambyses II 530-522	
			Hystaspes (8)
			Darius I (9)

As illustrated in the above chart, the Astyages of Herodotus' account is Cambyses I, the son of Cyrus I (Cyaxares). The reign of Cyaxares (Cyrus I) extended from 624 BC to 584 BC. The third year of his reign was 621 BC, more than twenty years before the captivity of 597 BC in which Mordecai was taken to Babylon. Thus, it was not possible for Cyaxares (Cyrus I) to be the Ahasuerus of the book of Esther.

Cyrus I (Cyaxares) was succeeded by his son Cambyses I (Astyages). Cambyses I ascended to the throne in 584 BC. If Mordecai had been a young man in his twenties when he was taken captive in 597 BC, he would have been about forty years of age in the third year of Cambyses I. This fits the time frame that has been established by the chronological records in the book of Esther. The reign of his son Cyrus II (the Great) does not fit the time frame as Mordecai would have been too old to be a cousin to the young Esther. Thus, **the scriptural and historical evidence points to Cambyses I as the Ahasuerus of the time of Esther**.

It is evident that Cambyses I is both the Ahasuerus of the book of Esther and the Astyages of Herodotus' account. Herodotus records that when Media made peace with Lydia in 585 BC, the Lydian princess Aryenis was given in marriage to Astyages (Cambyses I), son of Cyaxares (Cyrus I), to seal the peace between the two kingdoms. We may conclude that Aryenis is the Vashti of the book of Esther. Cambyses I removed her from being queen in 581 BC, the third year of his reign (Esther 1:3, 19). He became the husband of Esther in 577 BC, the seventh year of his reign (Esther 2:16-17).

It is possible that Vashti gave birth to Cyrus during her three years as queen. It is also possible that Cyrus was born to Esther, who was queen for many more years than Vashti. In view of the prophecies concerning Cyrus, it would seem logical to conclude that he was the son of Esther. If not, as a young prince he would nevertheless have grown up under the influence of Queen Esther, who reigned during his formative years. It is evident that he was acquainted with the history of Judah when he came to the throne, as his proclamation to rebuild Jerusalem was made in the first year of his reign.

The book of Esther does not make any reference to the birth of Cyrus. It does record the attempt of Haman to destroy the Jewish exiles before Cyrus came to the throne. This conspiracy was undoubtedly inspired by Satan to wipe out the line of Judah, from which the Messiah was prophesied to come. Knowing that such attempts would be made, God had intervened in advance by guiding the events that led to Esther being chosen by the king to replace Vashti. When Haman's plot became known, God intervened by giving Esther wisdom in how to approach the king and by granting her favor in the eyes of the king. As a result, Haman's murderous plot was thwarted and the evil he had desired to inflict on the Jews came back on his own head. Without the intervention of God to preserve His people, there would have been no remnant to return to the land of Judah when the proclamation was issued by Cyrus.

The book of Ezra begins with a description of the proclamation of Cyrus, which marked the beginning of the fulfillment of the prophecy in Daniel nine.

Part Two

The Beginning of the Seventy Weeks As Recorded by Ezra

In his account of Cyrus' decree, Ezra focuses on the rebuilding of the Temple. As a descendant of the high priests, his principle concerns were the preservation of the law of God and the restoration of the Temple service. In reading the account in Ezra chapter one, it is important to remember that the decree also included the restoration of the city of Jerusalem (Isa. 44:28). This was part of the prophecy that God had given through Isaiah.

> "And **in the first year of Cyrus king of Persia**, that the Word of the LORD by the mouth of Jeremiah might he fulfilled, the LORD stirred up the spirit of Cyrus king of Persia, so that he made a proclamation throughout all his kingdom, and put it also in writing, saying, 'Thus says Cyrus king of Persia, "The LORD God of heaven has given me all the kingdoms of the earth. And **He has charged me to build Him a house at Jerusalem, which is in Judah**. Whoever there is among you of all His people, may his God be with him, and let him go up to Jerusalem, which is in Judah, and build the house of the LORD God of Israel—He is the God Who is in Jerusalem" ' " (Ezra 1:1-3).

The first year of Cyrus II (the Great) by Persian reckoning was 539 BC. Cyrus II's reign over Babylon extended from 539 BC to 529 BC. Despite his royal decree to rebuild the Temple at Jerusalem, there was great persecution against the Jews who were engaged in the work. The conspiracy to hinder the Jews' effort to rebuild the Temple is recorded in Ezra 4:1-5.

> "And when the adversaries of Judah and Benjamin heard that the children of the exile were building the temple to the LORD God of Israel, then they came to Zerubbabel and to the chief of the fathers, and said to them, 'Let us build with you, for we seek your God, even as you. And we have sacrificed to Him since the days of Esar-haddon king of Assyria, who brought us up here.'
>
> "But Zerubbabel, and Jeshua, and the rest of the chief of the fathers of Israel, said to them, 'You have nothing to do with us to build a house unto our God. But we ourselves together will build unto the LORD God of Israel, as king Cyrus the king of Persia has commanded us.' **Then the people of the land weakened the hands of the people of Judah, and**

> **troubled them in building**. And they hired counselors against them to frustrate their purpose **all the days of Cyrus king of Persia, even until the reign of Darius king of Persia**."

This period of persecution spanned the reigns of three kings: Cyrus II, Cambyses II and Darius I. Cambyses II, the only king who reigned between Cyrus II and Darius I, is referred to in Ezra 4:6 by the title Ahasuerus. "And in the reign of Ahasuerus, in the beginning of his reign, they wrote an accusation against the people of Judah and Jerusalem."

The remaining verses in Ezra 4 describe the persecution that took place during the reign of Darius I. In verse 7, Darius is referred to by the title Artaxerxes.

> "And in the days of Artaxerxes, Bishlam, Mithredath, Tabel and the rest of their companions, wrote to Artaxerxes king of Persia. Now the letter was written in the Syrian tongue and interpreted in the Syrian tongue. Rehum the chancellor and Shimshai the scribe wrote a letter against Jerusalem to Artaxerxes the king in this way. Then wrote Rehum the chancellor and Shimshai the scribe, and the rest of their companions, the judges, and the emissaries, the consuls, the officials, the Erechites, the Babylonians, Elamites of Susa, and the rest of the nations whom the great and noble Osnappar brought over and set in the cities of Samaria, and in the rest of the province beyond the River—and now, this is the copy of the letter which they sent to him, to Artaxerxes the king:
>
> " 'Your servants the men of the province beyond the River, and so now, let it be known to the king that the Jews who came up from you to us have come to Jerusalem, and are **building the rebellious and the evil city, and have set up its walls, and have joined the foundations**. Let it be known to the king that **if this city is built and the walls set up**, then they will not pay toll, taxes, or custom, and you shall endanger the revenue of the kings. Now because we have eaten the salt of the palace, and it was not right for us to see the king's dishonor, therefore we have sent and notified the king, so that search may be made in the book of the records of your fathers, and you shall find in the book of the records, and shall know that this city is a rebellious city, hurtful to kings and provinces, and that they have incited sedition in it in the past, for which cause that city was destroyed. We notify the king that **if this city is built and the walls of it set up**, then you shall have no portion beyond the River' " (Ezra 4:7-16).

Ezra's record of the letter that was sent to Artaxerxes (Darius I) from the Jews' enemies demonstrates that the Jews in Jerusalem were engaged in building not only the Temple but also the walls of the city. This detailed record confirms that the decree of Cyrus included the restoration of the city of Jerusalem as well as the Temple, exactly as prophesied by Isaiah.

After receiving the letter, Artaxerxes (Darius I) ordered a search of the archives to determine whether the charges against Jerusalem were valid. Finding that there had been a history of rebellion against former kings who had gained dominion over Jerusalem, he ordered a stop to the rebuilding of the city.

> "The king sent an answer to Rehum the chancellor, and to Shimshai the scribe, and to the rest of their companions who dwell in Samaria, and to the rest beyond the River: 'Peace! And now, the letter which you sent to us has been plainly read before me. And I decreed, and search has been made, and it is found that this city has risen up against kings in the past, and rebellion and revolt have been made in it. There have been mighty kings also over Jerusalem, who have ruled over all the country beyond the River. And toll, taxes, and custom were paid to them. Now make a decree to **cause these men to cease, and that this city be not built** until the decree shall be given from me. And take heed that you do not fail to do this. Why should damage increase to the hurt of the kings?'
>
> "And when the copy of King Artaxerxes' letter was read before Rehum, and Shimshai the scribe, and their companions, they hurried to Jerusalem unto the Jews, and made them cease by force and power. **Then the work of the house of God at Jerusalem ceased. So it ceased to the second year of the reign of Darius king of Persia**" (verses 17-24).

The decree of Artaxerxes (Darius I) caused all construction in Jerusalem to cease, the work on the Temple as well as the work on the wall. As no further work was done until the second year of Darius, it is evident that he had received the letter from the Jews' enemies in the first year of his reign, which was 521 BC.

Construction on the Temple and the wall was halted from 521 to 520 BC. In 520 BC, God inspired the prophets Haggai and Zechariah to stir up the people to finish rebuilding the Temple, and they set to work. Their opponents immediately reported to Darius that the Jews were again building in Jerusalem and were claiming that this work was authorized by Cyrus, king of Babylon. After a search of the archives in Babylon revealed the decree of Cyrus, Darius ordered the Jews' enemies to cease from their opposition. The rebuilding of the Temple then proceeded without interruption.

Ezra records that the Temple was completed and dedicated on Adar 3 in the sixth year of Darius (Ezra 6:15), which was 515 BC. Adar was the twelfth and last month of the year. Thus the Temple was set up in time for the observance of Passover and the Feast of Unleavened Bread in the first month of the new year. This observance, recorded in Ezra 6:19-22, is followed by the account in Ezra seven of Ezra's journey to Jerusalem. Note the words that begin verse one. "**Now after these things**, in the reign of Artaxerxes king of Persia, Ezra the priest the son of Seraiah, the son of Azariah, the son of Hilkiah…" (Ezra 7:1).

This phrase reveals the chronological sequence of events, but it does not indicate the length of time that passed between these events. In reading this passage, it might appear that a very short period of time elapsed between the events in this chapter and the preceding chapter. However, similar chapter breaks can be found in the book of Ezra where the events were separated by a number of years.

Some scholars propose that the Artaxerxes of Ezra seven was Darius I. If this were the case, Ezra would have arrived in Jerusalem a few months after the completion of the Temple. This timing might appear to be logical as he brought with him many priests and Levites to serve at the Temple and many vessels for the Temple service. However, dating Ezra's arrival to the seventh year of Darius I is contradicted by the book of Nehemiah, which records that Ezra was in Jerusalem during the year that the wall of the city was dedicated (Neh. 12:27, 36). Nehemiah's account of the building of the wall reveals that the Temple was in service before the wall was completed (Neh. 6:10-15). The Temple was finished in the sixth year of Artaxerxes (Darius I), but Nehemiah's work on the wall did not begin until the twentieth year of Artaxerxes (Neh. 5:14). Since the building of the wall followed the restoration of the Temple, the earliest that the building of the wall could have begun is the twentieth year of Darius I. It is therefore not valid to interpret the seventh year of the Artaxerxes of Ezra seven as the seventh year of Darius I.

In order to determine the identity of the Artaxerxes who ruled Persia when Ezra made his journey to Jerusalem, we must first establish the chronology of the events in Nehemiah's account. In his account, Nehemiah records that Ezra was present in Jerusalem for an observance of the fall festival season as well as for the dedication of the wall. The details Nehemiah provides in his account of those days make it possible to determine the period of time Ezra was in Jerusalem.

As we read Nehemiah's account, it is important to understand that the books of Ezra and Nehemiah were originally one book. Although they are now separate books, some of the accounts in the two books are similar, giving different perspectives of the same events, as in the issue of intermarriage with foreigners. This similarity is most obvious in Ezra's and Nehemiah's accounts of the exiles who returned with Zerubbabel, as the wording in the two accounts is nearly identical. The fact that the two books record some of the same events is helpful in determining the order of events in Ezra's and Nehemiah's accounts.

Examining the Chronological Records in The Book of Nehemiah

The events that are recorded in the book of Nehemiah begin in the twentieth year of Artaxerxes (Neh. 1:1; 2:1). In that year, Nehemiah received a report that the wall of Jerusalem was still broken down, leaving the city open to attack. The exiles who had returned to the land of Judah were in great affliction (Neh. 1:2-3). Grieved by this news, Nehemiah set himself to fast and pray, supplicating God to show mercy to His people. In his prayers, Nehemiah also asked God to grant him favor in the eyes of the king as he requested permission to leave his duties in Persia and return to Jerusalem to rebuild the wall (verses 5-11).

God answered Nehemiah's prayers and moved the king to appoint him governor of Judah and to grant him all the materials that were needed for rebuilding the wall (Neh. 2:6-8). Nehemiah traveled to Jerusalem in the company of the king's guards and delivered the king's authorization to the governors of the lands bordering Judah (verse 9). Before speaking to the inhabitants of Jerusalem and Judah, he surveyed every section of the wall of the city to assess the extent of the damage (verses 12-16).

Nehemiah chapter three records the beginning of the construction and gives a detailed list of the men who set to work on the wall, beginning with the priests who were living in Jerusalem. The fact that there were many priests in the city confirms that the building of the wall was begun after the return of Zerubbabel and the restoration of the Temple. If the priests had not been serving at the Temple and receiving tithes of the produce of the land, they would have had no means of sustenance and would not have been dwelling in the city of Jerusalem. (This fact is confirmed by Nehemiah 13:10.) Additional evidence that the Temple was in service is found in Nehemiah 6, which records Sanballat's plot to deceive Nehemiah into seeking sanctuary at the Temple (verses 10-12).

Nehemiah's list of the builders of the wall also shows that goldsmiths, apothecaries and merchants were dwelling in Jerusalem (Neh. 3:8, 32). These were not the poor of the land whom Nebuchadnezzar had left behind when he carried the people of Judah captive to Babylon (II Kings 25:8-12). Thus there is an abundance of evidence to confirm that the building of the wall took place after the return of Zerubbabel and the exiles.

As recorded in the book of Ezra, the return of Zerubbabel took place in the year that the proclamation of Cyrus was issued, which was 539 BC. Cyrus appointed Zerubbabel governor of Judah and commissioned him to rebuild the Temple. The materials that were needed were ordered upon his arrival in Jerusalem, and the laying of the foundation began in the spring of 538 BC.

The prophecies of Haggai and Zechariah show that Zerubbabel was still serving as governor of Judah in 515 BC when the Temple was completed (Hag. 1:1, 14; 2:1-4; Zech. 4:9). It is evident that Zerubbabel's years as governor extended for a period of time after the completion of the Temple, as Nehemiah records that tithes were brought to the Temple storehouses "in the days of Zerubbabel, and in the days of Nehemiah" (Neh. 12:47). The order of the two names in this record confirms that Nehemiah's governorship followed that of Zerubbabel.

The scriptural account gives no indication that an interim of years passed between Zerubbabel's governorship and Nehemiah's governorship. To the contrary, other records in the book of Nehemiah indicate that there was no lapse of time between the two. Let us examine the account in Nehemiah 12, which records the names of the high priests who served at Jerusalem from the beginning of the return under Zerubbabel (see Supplement One, p. 186).

The first high priest to serve after the return from exile was Joshua (spelled Jeshua in Nehemiah 12:1). Joshua, who is named in the prophecies of Haggai and Zechariah, returned with Zerubbabel and served as high priest during Zerubbabel's years as governor (Neh. 7:7; Ezra 3:8; 5:2; Hag. 1:1; 2:4). As high priests served until death, the number of years that each one served may be estimated by using the generational difference, which is 30-35 years. By this calculation, Joshua would have served until about 505 BC. He was succeeded by his son Joiakim.

Nehemiah 12 lists the names of the priests who served with Joshua (verses 1-7) and the names of their sons, the next generation of priests, who served with Joshua's son Joiakim (verses 12-21). These records are most significant in view of Nehemiah's closing words in this passage. "**These were in the days of Joiakim the son of Jeshua, the son of Jozadak, and in the days of Nehemiah the governor, and of Ezra the priest, the scribe**" (Neh. 12:26).

There is no mistaking the identity of the three who are named in this verse. Although the names Nehemiah and Ezra can be found in reference to other individuals in the scriptural accounts, the titles that accompany the names in this record are explicit and establish beyond any doubt that Ezra the scribe and Nehemiah the governor were contemporary with Joiakim and the priests who served during his high priesthood. A comparison of the names of the priests in verses 8 and 9 with the names in verses 24 and 25 verifies that some of the priests who served with Joshua continued to serve during the priesthood of Joiakim. Other verses in Nehemiah's account reveal that some of the priests who served with Joiakim continued to serve in the high priesthood of his son Eliashib. This overlapping of priests from one high priesthood to the next is due to the fact that the priests began serving when they were thirty years old whereas the high priests were about twice that age when they took office. (The high priesthood was passed from father to son upon the death of the high priest who held the office.) Like some of the priests who served with Joiakim, Ezra and Nehemiah lived to see the high priesthood of Joiakim's son Eliashib (Neh. 13:28).

These scriptural records leave no room to place Ezra or Nehemiah in the reign of Artaxerxes I or any king who followed him. None of the priests who had outlived Joshua to serve under Joiakim would have lived to see the seventh year of Artaxerxes I. The fact that a number of them were alive in the days of Nehemiah limits the events in his book to a period extending from the high priesthood of Joiakim to the high priesthood of Eliashib.

The scriptural accounts indicate that Nehemiah came to Jerusalem shortly after Joiakim's high priesthood began, which would place Nehemiah's arrival about 500 BC (based on the estimated time of Joshua's death). Historical records of the reigns of the Persian kings reveal that Darius I, during whose reign the Temple was completed, was still ruling Persia at this time. In fact, the twentieth year of his reign was 502 BC, which coincides with the time frame that has been established by the scriptural accounts. It is therefore evident that Darius I is the Artaxerxes of the book of Nehemiah. Darius I, the king who appointed Nehemiah governor of Judah, remained on the throne during the entire twelve years of Nehemiah's governorship, which extended from 502 BC to 490 BC.

During his years as governor, Nehemiah succeeded in accomplishing his mission to rebuild the wall of Jerusalem. The subversive devices of Sanballat and his cohorts, which continued through all the years of building, had hindered the workers but failed to stop the work (Neh. 4).

Nehemiah 6 records the last attempts of Sanballat to prevent the completion of the construction. At that time, the wall was finished but the gates were not yet in place (verse 1). Sanballat immediately set about to keep Jerusalem from being enclosed. He knew that the gates could be closed and locked to keep him and his companions out. The people of Jerusalem had been open to his influence for many years, and he did not want to lose his position of power.

Sanballat made four attempts to draw Nehemiah away from the work, but Nehemiah was wise to his devices and declined to meet with him (verses 2-4). Sanballat then threatened to make accusations against Nehemiah to the king. Nehemiah responded that these accusations had been invented in Sanballat's own mind (verses 5-9). Nehemiah refused to be intimidated even by a threat against his life (verses 10-12). He did not allow any of Sanballat's conspiracies to interfere with the work of setting up the gates. The work continued, and fifty-two days from the time that the wall was finished, all the gates were in place (verses 1, 15). The account states that the work was completed on Elul 25 but does not specify the year. It could not have been later than the tenth year of Nehemiah's governorship as in his eleventh and twelfth years Elul 25 fell on the weekly Sabbath.

Nehemiah seven records that when the gates were in place, Hanani and Hananiah were put in charge of the city and entrusted with overseeing the opening and closing of the gates. They were also responsible for setting watches to ensure the safety of the inhabitants (verses 1-3).

As the end of Nehemiah's governorship approached, the Temple was in service and the city was protected by a secure wall, but the restoration of Jerusalem was not yet complete. The houses that were destroyed by

Nebuchadnezzar and his army had not been rebuilt. Nehemiah 7 describes the condition of Jerusalem. "**And the city was large and great, but the people in it were few, and the houses not built**" (verse 4).

At this time, God inspired Nehemiah to take a census of the people by genealogy for the purpose of resettling a portion of them in the city of Jerusalem. "And my God put into my heart to gather together the nobles, and the rulers, and the people, so **that they might be counted by genealogy**. And I found a register of the genealogy of those who came up at the first…" (verse 5).

The remaining verses in Nehemiah seven record the family names of the exiles who had returned with Zerubbabel, and the number from each family. The total number of exiles was 42,360. Many in this number were aged when they returned from exile (Ezra 3:12) and had died in the years of Zerubbabel's governorship. Others, who were younger at the time of their return, had married and added new descendants to their family lines.

When the census was complete, one tenth of the people who were dwelling in cities throughout the land of Judah were selected by lot to become inhabitants of Jerusalem. This event is described in Nehemiah 11, verses 1-2. "And the rulers of the people lived at Jerusalem. And the rest of the people cast lots to bring one of every ten to live in Jerusalem, the holy city, and nine parts in other cities. And the people blessed all the men who willingly offered themselves to live at Jerusalem."

In listing those who dwelt in Jerusalem, Nehemiah records that Seraiah, who had served in the high priesthood of Joshua, was "the ruler of the house of God" (verse 11). His name is also listed in the record of the covenant that was made by the people (Neh. 10:2). These records add to the evidence that limits the events in the book of Nehemiah to a few decades after the high priesthood of Joshua.

When those who were selected to dwell in Jerusalem had built their houses, the restoration of the city was complete. This event was the final act in the fulfillment of Cyrus' proclamation as prophesied by Isaiah. "[I am the LORD] Who makes the word of His servant sure, and makes good the counsel of His messengers; Who says to Jerusalem, '**She shall have people**;'… Who says of Cyrus, 'He is My shepherd, and shall do all My pleasure; even saying to Jerusalem, "**You shall be built**;" and to the temple, "**Your foundation shall be laid**" ' " (Isa. 44:26, 28).

When Nehemiah returned to the king at the end of his governorship, the first division of the seventy-week prophecy was complete. The fulfillment of the "seven weeks" (seven *heptads*, which equates to 7 x 7 years) had begun in the first year of Cyrus and had ended in the thirty-second year of Darius I, which was the year that Nehemiah's governorship ended. This period of time extended from 539 BC to 490 BC, which is exactly 49 years. The following chart illustrates the sequence of events that took place in the fulfillment of the 49 years.

The Fulfillment of the 49 Years — 539 BC-490 BC

PROCLAMATION OF CYRUS II TO REBUILD JERUSALEM	539	DAN 9:25; ISA 44:28; EZRA 1:1-4
RETURN UNDER ZERUBBABEL	539	EZRA 1:5-11
ALTAR OF BURNT OFFERING SET UP ON FEAST OF TRUMPETS	539	EZRA 3:1-3
FEAST OF TABERNACLES OBSERVED	539	EZRA 3:4-6
FOUNDATION OF TEMPLE LAID	538	EZRA 3:8-13
15 YEARS OF OPPOSITION BEGIN	538	EZRA 4
CAMBYSES II BEGINS REIGN	529	
DARIUS I BEGINS REIGN	521	
CONSTRUCTION OF TEMPLE RESUMES (SECOND YEAR OF DARIUS I)	520	EZRA 4:24; 5:1-2
COMPLETION OF TEMPLE (SIXTH YEAR OF DARIUS I)	515*	EZRA 6:14-18
NEHEMIAH APPOINTED GOVERNOR OF JUDEA (TWENTIETH YEAR OF DARIUS I)	502	NEH 2:1-6; 5:14
WORK ON THE WALL BEGINS	502	NEH 2:18
WALL FINISHED TO HALF ITS HEIGHT; THREAT OF ATTACK, ARMED GUARD IS SET	c. 497	NEH 4:6-23
UPPER HALF OF WALL COMPLETED	c. 492	NEH 6:1
DOORS SET UP; WORK COMPLETED ON ELUL 25	c. 492	NEH 6:1-15
HANANI AND HANANIAH GIVEN CHARGE OVER JERUSALEM	c. 492	NEH 7:2-3
JERUSALEM REPOPULATED, HOUSES REBUILT	c. 491	NEH 7:4-5; 11:1-2
NEHEMIAH LEAVES JERUSALEM AT END OF GOVERNORSHIP	490	NEH 13:6

*515/514 BC was a sabbatical year

A number of years after the end of Nehemiah's governorship, Ezra made his journey to Jerusalem with a large company of priests, Levites and Nethinim for the Temple service. What were the circumstances that moved Ezra to bring these priests and assistants to Jerusalem at that time? The answer is revealed in Nehemiah's account of the decadence that the people of Jerusalem fell into after he left. The sins of the people are recorded in Nehemiah 13.

> "And before this, Eliashib the priest, who was set over the storerooms of the house of our God, was allied with Tobiah. And he had prepared for himself a large room where they formerly laid the grain offering, the frankincense, and the vessels, and the tithes of the grain, the new wine, and the oil, which were commanded to be given to the Levites, and the singers, and the gatekeepers, and the offerings of the priests. **But in all this time I was not at Jerusalem**, for in the thirty-second year of Artaxerxes king of Babylon, I came to the king. And after some days I asked permission to leave the king.
>
> "And **I came to Jerusalem and understood the evil which Eliashib did** for Tobiah in preparing him a room in the courts of the house of God. And it grieved me very much. And I threw all the household goods of Tobiah out of the room. Then I commanded, and they cleansed the rooms. And there **I brought again the vessels of the house of God with the grain offering and the frankincense**. And I perceived that the portions of the Levites had not been given to them; for the Levites and the singers, who did the work, had gone back, each one to his field" (verses 4-10).

This passage in Nehemiah's account shows that the Levites and singers were not carrying out their duties at the Temple. They had been forced to leave because the people had stopped bringing tithes to the Temple. The following passage confirms that the worship of God at the Temple had ceased and the Temple was no longer in service: "And I contended with the rulers and said, '**Why is the house of God forsaken?**' And I gathered them together and set them in their place. And all Judah brought the tithe of the grain and the new wine and the oil into the treasuries" (verses 11-12).

Nehemiah contended with the rulers because it was their responsibility to oversee the collection of the tithes from the people. After ensuring that the Temple storehouses would be replenished, he gathered the Levites and singers together and set them in their places at the Temple. Since they could not remain at the Temple to serve unless they were receiving their daily portions of the tithes, Nehemiah put faithful men in charge of the storehouses to distribute the portions. "And I made treasurers over the treasuries, Shelemiah the priest, and Zadok the scribe, and of the Levites, Pedaiah. And next to them was Hanan the son of Zaccur, the son of Mattaniah, for they were counted faithful, and their office was to distribute to their brethren" (verse 13).

Nehemiah's account of the forsaking of the Temple service shows the deplorable condition that had come about during his absence. He does not specify the number of years that had passed since his governorship ended, but it is evident that it was a relatively short period of years as

Hanan, a descendant of Mattaniah, was among the Levites appointed over the storehouses. Hanan's grandfather Mattaniah is listed among the Levites who served in the high priesthood of Joshua (Neh. 12:8). This places Hanan in the generation of Levites who began serving in the last years of Joiakim and continued to serve in the high priesthood of Eliashib. The account of the falling away indicates that Eliashib held the office of high priest when Nehemiah returned to Jerusalem although this is not specifically stated. (Even before he held the office, the title was applied to his name to distinguish him from other priests in the scriptural accounts who were named Eliashib. See Nehemiah 3:1, 20 and Ezra 10:24, 27, 36.)

The above verses in Nehemiah 13 describe the steps that Nehemiah took to restore the worship of God at the Temple. His account of the restoration of the Temple service reveals the reason for the entourage that Ezra brought to Jerusalem. Ezra records that he assembled a large number of priests to travel with him to the land of Judah (Ezra 8:1-14). When a roll call showed that no Levites were among the number, he sent a request to the chief men in Babylon to provide Levites and Nethinim to accompany him to Jerusalem (verses 15-17). Ezra's purpose was to bring a good number of faithful priests and assistants to ensure that the daily performance of the Temple service would continue throughout the year.

The account in Ezra eight records that Ezra also brought vessels for the Temple service, which were weighed into the hand of Meremoth by the priests who had carried them to Jerusalem (verses 26-34). Meremoth is listed in Nehemiah 12:3 as one of the priests who had served in the days of Joshua. Verse 15 shows that he continued to serve in the days of Joiakim, as did his son. (Meremoth, in verse 3, and Meraioth, in verse 15, are translated from the same Hebrew word (*Hebrew and English Lexicon of the Old Testament*, page 599).

After delivering the vessels to the priests at the Temple, Ezra delivered the commissions he had received from the king to the governors of the adjoining lands (Ezra 8:36). These commissions are described in Ezra 7:21-24. The governors responded to the king's commands by furnishing all the supplies that were needed for performing the Temple service.

The final chapters in the book of Ezra cover the issue of intermarriage with foreign wives. Ezra nine records the report that Ezra received from the princes of Judah, and the astonishment that struck him when he learned that this grievous sin had been committed by a great number of the people, including many of the rulers (verses 1-2). Overcome with grief, he tore his clothing and pulled out his hair (verse 3). After recovering from the shock of their blatant disobedience to God's commands, he fell to his knees and prayed, confessing to God the great sin of the remnant who had been delivered from captivity (verses 5-15). Too ashamed to enter the house of God, Ezra wept and prayed outside in plain view of the people. The response of the crowd who gathered around him shows that many of the people had begun to repent of their sin. "Now while Ezra prayed, and made confession, weeping and casting himself down before the house of God, **there gathered to him out of Israel a very great congregation of men and women and children, for the people wept with a great weeping**" (Ezra 10:1).

The following verses in Ezra 10 record the words of Shechaniah, a priest of the line of Elam. As a priest, he understood that the sin of intermarriage was a matter for the high priesthood to resolve. The high priest Eliashib, whose own grandson was guilty of intermarriage, had failed in his responsibility to enforce the commands of God. Although Ezra did not hold the office of high priest, he was a descendant of the high priests. The sin of intermarriage needed to be corrected, and Ezra was the one to whom the responsibility had fallen.

> "And Shechaniah the son of Jehiel, of the sons of Elam, answered and said to Ezra, 'We have been unfaithful to our God and have married strange women from the people of the land. Yet now there is hope for Israel concerning this thing. And now therefore, let us make a covenant with our God to put away all the women, and such as have been born of them, according to the counsel of the LORD, and of those who tremble at the commandment of our God. And let it be done according to the law. Arise, for this matter belongs to you. We also will be with you. Be of good courage and do it.' Then Ezra arose and made the chief priests, the Levites, and all Israel to swear that they would do according to this word. And they swore" (Ezra 10:2-5).

Ezra's account of Shechaniah's words is significant in that it links the events in Ezra 10 with the covenant that is recorded in Nehemiah 9 and 10. The date of the covenant is recorded in the first verse of Nehemiah 9. "And on the **twenty-fourth day of this month**, the children of Israel were gathered with fasting and with sackcloth, and with earth upon them."

The covenant was made on the twenty-fourth day of the seventh month—two days after the last holy day of the fall festival season. The observance of the holy days is recorded in Nehemiah 8. On the first holy day, the Feast of Trumpets, Ezra began to read the Book of the Law to the people (verses 2-3). It is evident that God's commands concerning intermarriage were read to them because the people wept after hearing the law (verses 8-9). They were forbidden to weep on that day, however, as it was a day for rejoicing (verses 9-12). They then began to rejoice and continued to rejoice for the remaining days of the festival season (verses 13-18).

After the festival season had ended, they gathered together to confess their sins. Nehemiah nine records their repentance and the prayers of the Levites for God's mercy to be showed to His people. "And the seed of Israel separated themselves from all strangers, and stood and confessed their sins and the iniquities of their fathers" (verse 2).

The sin of intermarriage was foremost in the minds of the people at this time. Many who had intermarried had already put away their foreign wives, but the process of separation was not yet complete. This fact is demonstrated by the use of the imperfective verb in the Hebrew text. The imperfective form is used for action that is *in progress*.

The Book of the Law was read on that day, and the people continued to confess as they learned of other commands they had violated (verse 3). The Levites led the people in the worship of God (verses 4-5). As in former times of national repentance, the great mercy of God was extolled in prayer, beginning with the deliverance of His people from their bondage in Egypt (verses 6-12). The prayer of the Levites described the giving of the Law at Mt. Sinai and the sustenance that God had provided during the forty years in the wilderness (verses 13-21). Their prayers also recounted the victories that God had given His people in order that they might inherit the land (verses 22-25), and the disobedience and rebellion of the people when they had enjoyed the abundance of the land for many years (verses 26-31).

After praising God for His great mercies despite their many transgressions against His laws, the Levites appealed to Him to extend mercy once more as they pledged to be faithful in keeping His commandments. The last verse in Nehemiah nine records the initiation of the covenant to which they bound themselves by an oath. "And because of all this **we are making a sure covenant** and writing it, and our princes, Levites, and priests are sealing it" (verse 38).

This is the covenant that is described in the account in Ezra 10 of Shechaniah's words, which encouraged Ezra to take action to resolve the problem of intermarriage. The oath that Ezra bound upon the people is the oath of the covenant that is recorded in Nehemiah 10.

> "And the rest of the people, the priests, the Levites, the gatekeepers, the singers, the temple servants, and **all those who had separated from the people of the lands** to the law of God, their wives, their sons, and their daughters (everyone who had knowledge, and who had understanding), they have joined with their brethren, their nobles, and have **entered into a curse and into an oath to walk in God's law**, which was given by Moses the servant of God, and **to observe to do all the commandments of the LORD our Lord, and His ordinances and His statutes; and that we would not give our daughters to the people of the land nor take their daughters for our sons**" (verses 28-30).

These verses in Nehemiah's account record the pledge of the people to obey God's command forbidding intermarriage. However, the account in the book of Ezra makes it clear that the oath of the covenant was a pledge not only to refrain from future intermarriage but also to separate from foreign wives in existing marriages (Ezra 10:2-5).

The book of Ezra describes the process of separation, which took three months to complete. Although the covenant was made in the seventh month, the process of separation did not begin until the first day of the tenth month (Ezra 10:16). The reason for the delay is that after the fall festival season ended, the rains began and continued through the eighth and ninth months (verses 9 and 13). These two months were the time for planting barley and wheat for the next year's harvest. By the tenth month, the planting was finished and the process of separation could begin. To aid in understanding the events that are recorded in the accounts of Ezra and Nehemiah concerning the issue of intermarriage, a harmony of the two separate accounts is presented below.

The People Confess Their Transgressions of God's Law

Ezra 10

1. Now while Ezra prayed, and made confession, weeping and casting himself down before the house of God, there gathered to him out of Israel a very great congregation of men and women and children, for the people wept with a great weeping.
2. And Shechaniah the son of Jehiel, of the sons of Elam, answered and said to Ezra, "**We have been unfaithful to our God and have married strange women from the people of the land**. Yet now there is hope for Israel concerning this thing.

Nehemiah 9

1. And on the twenty-fourth day of this month, the children of Israel were gathered with fasting and with sackcloth, and with earth upon them.
2. **And the seed of Israel separated themselves from all strangers, and stood and confessed their sins** and the iniquities of their fathers.
3. And they stood up in their place and read in the Book of the Law of the LORD their God a fourth part of the day. And another fourth part they confessed and worshiped the LORD their God.

The Prayer of the Levites
Nehemiah 9:4-37

"And Jeshua, Bani, Kadmiel, Shebaniah, Bunni, Sherebiah, Bani and Chenani stood upon the stairs of the Levites and cried with a loud voice to the LORD their God. And the Levites, Jeshua, and Kadmiel, Bani, Hashabniah, Sherebiah, Hodijah, Shebaniah, and Pethahiah, said: 'Stand up and bless the LORD your God forever and ever. And blessed be Your glorious name, which is exalted above all blessing and praise. You, even You, are LORD alone. You have made heaven, the heaven of the heavens, with all their host, the earth and all things upon it, the seas and all in them, and You preserve them all. And the host of heaven worships You. You are the LORD, the God Who chose Abram and brought him out of Ur of the Chaldees, and gave him the name of Abraham, and found his heart faithful before You, and made a covenant with him to give the land of the Canaanites, the Hittites, the Amorites, and the Perizzites, and the Jebusites, and the Girgashites, to give it to his seed. And You have performed Your words, for You are righteous.

" 'And You saw the affliction of our fathers in Egypt, and heard their cry by the Red Sea, and performed signs and wonders upon Pharaoh and upon all his servants and upon all the people of his land, for You knew that they were acting arrogantly against them. So You made a name for Yourself, as it is this day. And You divided the sea before them, so that they went through the midst of the sea upon the dry land. And their pursuers You hurled into the deep, like a stone into the mighty waters. And You led them in the day by a pillar of cloud, and in the night by a pillar of fire to give them light in the way in which they should go. And You came down on Mount Sinai, and spoke with them from heaven, and gave them just ordinances and laws of truth, good statutes and commandments. And You made known to them Your holy Sabbath and provided them commandments, statutes, and a law, by the hand of Moses Your servant. And You gave them bread from heaven for their hunger and brought forth water for them out of the rock for their thirst. And You told them that they should go in to possess the land which You had lifted up your hand to give them.

" 'But they and our fathers acted proudly and hardened their necks, and did not hearken to Your commandments. And they refused to obey; neither were they mindful of Your wonders which You did among them. But they hardened their necks, and in their rebellion appointed a captain to return to their bondage. But You are a God ready to pardon, gracious and merciful, slow to anger, and of great kindness, and did not forsake them. Yea, when they had made them a molten calf, and said, "This is your god who brought you up out of Egypt," and had worked great provocations, yet You in Your great mercies did not forsake them in the wilderness. The pillar of the cloud did not depart from before them by day to lead them in the way, nor the pillar of fire by night to show them light and the way in which they should go.

" 'You also gave Your good spirit to instruct them, and did not withhold Your manna from their mouth, and gave them water for their thirst. Yea, forty years You sustained them in the wilderness. They lacked nothing; their clothes did not become old, and their feet did not swell. And You gave them kingdoms and people, and divided them into districts. And they possessed the land of Sihon, and the land of the king of Heshbon, and the land of Og, king of Bashan. And You multiplied their children like the stars of the heavens and brought them into the land concerning which You said to their fathers that they should go in to possess it. And the children went in and possessed the land, and You subdued the people of the land before them, the Canaanites, and gave them into their hands, with their kings and the people of the land, so that they might do with them as they would. And they took strong cities and a rich land, and possessed houses full of all goods, wells already dug, vineyards and olive groves, and fruit trees in abundance. And they ate and were filled, and became fat, and delighted themselves in Your great goodness.

" 'But they were disobedient and rebelled against You, and cast Your law behind their backs. And they killed Your prophets who testified against them to turn them to You, and they worked great provocations. Therefore You delivered them into the hand of their enemies, who troubled them. And in the time of their trouble, they cried to You, and You heard from heaven. And according to Your manifold mercies, You gave them deliverers, who saved them out of the hand of their enemies. But after they had rest, they did evil again before You. Therefore, You left them in the hand of their enemies, so that they had rule over them. Yet when they returned and cried to You, You heard from heaven. And many times You delivered them according to Your mercies, and testified against them that You might bring them back to Your law. Yet they acted arrogantly and did not hearken to Your commandments, but sinned against Your ordinances (which if a man do, he shall live in them), and presented a stubborn shoulder, and hardened their neck, and would not hear. Yet for many years You had patience with them, and admonished them by Your spirit, through Your prophets, but they would not give ear. And You gave them into the hand of the people of the lands. But in Your great mercies, You did not completely destroy them nor forsake them, for You are a gracious and merciful God.

" 'Now therefore, our God, the great, the mighty, and the awesome God, Who keeps covenant and mercy, let not all the trouble seem little before You that has come upon us, on our kings, on our rulers, and on our priests, and on our prophets, and on our fathers, and on all Your people since the time of the kings of Assyria to this day. But You are just in all that is brought upon us, for You have dealt truthfully, but we have done wickedly. And our kings, our rulers, our priests, and our fathers have not kept Your law, nor hearkened to Your commandments and Your warnings with which You testified against them. They have not served You in their kingdom, and in Your great goodness which You gave them, and in the large and rich land which You gave before them, neither did they turn from their evil ways. Behold, we are servants this day. And the land that You gave to our fathers to eat its fruit, and its goodness, behold, we are servants in it. And it yields much increase to the kings whom You have set over us because of our sins. And they are ruling over our bodies and over our livestock at their pleasure, and we are in great distress. And because of all this we are making a sure covenant and writing it, and our princes, Levites, and priests are sealing it.' "

The People Enter Into a Covenant

Ezra 10

3. **And now therefore, let us make a covenant with our God to put away all the women, and such as have been born of them**, according to the counsel of the LORD, and of those who tremble at the commandment of our God. And let it be done according to the law.
4. Arise, for this matter belongs to you. We also will be with you. Be of good courage and do it."

Nehemiah 9

38. **And because of all this we are making a sure covenant and writing it, and our princes, Levites, and priests are sealing it."**

The Covenant is Sealed with an Oath

Ezra 10

5. Then Ezra arose and **made the chief priests, the Levites, and all Israel to swear** that they would do according to this word. And they swore.

Nehemiah 10

1. And **those who sealed it were, Nehemiah, the governor**, the son of Hachaliah, and Zedekiah,
2. Seraiah, Azariah, Jeremiah,
3. Pashhur, Amariah, Malchijah,
4. Hattush, Shebaniah, Malluch,
5. Harim, Meremoth, Obadiah,
6. Daniel, Ginnethon, Baruch,
7. Meshullam, Abijah, Mijamin,
8. Maaziah, Bilgai, and Shemaiah. **These were the priests.**
9. **And the Levites** were both Jeshua the son of Azaniah, Binnui of the sons of Henadad, Kadmiel,
10. And their brothers....

14. The **chief of the people** were....

28. **And the rest of the people**, the priests, the Levites, the gatekeepers, the singers, the temple servants, and all those who had separated from the people of the lands to the law of God, their wives, their sons, and their daughters (everyone who had knowledge, and who had understanding),
29. They have joined with their brethren, their nobles, and have **entered into a curse and into an oath to walk in God's law**, which was given by Moses the servant of God, and to observe to do all the commandments of the LORD our Lord, and His ordinances and His statutes;
30. And **that we would not give our daughters to the people of the land nor take their daughters for our sons**.

The Separation From Foreign Wives
Ezra 10:7-17

> "And they made a proclamation throughout Judah and Jerusalem to all the children of the captivity to gather themselves unto Jerusalem, and that whoever would not come within three days, according to the counsel of the rulers and the elders, all his substance should be forfeited, and he himself separated from the congregation of the exiles. Then all the men of Judah and Benjamin gathered themselves to Jerusalem within the three days. It was the ninth month, on the twentieth day of the month. And all the people sat in the street before the house of God, trembling because of this matter, and because of the great rain.
>
> "And Ezra the priest stood up and said to them, 'You have been unfaithful, and have married strange women to increase the guilt of Israel. Now confess to the LORD God of your fathers, and do His pleasure. And separate yourselves from the people of the land and from the foreign women.' Then all the congregation answered and said with a loud voice, 'As you have said, so we must do. But the people are many, and it is a time of much rain, and we are not able to stand outside. And the work is not of one or two days, for we have transgressed greatly in this matter. Let our rulers of all the congregation stand, and let all those who have married strange women in our cities, come at set times, and with them the elders of every city and its judges, until the fierce wrath of our God for this matter has turned from us.'
>
> "Only Jonathan the son of Asahel and Jahaziah the son of Tikvah made a stand against this. And Meshullam and Shabbethai the Levite supported them. And the children of the captivity did so. And Ezra the priest, with certain heads of the fathers, after the house of their fathers, and all of them by their names, were separated. And they sat down in the first day of the tenth month to examine the matter. And they were finished with all the men who had married foreign women by the first day of the first month."

The separation of those who had intermarried from their foreign wives brought a resolution to the existing problem, and the oath of the priests and the people to refrain from future intermarriages ensured that they would not slip back into this sin.

The sin of intermarriage was not the only issue that needed to be resolved. The sin of Sabbath-breaking had also set in after Nehemiah's governorship ended. The account in Nehemiah 13 records that the people of Judah had fallen into the practices of the people in the neighboring lands and were laboring on the Sabbath day. They were not only working in their fields but also hauling their produce to Jerusalem to sell on the Sabbath day. The people of Jerusalem were buying their wares as well as those of the foreign merchants who came to the city.

> "In those days **I saw in Judah some treading winepresses on the Sabbath, and bringing in sacks of grain, and loading donkeys and also wine, grapes, and figs, and all kinds of burdens which they brought into Jerusalem on the Sabbath day**. And I admonished them **on the day in which they sold food**. And men of Tyre dwelt therein, who brought fish and all kinds of goods, and **sold them on the Sabbath to the children of Judah and in Jerusalem**.
>
> "And I contended with the nobles of Judah and said to them, '**What evil thing is this that you do and defile the Sabbath day?** Did not your fathers do this, and did not our God bring all this evil upon us and upon this city? Yet you bring more wrath upon Israel by defiling the Sabbath.'
>
> "And it came to pass when the evening shadows fell on the gates of Jerusalem before the Sabbath, **I commanded that the gates should be shut and that they should not be opened until after the Sabbath**. And I set some of my servants at the gates, so that there should be no burden brought in on the Sabbath day. And the merchants and sellers of all kinds of goods stayed the night outside Jerusalem once or twice. And I warned them and said to them, 'Why do you stay around the wall? If you do so again, I will lay hands on you.' From that time on they did not come any more on the Sabbath" (Neh. 13:15-21).

The grievous sin of buying and selling on the Sabbath threatened to bring the wrath of God upon the people of Jerusalem and Judah. It was vital that the problem be corrected. What was needed was a pledge by the people to obey the law of God by refraining from buying and selling on the Sabbath day. This pledge is recorded in the account of the covenant in Nehemiah 10. "**And if the people of the land should bring goods or any food on the Sabbath day to sell it, that we would not buy it from them on the Sabbath or on a holy day**, and that we would forego the seventh year's produce and the exacting of every debt" (verse 31).

In correcting the sin of Sabbath-breaking, Nehemiah commanded the Levites to cleanse themselves and to sanctify the Sabbath day by keeping the gates barred to merchants from the surrounding lands. "And I commanded the

Levites that they should **cleanse themselves**, and that they should come and **keep the gates, to sanctify the Sabbath day**" (Neh. 13:22).

This passage ties in with the account of the dedication of the wall of Jerusalem, which reveals that the priests and Levites purified not only themselves but also the gates and the wall, which had been defiled by the trafficking of merchants on the Sabbath day. As the people had pledged to obey God by observing the Sabbath day, they also were purified at this time. All these purifications are recorded in the account of the dedication of the wall in Nehemiah 12. "**And the priests and the Levites purified themselves. And they purified the people, and the gates, and the wall**" (verse 30).

In his account of the dedication of the wall, Nehemiah records that the procession of the priests was headed by Ezra the scribe (verse 36). Many of the priests who participated in the ceremonies at the dedication of the wall are listed in earlier verses in Nehemiah 12. Those who had begun to serve in the days of Joshua include Jeremiah, who is listed in verses 1 and 12; Ezra (not the same as Ezra the scribe), who is listed in verses 1 and 13; Miniamin, who is listed in verses 5 and 17; and Shemaiah, who is listed in verses 6 and 18. Those who began serving in the high priesthood of Joiakim include Hananiah, who is listed in verse 12; Ezra's son Meshullam, who is listed in verse 13; Jehohanan, who is listed in verse 13; Uzzi, who is listed in verse 19; and Nethaneel, who is listed in verse 21.

A number of these priests are also listed in the account of the covenant in Nehemiah 10. Azariah, who is listed among the priests at the dedication of the wall (Neh. 12:33) was also present at the sealing of the covenant (Neh. 10:2). Other priests who were present at both the sealing of the covenant and the dedication of the wall include Jeremiah, Meshullam, Shemaiah and Hananiah (Neh. 10: 2, 7, 8, 23). It is therefore evident that the two events took place within the same time frame.

It is significant that Nehemiah's account of the dedication of the wall records the appointment of overseers for the Temple storehouses. This record removes any doubt as to the time of the dedication of the wall. "And at that time **some were chosen over the rooms for the treasuries**, for the offerings, for the firstfruits, and for the tithes, to gather into them out of the fields of the cities the portions appointed by the law for the priests and Levites, **for Judah rejoiced for the priests and for the Levites who served**" (Neh. 12:44).

The appointments over the storehouses are also described in the account in Nehemiah 13 of the restoration of the Temple service (verses 10-13). The fact that the appointments were part of the restoration of the Temple service clearly demonstrates that the dedication of the wall did not take place during Nehemiah's governorship but during his second visit to Jerusalem.

The book of Nehemiah places both the sealing of the covenant and the dedication of the wall during the time of Nehemiah's second visit to Jerusalem. Since Ezra was in Jerusalem at the time of both events, it is evident that his visit coincided with Nehemiah's return. As the book of Nehemiah records that a number of priests who had served in the high priesthood of Joshua were still living at that time, it could not have been during the reign of Artaxerxes I. (The priests who had served with Joshua were at least in their 20s in 539 BC and would have been in their late 90s by the first year of Artaxerxes I, which was 464 BC. By his seventh year, even the youngest priest would have been more than one hundred years old.) Thus, the scriptural records limit the time of Ezra's visit to a period of two decades after the end of Nehemiah's governorship in 490 BC, which places Ezra's visit no later than 470 BC.

Nehemiah's twelve years of governorship in Jerusalem ended four years before the death of Darius I. Darius I was succeeded by Xerxes I, who reigned from 485 BC to 464 BC. The reign of Xerxes I extended for two decades, spanning the time limit that the scriptural records establish for Ezra's visit to Jerusalem (no later than 470 BC). It is therefore evident that Ezra made his journey during the reign of Xerxes I. The fact that Ezra dates his journey to the seventh year of the king enables us to determine that his visit took place in 478 BC.

The Historical Setting of Ezra's Journey to Jerusalem

Scholars have traditionally argued that Ezra's journey to Jerusalem could not have taken place during the reign of Xerxes I as it was a time of war. Xerxes, son of Darius I, was continuing the war that his father had begun against the Greek city states. In 492 BC, six years before Xerxes took the throne, Darius I had invaded Greece and succeeded in subduing Thrace and Macedonia. His second invasion, however, ended in defeat at the Battle of Marathon in 490 BC, and his army returned to Persia.

When Xerxes I came to the throne in 485 BC, he continued his father's policy of aggression toward the Greeks. In 480 BC, Xerxes demanded total submission of all Greek states. Subsequently, with an army of 180,000 men, he attacked Greece from the north through Thrace and Macedonia. The Greek army retreated to the pass of Thermopylae and took up defensive positions. The Persian army, however, was victorious, and obliterated three hundred Spartans and seven hundred Thespians. The Persians occupied Attica and proceeded to destroy the city of Athens.

Later that year, the tide began to shift in favor of the Greeks. After an indecisive battle with the Persian fleet, the Greek fleet retreated to the Saronic Gulf. When the Persians received intelligence that the Greek fleet was about to escape their entrapment by night, the Persian fleet rushed into the gulf, became entangled in the narrows and was soundly defeated by the Greek fleet in the Battle of Salamis. This defeat in 480 BC made it impossible for Xerxes to continue the conflict, and he returned to Sardis with a third of the army. Direct conduct of the war was transferred to his general, Mardonius.

By 479 BC, Mardonius was on the march south. Again the Persians met with disaster. The Persian army was attacked at Plataea by an allied army of Greek states led by the Spartan general Pausanias and was soundly defeated. Mardonius was killed and the Persian army retreated. The Battle of Plataea in late August of 479 BC was the last Persian invasion of the Greek peninsula.

Shortly before this decisive battle, the Greeks launched a fleet against the Persians on the Isle of Samos, which is situated north of the Isle of Patmos off the coast of Turkey. The Persians fled to Cape Mycale on the Ionian coast, beached their ships and took up defensive positions. The Greeks attacked, destroying the main Persian forces in Ionia as well as the Mediterranean fleet. This battle brought an end to Persian rule over Greek Ionia.

The decisive battles of Plataea and Mycale, which took place concurrently in August of 479 BC, forced Xerxes to withdraw from his war with Greece and tarnished his image as head of the Medo-Persian Empire. Unrest had already been building in the empire due to the heavy taxation that had been imposed to support the king's army. News of their defeat sparked even more discontent. To stabilize the situation and minimize the threat of insurrection in his provinces, Xerxes enlisted the support of ethnic groups that were known to be loyal, including the Jewish population. While serving as viceroy in Babylon before his reign, Xerxes had become well acquainted with the Jews. He therefore enlisted the aid of Ezra, who was highly respected among both Jews and Persians. This was the reason for Ezra's visit to Jerusalem in the spring of 478 BC, a few months after the end of the war.

The need for support and stability in his outlying provinces led Xerxes to delegate broad powers to Ezra not only in the land of Judah but in all the lands beyond the Euphrates that were part of his dominion. This act was providential in that it turned the tables against the corrupting influences of the inhabitants of the lands that surrounded Judah. Instead of drawing the people of Judah away from the laws of God, the other nations were required to learn and to practice His laws. In fact, obedience to the laws and commandments of God was enforced by the king's ordinance (Ezra 7:25-26). These measures served to restrain the evil influences that had led to intermarriage, Sabbath-breaking and forsaking the worship of God at the Temple—all the sins listed in Nehemiah 13—which had required the intervention of Nehemiah and Ezra. The correction of these sins brought the people of Judah back into covenant with God and thereby preserved the remnant from which the Messiah was prophesied to come.

To encourage continuing obedience by the people, Ezra brought to Jerusalem copies of the Book of the Law and faithful priests who would read the words and teach the meaning to the people. He also promoted the continuation of the Temple service by bringing Levites and others to assist the priests in carrying out God's commands for sacrifices and offerings. That is the purpose for which Ezra led his entourage of about 2,000 priests, Levites, Nethinim, singers and porters to Jerusalem in the seventh year of Xerxes I.

Ezra's journey to Jerusalem took place twelve years after the completion of the first division of the seventy-week prophecy, and approximately seventy years before the beginning of the second division of the prophecy. The 62 weeks, or 434 years, began in the fall of 409 BC and ended in the fall of 26 AD with the beginning of Christ's ministry.

Part Three

Understanding the Chronology of the Sixty-Two Weeks

Many biblical scholars and theologians teach that the 62 weeks of Daniel's prophecy ended in 27 AD. This chronology is based on counting backward 3½ years from a crucifixion in the spring of 31 AD. However, a crucifixion in 31 AD is contradicted by the Gospel accounts and by the intercalary cycle of the Hebrew Calendar (see Introduction). The Gospel writers reveal that the Passover fell on Wednesday in the year that Christ was crucified; but according to the Hebrew Calendar, the Passover of 31 AD fell on Monday, which eliminates any possibility that the crucifixion occurred in that year. The only years during Christ's ministry in which the Passover fell on Wednesday were 27 AD and 30 AD. Since 27 AD was in the early phase of His ministry, it is excluded as a possibility, leaving 30 AD as the only historically valid date for the crucifixion. Many other scriptural and historical records confirm that the Passover of 30 AD fell on Wednesday, April 5.

In addition to the error of dating the crucifixion to 31AD, some commit a second error in calculating the 62 weeks. Instead of counting backward from the crucifixion to the beginning of Christ's ministry, they include His ministry in the 62 weeks and date the end to His crucifixion on the Passover day.

In dating the end of the 62 weeks to the Passover season, they overlook the fact that the 70 weeks of Daniel nine are sabbatical cycles (*heptads*) which run from fall to fall. Thus the Hebrew text rules out dating the 62 weeks to the spring of the year. Furthermore, the prophecy in Daniel nine states that the Messiah would be "cut off" *after* the 62 weeks—not during (verse 26). The Hebrew preposition that is translated "after" does not allow the "cutting off" to be linked to the 62 weeks. Below is an illustration of the meaning of this Hebrew preposition as diagrammed by Waltke in *An Introduction to Biblical Hebrew Syntax.* (His diagram includes a number of Hebrew prepositions, but this illustration is limited to the one used in Daniel 9:26.) The spelling of the preposition is found in Owens' *Analytical Key to the Old Testament*.

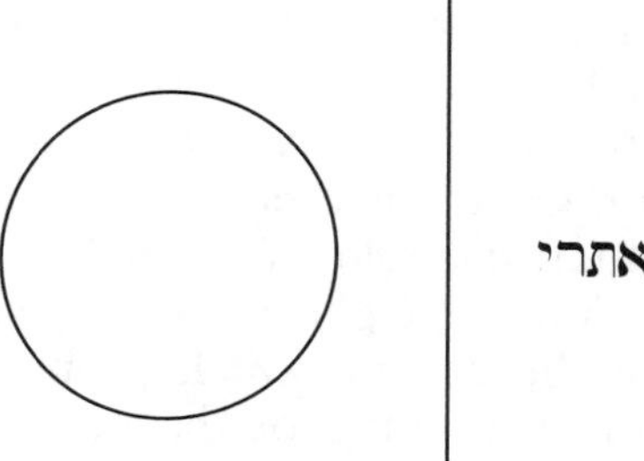

The line and the space between the circle and the preposition represent a space of time between the preposition and its object, ruling out any link between the ending of the 62 weeks and the Messiah's being "cut off," which occurred **after 62 weeks**.

Jesus' Ministry Began in the Fall of 26 AD At the Beginning of a Jubilee Year

In addition to the above evidence in the Hebrew text, the prophecy states that the 62 weeks would end with "**the coming** of an anointed one" (see Owens, Dan. 9:25)—not with His being "cut off."

Although a Jubilee year begins in the fall on the Day of Atonement, Jesus did not publicly announced Himself as the Anointed One until well *after* the Jubilee year had begun. Rather, His proclamation coincided with His public reading of the prophecy of Isaiah 61 at the synagogue in Nazareth during the Jubilee year 26/27 AD:

> "And He came to Nazareth, where He had been brought up; and according to His custom, He went into the synagogue **on the Sabbath day** and stood up to read. And there was given Him the book of the prophet Isaiah; and when He had unrolled the scroll, He found the place where it was written, 'The Spirit of the Lord is upon Me; for this reason, He has anointed Me to preach the gospel to the poor; He has sent Me to heal those who are brokenhearted, to proclaim pardon to the captives and recovery of sight to the blind, to send forth in deliverance those who have been crushed, **to proclaim the acceptable year of the Lord**.' And after rolling up the scroll and delivering it to the attendant, He sat down; and the eyes of everyone in the synagogue were fixed on Him. Then He began to say to them, '**Today, this scripture is being fulfilled in your ears**' " (Luke 4:16-21).

Jesus' baptism and forty-day fast and temptation were the key events that marked the actual beginning of His ministry in 26/27 AD, thus fulfilling the prophecy of the exact time that the Messiah would come: "Know therefore and understand that from the going forth of the commandment to restore and to build Jerusalem, to Messiah the Prince, shall be **seven weeks** [the first segment of 49 years], and **sixty-two weeks** [the second segment of 434 years]" (Dan. 9:25).

As each of the 62 weeks was a *heptad* composed of seven sabbatical years, this division of Daniel's prophecy extended over a period of 434 years (62 x 7 = 434). Counting backward from the fall of 26 AD, we can determine that the 434 years began in the fall of 409 BC. (One year must be subtracted when calculating from AD to BC.)

Unlike the first division of 49 years, which was a period of restoration after seventy years of desolation, the second division of 434 years was a period of judgment marked by invasion and foreign domination after the people and the priests fell back into sin. Ezra's visit to Jerusalem in 478 BC had helped to reinforce and complete the reforms that Nehemiah had begun, but the repentance of the people at that time did not end the pattern of disobedience that had stained the history of Israel since their Exodus from Egypt.

The Book of Malachi and John the Baptist

God's warnings to His people—and especially the priests who had violated His laws—are recorded in the book of Malachi, which pronounced a curse upon those who failed to take heed and repent of their evil ways (Mal. 1:6-8; 2:1-3).

However, God also inspired Malachi to *commend* the faithful priests—the descendants of Levi/Aaron, depicting John the Baptist's father Zacharias: "The law of truth was in his mouth, and iniquity was not found in his lips. He walked with Me in peace and uprightness…" (Mal. 2:6). Luke records that Zacharias and his wife Elizabeth "were both righteous before God, walking blamelessly in all the commandments and ordinances of the Lord" (Luke 1:6).

At the same time, Malachi was inspired to prophesy about their priestly son, John the Baptist: "The law of truth was in his mouth, and iniquity was not found in his lips. He walked with Me in peace and uprightness, and turned away many from iniquity, **for the priest's lips should keep knowledge, and the people should seek the law at his mouth; for he is the messenger of the LORD of hosts**" (Mal. 2:6-7).

God inspired Malachi to add several specific prophecies directly concerning John the Baptist, revealing that he would prepare the way for the coming of the Messiah: " 'Behold, **I will send My messenger**, and **he will prepare the way before Me**. And the Lord, Whom you seek, shall suddenly come to His temple, **even the Messenger of the covenant**, in Whom you delight. Behold, He comes,' says the LORD of hosts" (Mal. 3:1)

This prophecy was fulfilled more than four centuries later when John the Baptist prepared the way for the prophesied Messiah and brought many in Judea to repentance: "Now in those days John the Baptist came preaching in the wilderness of Judea, and saying, 'Repent, for the kingdom of heaven is at hand.' For this is he who was spoken of by Isaiah the prophet, saying, 'The voice of one crying in the wilderness, "Prepare the way of the Lord, make straight His paths" ' " (Matt. 3:1-3).

A Future Elijah—John the Baptist

The book of Malachi ends with a prophecy of a future Elijah who would turn the hearts of the people to the commandments that God had delivered to Moses for all their generations: "Remember the law of Moses My servant, which I commanded to him in Horeb for all Israel, with the statutes and judgments. **Behold, I will send you Elijah the prophet** before the coming of the great and dreadful day of the LORD. And he shall turn the heart of the fathers to the sons, and the heart of the sons to their fathers, lest I come and strike the earth with utter destruction" (Mal. 4:4-6).

The angel Gabriel announced to Zacharias that he and his wife, Elizabeth, would have a son, John the Baptist, who would come in the power of Elijah. "Fear not, Zacharias, because your supplication has been heard; and your wife Elizabeth shall bear a son to you, and you shall call his name John. And he shall be a joy and exultation to you; and many shall rejoice at his birth. **For he shall be great before the Lord**. And he shall never drink wine or strong drink in any form, but he shall be filled with the Holy Spirit even from his mother's womb. And many of the children of Israel shall he turn to the Lord their God. And **he shall go before Him *in the spirit and power of Elijah*, to turn the hearts of the fathers to the children, and the disobedient to the wisdom of the righteous, to make ready a people prepared for the Lord**" (Luke 1:13-17).

There is no question that John the Baptist fulfilled Gabriel's promise. In the beginning of His ministry, Jesus Himself declared that John the Baptist was fulfilling the role of the Elijah prophesied by Malachi. After Peter, James and John witnessed the vision on the mount of transfiguration, Jesus fully explained that John the Baptist was, indeed, the Elijah that was to come:

> "Now as they were descending from the mountain, Jesus commanded them, saying, 'Tell the vision to no one until the Son of man has risen from the dead.' Then His disciples asked Him, saying, **'Why then do the scribes say that Elijah must come first?'** And Jesus answered and said to them, **'Elijah shall indeed come first and restore all things. But I tell you that Elijah has already come**, and they did not recognize him; but they did to him whatever they desired. In like manner also, the Son of man is about to suffer from them.' Then the disciples understood that **He was speaking to them about John the Baptist**" (Matt. 17:9-13).

In doing so, Jesus also emphasized that John's ministry was founded upon the Law and the Prophets: "For **all the prophets and the law prophesied until John**. And if you are willing to receive it, **he is Elijah who was to come**. The one who has ears to hear, let him hear" (Matt. 11:13-15).

Jesus' use of the phrase "all the prophets and the law" includes the book of Malachi and signifies the completion of the Old Testament Scriptures as prophesied by Isaiah: "Bind up the testimony, seal the law among My disciples.... To the law and to the testimony! If they do not speak according to this Word, it is because there is no light in them" (Isa. 8:16, 20).

The process of binding and sealing was begun in the days of Ezra when the Old Testament Scriptures were "bound up" or compiled—with the exception of the book of Malachi, which had not yet been written. The book of Malachi, the last book of the Old Testament, was added later by the *So-*

pherim and the entire collection of Scriptures was canonized, or "sealed." These Scriptures were divided into three categories: the Law, the Prophets and the Writings. In its general sense, the term "the Law" is not restricted to the Book of the Law, but may also apply to the Prophets (Isa. 30:9-10). Thus, the sealing of "the Law" refers to the complete collection of Scriptures.

The canonization or "sealing" of the Scriptures was a **major historical event**. It could not take place until the book of Malachi was written with its prophecies concerning John the Baptist as the one who would herald the Messiah. Thus, a timeline is established between the sealing of the Scriptures and the beginning of Jesus' ministry. The context of the prophecy concerning the sealing confirms this connection:

> "**Bind up the testimony, seal the law** among My disciples.... To the law and to the testimony! **If they do not speak according to this Word, it is because there is no light in them**.... The people who walked in darkness **have seen a great light**; they who dwell in the land of the shadow of death, **upon them the light has shined**" (Isa. 8:16, 20; 9:2).

Although the book of Malachi is dated to the 400s BC, there is no historical record of the specific year that it was written. In view of Isaiah's prophecies, there is sound scriptural basis for concluding that the book of Malachi was written in 409 BC and marked the beginning of the sixty-two weeks (434 years). Since the book of Malachi contains a prophecy of the ministry of John the Baptist, which took place at the end of the 434 years (26 AD), it is fitting that God would inspire it to be written at the beginning of the 434 years, in 409 BC. The title of the book itself points to the work of John the Baptist as the one who would herald the promised Messiah. The name Malachi means "my messenger." The book begins with a call to repentance and ends with the prophecy of the messenger who would come in the spirit of Elijah to turn the hearts of the people back to their God. The Messiah Himself declared that this prophecy was fulfilled by John the Baptist.

There is additional support in Scripture for dating the prophecy of Malachi to the beginning of the sixty-two weeks. Malachi's prophecy was, in effect, a decree from God: "Behold, **I will send My messenger**..." (Mal. 3:1). As this decree was fulfilled at the end of the sixty-two weeks, a parallel is established with the fulfillment of the first segment of the seventy weeks, which began with a decree and ended with the fulfillment of that decree. This parallelism is illustrated below.

First segment: The seven weeks began with **the decree of Cyrus** and ended with the rebuilding of Jerusalem under Nehemiah, which completed **the fulfillment of the decree.**

Second segment: The sixty-two weeks began with **the decree of God** in the book of Malachi—"Behold, I will send My messenger"—and ended with **its fulfillment through the ministry of John the Baptist and the appearance of the Messiah.**

The book of Malachi reveals that the time span between the end of the seven weeks in 490 BC and the beginning of the sixty-two weeks in 409 BC was a period of increasing corruption within the priesthood after it was restored by Ezra and Nehemiah. Malachi's message is directed to a priesthood that had lost its reverence for God and defiled His altar by sacrificing diseased and defective animals (Mal. 1:6-8, 12-14). This is the decadent condition that moved God to issue His warnings in the book of Malachi at the beginning of the sixty-two weeks. The failure of the priests and the people to heed these warnings and repent led God to forsake His Temple in Jerusalem and allow the city to be overrun by foreign armies many times during the sixty-two weeks, or 434 years, which extended from 409 BC to 26 AD.

As the book of Malachi is the last of the Old Testament writings, there are no scriptural records of the battles that were waged by these foreign armies during the 434 years. There are, however, the visions that are recorded in the book of Daniel which describe the last years of the Medo-Persian Empire and the rise of Alexander the Great, who died at the height of his power and left his empire to be divided by his four generals. Using the records of ancient history, we can reconstruct these and other events that took place during the second division of the seventy weeks.

Major Events in the Fulfillment of the Sixty-two Weeks (409 BC – 26 AD)

The sixty-two weeks, or 434 years, began in 409 BC, which was the sixteenth year of Darius II. Upon his death in the spring of 404 BC, his son Artaxerxes II (Mnemon) took the throne. During his reign the stability of the empire was threatened by major insurrections. A rebellion by his brother Cyrus had to be crushed. Then an insurrection by Datames, the governor of Cappadocia in Asia Minor, spread to the western satrapies (366-360 BC) before it was stopped. As a result, Egypt became more or less independent.

Artaxerxes II ruled until his death in 359 BC and was succeeded by his son Artaxerxes III. Although Artaxerxes III was able to restore royal authority over the satraps, the empire was greatly weakened. Upon his death in 339 BC, Arses took the throne and reigned from 338 to 336 BC. He was followed by Darius III, the last of the Medo-Persian kings, who died while being pursued by Alexander the Great in 330 BC. Darius III had attempted to turn back the army of Alexander but was defeated at the battles of Granicus (334 BC), Issus (333 BC) and Gaugamela near Arbela (331 BC). As prophesied in Daniel 8, no king of Medo-Persia was able to stand against the overpowering force of Alexander's army.

> "And as I was considering, behold, **a he-goat** came from the west, over the face of all the earth, and did not touch the ground. And the he-goat had a notable horn between his eyes. And he came to the **ram that had two horns**, which I had seen standing before the river, and **ran at him in the fury of**

> **his power**. And I saw him come close unto the ram, and he was moved with anger against him, and **struck the ram** and shattered his two horns. And **there was no power in the ram to stand before him. But he threw him down to the ground and stamped upon him**. And none could deliver the ram out of his hand" (Dan. 8:5-7).

Alexander began his conquest of Medo-Persia in 334 BC. As foretold in Daniel's vision, he fought fiercely and with amazing speed. With an army of 35,000 men, he crossed the Dardanelles and defeated the armies of the Persians. After capturing Sardis and the coastal cities of Ionia, he advanced eastward into Caria and Lycia before turning inland.

His army was reunited with the forces of his general, Parmenio, at Gordium and went on to Ancyra. They then turned southeast, passing through the Taurus Mountains to capture Tarsus, capital of Cilicia. Victorious in every battle with the Persians, they advanced toward Soli on the coast and then eastward through the Amanus Mountains to the Syrian coast.

In 333 BC, Darius III approached the rear of Alexander's army but was defeated in a stunning cavalry attack at Issus. Darius was forced to retreat after losing 110,000 of his men. Alexander chose not to pursue Darius and instead headed south into Phoenicia where he laid siege to Tyre, which fell in July, 332 BC. He went on to take Acco and two other Egyptian cities which surrendered without a battle. Gaza resisted but fell in September, 332 BC, after a siege of one month. It was during the siege of Gaza that Alexander met with the High Priest Jaddua, known as Simon the Just (see Supplement One. p. 186), who read the prophecies of Alexander's conquests in the book of Daniel. Alexander was so impressed that he did not disturb the Temple in Jerusalem.

Alexander went on to defeat the Nabateans before wintering in Egypt. In the spring of 331 BC he returned to Tyre. From there he advanced to Damascus and then to cities on the Euphrates and the Tigris before shattering the army of Darius III at Gaugamela in October, 331 BC. Alexander then captured Arbela and seized a large amount of treasure from the Persians. Babylon and Susa surrendered to him, but Persepolis resisted and was looted and burned.

In the spring of 330 BC, Alexander pursued Darius III through Media where Darius was murdered by the satrap Bessus. In 329 BC Alexander conquered Bactria and in 328 BC triumphed over the Iranians. These victories completed his conquest of the Medo-Persian Empire.

Alexander, however, was not ready to exchange his sword for the throne. The desire to conquer, which had driven him during his seven years on the battlefield, was still burning within him. He longed for new challenges and new territories to conquer. An opportunity came in 327 BC when he was invited to India to do battle against Porus. At the Battle of Hydaspes in 326 BC, he defeated Porus and then continued eastward to the Hyphasis River. When his troops refused to advance any farther to the east, he turned southward and followed the Hydaspes and Indus rivers, reaching the Indian Ocean in 325 BC. His fleet explored the coastal areas of the Indian Ocean on the way back to Persia while Alexander and his army returned through the Desert of Gedrosia. Alexander arrived at Susa in 324 BC, and after a short stay went on to Babylon. He died in Babylon on June 13, 323 BC, after falling ill with a fever. Alexander had ruled Medo-Persia for only seven years before his death at the age of thirty-two.

As prophesied by Daniel, the death of Alexander led to the division of the empire into four parts (Dan. 8:8, 22). It did not pass to his heir but to his generals (Dan. 11:4). Although there were four, only two played a major role in the fulfillment of the 434 years: Seleucus, who founded the Seleucid line of Syria; and Ptolemy, who founded the Ptolemaic line of Egypt. The descendants of these two generals became "the king of the north" and the "king of the south," whose battles are described in the detailed prophecy in Daniel 11. This prophecy, which extends down through the ages to the time of the end, foretold major events that took place in Jerusalem and Judea during the fulfillment of the 434 years. Verse 16 describes the invasion and desolation of Judea at the hand of the king of the north. This prophecy was fulfilled by Antiochus III (the Great) of Syria during a war with Ptolemy V of Egypt. The prophecy of a "raiser of taxes" in verse 20 was fulfilled when Seleucus IV of Syria sent Heliodorus to plunder the Temple of God in Jerusalem. The prophecy in verse 21 of a "vile person" was fulfilled in *type* by Antiochus IV (Epiphanes) who polluted the Temple in 167 BC causing the sacrifices to cease. Ultimately, this prophecy refers to the Antichrist at the time of the end (verses 35-36), of which Antiochus was only a forerunner. (See Part Four for an explanation of the detailed prophecy of Daniel 11, p 180.)

While the kings of Syria and Egypt were draining their resources in continuous warfare, Rome was steadily growing in power. In 63 BC the Roman general Pompey took control of Judea and left in charge the Maccabean high priest Hyrcanus and Antipater, a civil advisor. Judea was also placed under the supervision of the governor of Syria. By 40 BC, the Romans had made Herod king of Judea. Thus, Jesus was born into a nation dominated by the Roman Empire and carried out His ministry under the oppressive hand of Herod (Luke 13:31-32).

The beginning of Jesus' ministry marked the completion of the second division of the seventy-week prophecy, the "sixty-two weeks" of Daniel 9:25. The following chart illustrates major events that took place in the fulfillment of these sixty-two weeks, or 434 years. The fulfillment of the 62 prophetic weeks began in the fall of 409 BC and ended with the beginning of Christ's ministry in the fall of 26 AD.

The Fulfillment of the 434 Years — 409 BC-26 AD

SIXTEENTH YEAR OF DARIUS II	409	DAN 9:25
ARTAXERXES II MNEMON BEGINS REIGN	404	

ARTAXERXES III BEGINS REIGN	358	
ARSES BEGINS REIGN	338	
DARIUS III BEGINS REIGN	335	
ALEXANDER BEGINS CONQUEST OF MEDO-PERSIAN EMPIRE	334	DAN 8:2-7
DEATH OF DARIUS III; ALEXANDER RULES MEDO-PERSIAN EMPIRE	330	DAN 8:7; 11:3
END OF ALEXANDER'S EMPIRE	323	DAN 8:21-22
EMPIRE DIVIDED BY FOUR GENERALS: PTOLEMY—EGYPT, PALESTINE, PART OF ASIA MINOR SELEUCUS—SYRIA, ARMENIA, LAND EAST OF EUPHRATES LYSIMACHUS—BITHYNIA, THRACE, MYSIA CASSANDER—MACEDONIA, GREECE	323	DAN 11:4
ANTIOCHUS IV (EPIPHANES) OF SYRIA INVADES JERUSALEM	169	I Macc. 1:17-29
BEGINNING OF MACCABEAN REVOLT	168	
TEMPLE DEFILED, DAILY SACRIFICES CEASE ON 15TH KISLEV (WEDNESDAY, DECEMBER 6)	167	I Macc. 1:45-47
TEMPLE CLEANSED, DAILY SACRIFICES RENEWED ON 8TH TEBETH (FRIDAY, DECEMBER 25)	164	I Macc. 6:1-16
END OF MACCABEAN LINE	137	
POMPEY'S SIEGE OF JERUSALEM	63	
RISE OF HEROD TO POWER	40	
BIRTH OF JOHN THE BAPTIST	5 BC	LUKE 1
BIRTH OF JESUS	5 BC	MIC 5:2; ISA 9:6-7
JOHN THE BAPTIST'S MINISTRY BEGINS	26 AD	MATT 3
JESUS' MINISTRY BEGINS	26 AD*	ISA 9:1-2; LUKE 4:14-15

*25/26 AD was a sabbatical year; 26/27 AD was a year of jubilee

It is significant that Jesus began to reveal Himself as the Messiah during a jubilee year. The scriptural passage which He selected for His opening message in the synagogue at Nazareth has traditionally been reserved by the Jews for the Day of Atonement, and to this day is acknowledged to be a direct reference to the proclamation of a jubilee. However, Jesus read this passage on the Day of Pentecost—a mini-jubilee within a jubilee year. In Appendix Four of his publication *The Star of Bethleham*, Dr. Ernest L. Martin emphasizes the obvious connection of Luke 4:16 with the year of jubilee: "**These terms that Jesus was using** in His discourse at the synagogue at Nazareth were those **associated with Sabbatical Years (and with the Jubilee** which was a type of Sabbatical Year)…."

Dr. Martin also discusses the Jubilee in his book *The Teachings of Pentecost*:

> "Back in Leviticus 25 we read of the Jubilee. It is most interesting to read what would happen every 50th year: 'And you shall number seven sabbaths of years unto you, seven times seven years; and the space of the seven sabbaths of years shall be unto you forty and nine years. Then shall you cause the trumpet of the jubilee to sound on the tenth day of the seventh month, in the day of atonement shall you make the trumpet sound throughout all your land' (Leviticus 25:8-9).
>
> "Immediately someone would say this is the Day of Atonement, this is not Pentecost. You would be correct…. What is this year of Jubilee all about…? 'And you shall **hallow the fiftieth year, and proclaim liberty** throughout all the land unto all the inhabitants thereof: **it shall be a jubilee** unto you; and you shall return every man unto his possession, and you shall return every man unto his family' (Leviticus 25:10)."

Jesus' reading of Isaiah's prophecy includes the words "to set at liberty" and "the acceptable year of the Lord"—both of which are direct references to a jubilee. The exegete Albert Vanhoye wrote the following about Luke 4:16 in an essay titled *The Jubilee Year in the Gospel of Luke*, in which he dogmatically states that Jesus *was* proclaiming a jubilee:

> Saint Luke is not the only evangelist who records Jesus' visit to Nazareth "where he had been brought up" (Luke 4:16). Saint Mark and Saint Matthew also refer to this episode, although without mentioning the name of the town, referred to simply as "his home town" (Mark 6:1; Matt. 13:54). There are, however, several differences between the story told by Luke and those of Mark and Matthew. We have already implicitly indicated one, when we observed that Luke is the only one who gives the contents of Jesus' preaching. The other two evangelists limit themselves to saying that Jesus "began to teach in the synagogue" (Mark 6:2; cf. Matt. 13:54); but they do not say what he taught. Luke, on the other hand, tells how Jesus "stood up to read, and they handed him the scroll of the prophet Isaiah. Unrolling the scroll he found the place where it is written: The spirit of the Lord has been given to me…!" (Luke 4:16-18; Isa. 61:1). Very significantly, the last line of Isaiah read by Jesus says: "to proclaim *the Lord's year*

> *of favor*" (Luke 4:19; Isa. 61:2), and immediately afterwards Jesus' message was a declaration that precisely "this text" was being fulfilled on that day. The expression of Isaiah 61:2, "year of the Lord's favor," clearly refers to the prescriptions in the Book of Leviticus on the *jubilee year* (Lev. 25:10-13). Therefore at Nazareth, Jesus was proclaiming a Jubilee year.

Historical records in the works of Josephus provide additional evidence that Jesus' ministry began during a Jubilee. In Book XIV, Chapter XV, Paragraph 14, Josephus states that Herod's attack on Jerusalem took place in the third year after his coronation at Rome:

> When the rigour of winter was over, Herod removed his army, and came near to Jerusalem, and pitched his camp hard by the city. **Now this was the third year since he had been made king at Rome**; and as he removed his camp, and came near that part of the wall where it could be most easily assaulted, he pitched that camp before the temple, intending to make his attacks in the same manner as did Pompey. So he encompassed the place with three bulwarks, and erected towers, and employed a great many hands about the work, and cut down the trees that were round about the city; and when he had appointed proper persons to oversee the works, even while the army lay before the city, he himself went to Samaria, to complete his marriage, and to take to wife the daughter of Alexander, the son of Aristobulus; for he had betrothed her already, as I have before related.

The Romans made Herod king of Jerusalem in 40 BC. By Roman count "the third year since he [Herod] had been made king at Rome" was 38 BC. In Book XV, Chapter 1, Paragraph 2, Josephus reveals that the battle for Jerusalem occurred **in the spring of a sabbatical year**:

> At this time Herod, now he had got Jerusalem under his power, carried off all the royal ornaments, and spoiled the wealthy men of what they had gotten; and when, by these means, he had heaped together a great quantity of silver and gold, he gave it all to Antony, and his friends that were about him. He also slew forty-five of the principal men of Antigonus's party, and set guards at the gates of the city, that nothing might be carried out together with their dead bodies. They also searched the dead, and whatever was found, either of silver or gold, or other treasure, it was carried to the king; nor was there any end of the miseries he brought upon them; and this distress was in part occasioned by the covetousness of the prince regent, who was still in want of more, **and in**

> **part by the sabbatic year, which was still going on**, and forced the country to lie still uncultivated, since we are forbidden to sow our land in that year.

The events discussed by Josephus occurred in the spring of 38 BC, a sabbatical year that began on Atonement of 39 BC and extended to Atonement of 38 BC. A chart of sabbatical cycles from Herod's battle for Jerusalem down to the ministry of Christ will demonstrate that 25/26 AD was a sabbatical year. This chronology adds historical support to the scriptural evidence in Luke 4:16-18 that the following year, 26/27 AD, which was the first year of Jesus' ministry, was a Jubilee.

Land Sabbatical/Jubilee Cycles			
39-38	**BC**	**7**	**Sabbatical Year — 35**
38-37	BC	1	
37-36	BC	2	
36-35	BC	3	
35-34	BC	4	
34-33	BC	5	
33-32	BC	6	
32-31	**BC**	**7**	**Sabbatical Year — 42**
31-30	BC	1	
30-29	BC	2	
29-28	BC	3	
28-27	BC	4	
27-26	BC	5	
26-25	BC	6	
25-24	**BC**	**7**	**Sabbatical Year — 49**
24-23	**BC**	**1**	**Jubilee Year — 50**
23-22	BC	2	
22-21	BC	3	
21-20	BC	4	
20-19	BC	5	
19-18	BC	6	
18-17	**BC**	**7**	**Sabbatical Year — 7**
17-16	BC	1	
16-15	BC	2	
15-14	BC	3	
14-13	BC	4	
13-12	BC	5	
12-11	BC	6	
11-10	**BC**	**7**	**Sabbatical Year — 14**
10-9	BC	1	
9-8	BC	2	
8-7	BC	3	
7-6	BC	4	
6-5	BC	5	
5-4	BC	6	
4-3	**BC**	**7**	**Sabbatical Year — 21**

Land Sabbatical/Jubilee Cycles			
3-2	BC	1	
2-1	BC	2	
1-1	BC/AD	3	
1-2	AD	4	
2-3	AD	5	
3-4	AD	6	
4-5	**AD**	**7**	**Sabbatical Year — 28**
5-6	AD	1	
6-7	AD	2	
7-8	AD	3	
8-9	AD	4	
9-10	AD	5	
10-11	AD	6	
11-12	**AD**	**7**	**Sabbatical Year — 35**
12-13	AD	1	
13-14	AD	2	
14-15	AD	3	
15-16	AD	4	
16-17	AD	5	
17-18	AD	6	
18-19	**AD**	**7**	**Sabbatical Year — 42**
19-20	AD	1	
20-21	AD	2	
21-22	AD	3	
22-23	AD	4	
23-24	AD	5	
24-25	AD	6	
25-26	**AD**	**7**	**Sabbatical Year — 49**
26-27	**AD**	**1**	**Jubilee Year — 50** **First year of Jesus Christ's ministry**

The Gospel accounts reveal that during His ministry, which began in the fall of 26 AD, Jesus experienced far more persecution from the Jewish religious leaders than from the Roman authorities. In fact, the laws of Rome prevented the Jewish officials of His day from putting Him to death. To accomplish their purpose, they brought false charges of political crimes against Him, knowing that Rome imposed the death penalty for such crimes. They succeeded in convincing the Roman authorities of His guilt by hiring false witnesses to testify against Him. Their evil plot led to His crucifixion on the Passover day in 30 AD.

The crucifixion of Jesus in 30 AD fulfilled the prophecy in Daniel 9:26 that **the Messiah would be cut off *after* the completion of the sixty-two weeks**. Let us examine this verse and the following verse in Daniel nine, which describes the fulfillment of the *third division* of the seventy-week prophecy.

Part Four

Major Events in the Fulfillment of the Seven Years

The third and last division of the prophecy is the *seventieth* week, which represents a period of seven years. This period is separated from the second division of the prophecy by an indeterminate span of time. The events described in verse 26 of Daniel nine take place between the second division of 62 weeks and the third division of one week. The events in verse 27 take place during this final "week" of seven years.

> "**And after sixty-two weeks Messiah shall be cut off**, but not for Himself. And **the people of the prince who shall come shall destroy the city and the sanctuary**. But his end shall be with a flood, and **unto the end of the war** desolations are determined. And he **[the prince who invades Judea] shall confirm a covenant with many for one week**. And **in the midst of the week** he shall cause the sacrifice and the offering to cease, and upon the wing of abominations shall come one who makes desolate even until the consummation. And the fully determined end which is decreed shall be poured out upon the desolator" (verses 24-27).

These verses describe a time of war leading up to a covenant, or treaty, that will be established at the beginning of the seventieth week, or seven years. Midway through this seven-year period the treaty will be broken, and the abomination that brings desolation will be set up in the Temple of God at Jerusalem. The daily sacrifices, which apparently will be instituted at the beginning of the seven years, will cease at this time. All these events are described in the prophecy in Daniel 11.

Events to be Fulfilled by the Future Antichrist Daniel 11:21-45 and 12:1-4

Keep in mind that much of this lengthy prophecy has already been fulfilled *in type* by the Syrian dictator Antiochus IV Epiphanes (175-164 BC). Many of the details of the passage apply *only* to the time of Antiochus and to his desecration of the Temple in 167 BC; yet the passage also serves as a *foreshadowing* of the coming *Antichrist* and the "abomination of desolation." In particular, verses 36-45 (and parts of chapter 12) bring the prophecy into the modern era, dealing specifically with the coming Antichrist.

> "And a **contemptible one** [Antiochus/the future Antichrist or king of the North] shall stand up in his [Seleucus, Antiochus's brother] place, and they shall not give to him the majesty of the kingdom [Antiochus had no legitimate claim to it]; but he will come in a time of peace and seize the kingdom by flatteries [seductive speech]. And the overflowing forces will be swept from before him [he will sweep away all opposition], and they will be broken, and also the prince of the covenant [with whom he has an alliance].
>
> "And after the league is made with him he shall work deceitfully [secretly building a power base], for he shall come up and shall become strong with a small force. He shall enter peaceably, even into the rich places of the realm. And he shall do what his fathers have not done, nor his fathers' fathers. He shall distribute among them the prey, spoil and riches. And he shall devise his plots against the strongholds, but only for a time.
>
> "And he shall stir up his power and his courage against the **king of the south** [Ptolemy VI of Egypt/a future league of Muslim nations] with a great army. And the king of the south shall be stirred up to battle with a very great and mighty army; but he [Ptolemy] shall not stand, for they shall devise plots against him. Yea, those who eat his food [his most trusted companions] shall destroy him, and his army shall be swept away. And many shall fall down slain. And both these kings' hearts shall be to do evil, and they shall speak lies to each other at the same table [both will break the terms of the treaty they make]. But it shall not succeed, for still the end remains yet for the time appointed.
>
> "And he [Antiochus/the Antichrist] shall return to his land with great riches. And **his heart shall be against the holy**

> **covenant** [Antiochus hated the Jews' way of life based on the Scriptures—as will the coming Antichrist]. And he shall take action against it [initially, in 169 BC, Antiochus set up a garrison in Jerusalem and persecuted the Jews], and he shall return to his land. At the time appointed he [Antiochus] shall return and come against the south [Egypt]. But it shall not be in the latter time as it was in the former [when he had victory], for the ships of Kittim [the western coastlands of Rome] shall come against him [Antiochus]. And **he shall be cowed** [by the Romans] **and return, and** [in his rage of defeat] **have indignation against the holy covenant**. And he shall do his pleasure; he shall even return and **have regard to** [be in league with] **those** [apostate Jews] **who forsake the holy covenant**.
>
> "And forces from him will stand up on his part, and **they will profane the sanctuary** [Antiochus defiled the Temple by sacrificing swine on the altar], even the stronghold, and shall **take away the daily sacrifice** [the Antichrist will do this as well—Dan. 9:27], and they shall **set up the abomination that makes desolate**. [This was fulfilled *in type* in 167 BC when Antiochus placed an idolatrous bust of his god Zeus in the holy place; the coming Antichrist will apparently *seat himself* in the Temple "as God" (II Thess. 2:3-4), thus fulfilling Jesus' warning of a coming "abomination of desolation."] And he will corrupt by flattery those [apostate Jews] who do evil against the [holy] covenant, but the people who know their God shall be strong and do exploits [a reference to the Maccabean resistance movement].
>
> "And those who are wise among the people shall cause many to understand; yet they shall fall by the sword, and by flame, by exile, and spoil, many days [in the struggle for independence from Syrian rule; perhaps, as well, a reference to the coming Great Tribulation of Matthew 24:21]. Now when they stumble, they shall be helped with a little help, but many will join themselves unto them with flatteries. And some of those who understand shall fall, to refine and to purify them, and to make white, **to the time of the end**, **because it** [the ultimate, final fulfillment of the prophecy] **is yet even for the appointed time** [of the latter days]."

From this point, Daniel shifts away from Antiochus and begins to prophecy specifically concerning a *future* "king of the north"—the Antichrist.

> "And the king [of the north, the Antichrist, the "prince" of Daniel 9:26-27] shall do according to his will. And **he shall exalt and magnify himself above every god** [just as Paul warned, he will *sit* in the Temple proclaiming himself to *be* God], and shall speak astonishing things against the God of gods [manifesting that he is the Antichrist], and shall prosper until the indignation be accomplished [until the end of the seven-year period], for that which is decreed [prophesied] shall be done. He will not regard the gods of his fathers, nor the desire of women, nor regard any god, for he shall magnify himself above all. But in his place he shall honor the god of forces [the strongest fortresses]; and a god whom his fathers did not know shall he honor with gold and silver, and with precious stones and costly things. So he shall deal against the fortresses of the strongest with a strange [foreign] god, whom he shall acknowledge; and shall increase with glory. He shall cause them to rule over many and shall divide the land for a price.
>
> "And **at the time of the end**, the king of the south [a confederacy of Arab nations] shall push at [attack] him. And the king of the north [the Antichrist, the "beast" of Revelation 13] shall come against him like a whirlwind with chariots and with horsemen and with many ships; and he shall enter into the countries [war will spread throughout the Middle East] and shall overflow and sweep through. He shall also enter into the glorious land [of Israel], and many countries shall be overthrown. But these shall escape out of his hand: Edom and Moab, and the chief of the children of Ammon [Jordan]. And he shall stretch out his hand also upon the countries. And the land of Egypt shall not escape. But he shall have power over the treasures of gold and silver, and over all the precious things of Egypt. And the Libyans and the Ethiopians shall be at his steps. But tidings [of opposition] out of the east and out of the north [from the northeast—a massive Asian alliance led by Russia and China] shall alarm him. Then he will go forth with great fury to destroy and to utterly annihilate many [nuclear war]. And he shall plant his royal tents [his headquarters] between the seas in the glorious holy mountain [in Jerusalem]. Yet **he shall come to his end** [Christ will return to fight and defeat him], and none shall help him" (Dan. 11:21-45).

The prophecy of the abomination of desolation in Daniel 9:27 reveals that it will not be removed "until the consummation." The cataclysmic events that will take place at the time of the "consummation" are described in Matthew 24. The word "end" in Matthew 24:3 is translated from the Greek *sunteleia* and refers to the consummation of the plan of God for the end time. Thus, the Gospel of Matthew confirms that the events of the final 7 years will take place in the future.

In revealing to His disciples the events that will take place at the consummation, Jesus stated that the "abomination of desolation" will bring unprecedented suffering upon Jerusalem and the land of Israel—the Jewish "State of Israel" *and* the modern-day descendant nations of Israel. "Therefore, when you see **the abomination of desolation**, which was **spoken of by Daniel the prophet**, standing in the holy place (the one who reads, let him understand), then let those who are in Judea flee into the mountains.... **For then shall there be great tribulation**, such as has not been from the beginning of the world until this time, nor ever shall be again. And if those days were not limited, there would no flesh be saved; but for the elect's sake those days shall be limited" (Matt. 24:15-16, 21-22). This is the time of suffering described in Daniel 11:33.

Daniel continues in chapter 12 with this amazing prophecy:

> "And at that time [of the end of the age, the archangel] Michael shall stand up, the great prince who stands for [in defense of] the children of your people [Israel]. And **there shall be a time of trouble** [the Great Tribulation], **such as never was since there was a nation even until that time**. And at that time your people [Israel] shall be delivered [by Christ's direct intervention]—every one who shall be found written in the book. And [at the time of Jesus' return, at the first resurrection] many of those who sleep in the dust of the earth shall awake, some to everlasting life, and some to shame and everlasting contempt. And they who are wise shall shine as the brightness of the firmament, and they who turn many to righteousness shall shine as the stars forever and ever. But you, O Daniel, **shut up the words and seal the book, even to the time of the end**. Many shall run to and fro, and knowledge shall be increased" (Dan. 12:1-4).

The terrible suffering that the Antichrist brings upon the people of Israel will be followed by a series of ominous astronomical events which will terrify the people of all nations. "But **immediately after the tribulation** of those days, **the sun shall be darkened**, and **the moon shall not give her light**, and **the stars shall fall from heaven**, and the powers of the heavens shall be shaken" (Matt. 24:29).

After these heavenly signs, the return of Christ will be announced by a piercing trumpet blast that will be heard around the world. As He descends, the clouds that encircle Him will glow with the brilliant light of His glory. He will send His angels to gather His saints. "And **then shall appear**

the sign of the Son of man in heaven; and then shall all the tribes of the earth mourn, and they shall see the Son of man **coming upon the clouds of heaven with power and great glory**. And He shall send His angels with a **great sound of a trumpet**; and they shall **gather together His elect** from the four winds, from one end of heaven to the other" (Matt. 24:30-31).

The saints, who will be transformed to immortality, will rise to meet Him and will join Him in executing God's judgment upon all those who have given themselves to evil. "For the LORD takes pleasure in His people; He crowns the meek with salvation. **Let the saints be joyful in glory**.... Let the high praises of God be in their mouth, and a two-edged sword in their hand to execute vengeance upon the nations and punishments upon the people, to bind their kings with chains and their nobles with iron bands, **to carry out upon them the judgment written—this honor have all His saints**. O praise the LORD!" (Psa. 149:4-9).

The book of Revelation amplifies this time of judgment, which will culminate with the seven last plagues (Rev. 15:1). The seventh plague will cause an earthquake of enormous magnitude, "such as was not since men were on the earth, so mighty an earthquake, and so great" (Rev. 16:18). The earthquake will bring down Babylon the Great (verse 19), which represents the powerful religious, political and financial systems that underpin the business and commerce of this world (Rev. 18:1-3, 11-19).

The fall of Babylon the Great will signal the beginning of the Kingdom of God on earth under the rulership of Jesus Christ. "And I heard as it were the voice of a great multitude, and as the voice of many waters, and as the voice of mighty thunderings, saying, '**Hallelujah! For the Lord God Almighty has reigned**' " (Rev. 19:6).

After His coronation as King of kings, Christ will lead His army of the resurrected saints into battle against the armies of the world, who will gather in the Valley of Megiddo (Armageddon) near the city of Jerusalem. The Antichrist, called the "beast" in the book of Revelation, will be slain along with his chief accomplice, a religious leader called the "false prophet."

> "And I saw heaven open; and behold, a white horse; and He Who sat on it is called Faithful and True, and **in righteousness He does judge and make war**.... And He was clothed with a garment dipped in blood; and **His name is The Word of God**. And **the armies in heaven were following Him on white horses**; and they were clothed in fine linen, white and pure.... And I saw **the beast and the kings of the earth and their armies, gathered together to make war with Him** Who sits on the horse, and with His army. And **the beast was taken, and with him the false prophet** who worked miracles in his presence, by which he had deceived those who received the mark of the beast and those who worshiped his image. Those two were cast alive into the lake of fire, which

> burns with brimstone; and **the rest were killed by the sword** of Him Who sits on the horse, even the sword that goes out of His mouth; and all the birds were filled with their flesh" (Rev. 19:11, 13-14, 19-21).

The victory of Jesus Christ at Armageddon will be followed by a thousand years of rulership over all nations of the world. During this time, Satan will be bound and held in restraint so that he cannot deceive the nations. "Then I saw an angel descending from heaven, having the key of the abyss, and a great chain in his hand. And **he took hold of the dragon**, the ancient serpent, **who is the Devil and Satan, and bound him for a thousand years**. Then **he cast him into the abyss, and locked him up, and sealed the abyss over him, so that he would not deceive the nations any longer until the thousand years were fulfilled**; and after that it is ordained that he be loosed for a short time" (Rev. 20:1-3).

The saints who have been transformed to immortality in the first resurrection will be granted rulership with Christ during the thousand years. "And **I saw thrones; and they that sat upon them, and judgment was given to them**; and I saw the souls of those who had been beheaded for the testimony of Jesus, and for the Word of God, and those who did not worship the beast, or his image, and did not receive the mark in their foreheads or in their hands; and **they lived and reigned with Christ a thousand years**.... **Blessed and holy is the one who has part in the first resurrection; over these the second death has no power**. But they shall be priests of God and of Christ, and shall reign with Him a thousand years" (Rev. 20:4, 6).

Unlike the resurrection that is described in Ezekiel 37, which will be a restoration of the flesh to temporary physical life, the first resurrection will impart immortality to those who attain it. This is the superior resurrection that Paul describes in his epistle to the Hebrews (Heb. 11:35). Paul's words in this epistle concerning the trials that the saints of old experienced reveal that endurance is required to attain to the first resurrection. Whatever trials God allows to befall His saints, He has promised that His grace is sufficient. It is therefore a matter of faith on the part of each one that God calls to trust Him and rely on Him for strength to endure.

As we anticipate the calamitous events that will soon come to pass, let us hold fast to the faith that He has given us through His Word. Let us remain steadfast in every trial, fixing our eyes on the hope that He has set before us, that we may be counted among the faithful saints who will have part in the resurrection to immortality.

Supplement One

The following reconstruction of the **line of high priests** is based on extant records, with a focus on specific references in the books of Ezra and Nehemiah.

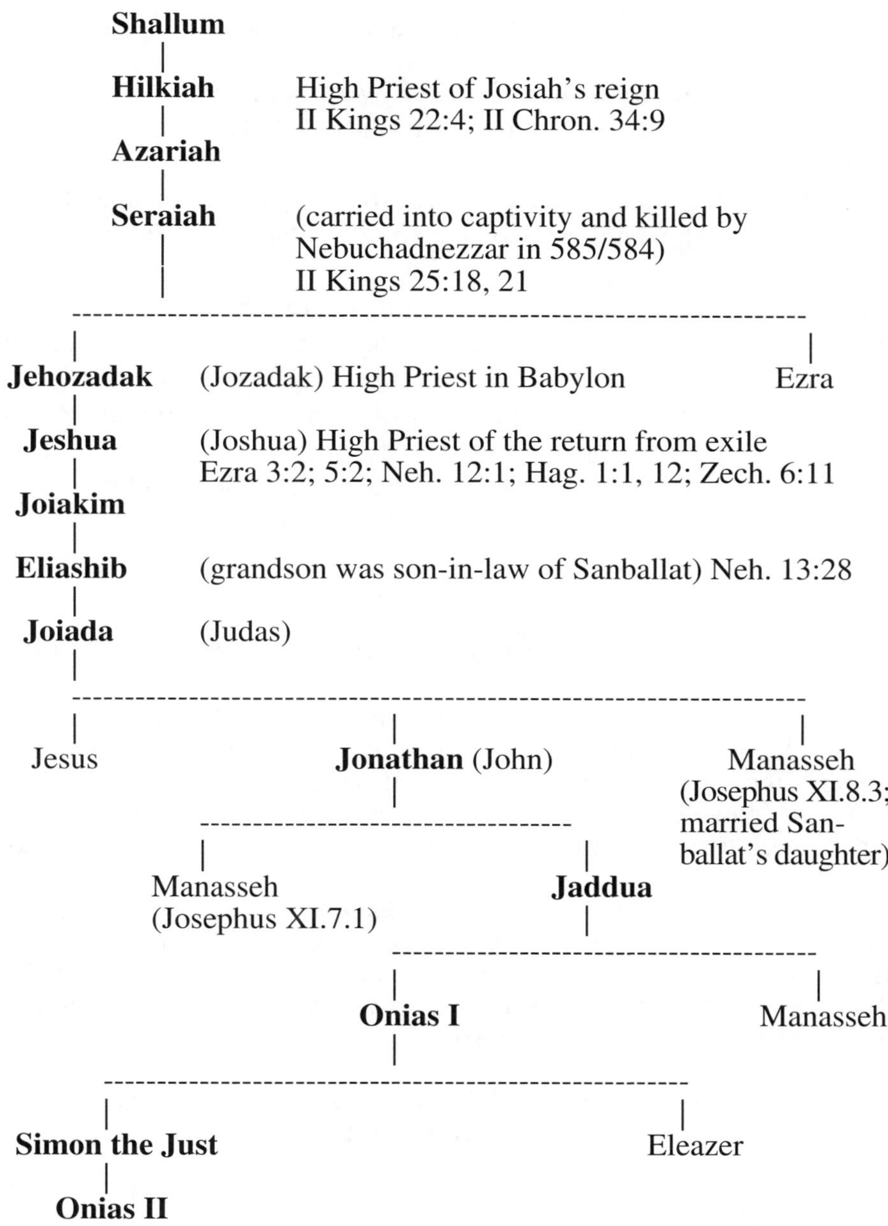

As noted in this reconstruction, Manasseh, one of three sons of Joiada, married the daughter of Governor Sanballat of Samaria. Although Manasseh was the rightful heir to the office of high priest, the office passed to his younger brother Jonathan because he apostatized to Samaria.

Supplement Two

The Invasion of Judea by Antiochus Epiphanes
A Chronology of Events (169-164 BC)

169 BC	Antiochus pushes north from Egypt and invades Jerusalem in the autumn; two years pass (I Macc. 1:17-29).
167 BC	Mysarch is sent by Antiochus Epiphanes to attack and occupy Jerusalem; the statue of Jupiter is set up on the altar of the Temple on December 6 (I Macc. 1:45-47). The Temple has been defiled and the daily sacrifices stop; three years pass.
164 BC	On December 25 the Temple is cleansed and the daily sacrifices are reinstituted (I Macc. 6:1-16).

Supplement Three

The Historical Setting of the Prophecy of Daniel Eight

The year is 539 BC. Daniel is in Babylon. Belshazzar is in the third year of his reign as king of Babylon, but his days are numbered. The Babylonian Empire is about to be conquered by Cyrus the Great, who will establish the Medo-Persian Empire in its place. Cyrus will soon issue his famous emancipation act initiating the return of Zerubbabel and the exiles to Jerusalem (Ezra 1:1-2:2).

The angel Gabriel appears to Daniel in the palace at Babylon and transports him in a vision to the Persian palace at Shushan in the province of Elam by the river Ulai. Shushan (also known as Susa) was about 200 miles due east of Babylon. The royal road began there and extended all the way to Sardis, a little northeast of Ephesus.

Gabriel Foretells the Rise of the Medo-Persian Empire—Daniel 8:2-4

> "And I saw in the vision, and it came to pass when I looked, I was at Shushan the palace, which is in the province of Elam. And in the vision I looked, and I was by the river Ulai. Then I lifted up my eyes, and looked. And behold, a ram [the symbol of Persia, verse 20] stood before the river [Ulai, now known as the Karun River, located in the extreme southwest section of Iran] having two horns [Media and Persia, verse 20], and the two horns were high, but one was higher than the other [Cyrus, king of Persia, became greater than his father, Astyages, king of Media], and the higher one came up last [Cyrus

> began joint reign with his father in 558 BC; Cyrus' sole reign began in 539 BC]. I saw the ram **pushing westward and northward and southward**, and no beast could stand before him, nor any that could deliver out of his hand. But he did according to his will and became great [Cyrus the Great]."

Cyrus, king of Anshan (also known as Pasargadae, a city of ancient Persia lying approximately 50 miles northwest of ancient Persepolis), pushed ***northwestward*** in 550 BC from this realm, conquering Ecbatana (also called Achmetha or Hamadan), the ancient capital of the Medes. He then pushed ***westward*** toward Asia Minor. Four years later, in 546 BC, Cyrus defeated Croesus, the last king of Lydia, bringing Asia Minor under the rule of the Persians. Seven years later, in 539 BC, Cyrus marched ***southward*** and conquered Babylon. Jerusalem was also brought under the control of the Medo-Persian Empire and remained so for the next two centuries.

With the fall of Babylon, the conquests of the Persian *ram* were complete. In less than twelve years, Cyrus had gained an empire that stretched from the Aegean Sea on the west to the Indus River Valley of India on the east. He controlled the most important trade routes in the world.

Gabriel Foretells the Fall of the Medo/Persian Empire—Daniel 8:5-7

> "And as I was considering, behold, a **he-goat** [Alexander, verse 21] came from the west, over the face of all the earth [conquered the entire civilized world], and did not touch the ground. And the he-goat had a **notable horn** [Alexander, the first king, verse 21] between his eyes. And **he came to the ram** [Medo-Persia, verse 20] **that had two horns** [the kings of Media and Persia, verse 20], which I had seen standing before the river, **and ran at him in the fury of his power**. And I saw him come close unto the ram, and he was moved with anger against him, and struck the ram [attacked Medo-Persia] and **shattered his two horns**. And there was no power in the ram to stand before him. But he threw him down to the ground and stamped upon him [completely defeated the Medo-Persians]. And none could deliver the ram out of his hand."

Alexander, a young Macedonian of the lineage of the ancient Amalekites, was only twenty-five when he began his conquest of the Medo-Persian Empire. As foretold in the vision of Daniel 8, he fought fiercely and with amazing speed. His conquests began in 334 BC when he crossed the Dardanelles with 35,000 men and routed the armies of the Persians. After capturing Sardis, he went on to take the coastal cities of Ionia. He advanced eastward into Caria and Lycia and then turned inland, victorious in every battle with the Persians.

At Gordium his army was reunited with the forces of his general Parmenio. They marched to Ancyra and then turned southeast, passing through the Taurus Mountains to Tarsus, capital of Cilicia. Undefeated, they marched toward Soli on the coast and then eastward through the Amanus Mountains to the Syrian coast.

By 333 BC, Darius III had reached Issus to Alexander's rear. A daring cavalry attack by Alexander killed 110,000 of the Persian army, forcing Darius to retreat. Instead of pursuing Darius, Alexander headed south into Phoenicia where he laid siege to Tyre for seven months, conquering it in July of 332 BC. He then proceeded toward Egypt. Acco surrendered without a fight, as did two other cities, but Alexander met fierce resistance at Gaza. A siege of one month ended with the capture of Gaza in September of 332 BC. (It was during the siege of Gaza in 332 BC that Alexander met with the High Priest Jaddua, known as Simon the Just.)

Alexander went on to defeat the Nabateans before wintering in Egypt. In the spring of 331 BC he returned to Tyre. From there he marched to Damascus and then to cities on the Euphrates and the Tigris before shattering the army of Darius III at Gaugamela on October 1, 331 BC. Alexander went on to Arbela where he seized a great deal of treasure from the Persians. Babylon and Susa surrendered without a fight. Persepolis, however, resisted and was subsequently looted and burned to the ground. In the spring of 330 BC Alexander pursued Darius III through Media (where Darius was murdered by the satrap Bessus). In 329 BC Alexander went on to conquer Bactria, and in 328 BC defeated the Iranians. These victories completed his conquest of the Medo-Persian Empire.

In 327 BC Alexander was invited to India to battle with Porus, whom he defeated in 326 BC at the Battle of Hydaspes. Alexander continued eastward as far as the Hyphasis River where his troops refused to advance farther. He then followed the Hydaspes and Indus Rivers southward, reaching the Indian Ocean in 325 BC. His fleet explored the coastal regions of the Indian Ocean on the way back to Persia while Alexander and his army returned through the Desert of Gedrosia. He arrived at Susa in 324 BC and remained there a while before going on to Babylon. Alexander died at Babylon in 323 BC after falling ill with a fever.

Gabriel Foretells the End of Alexander's Reign—Daniel 8:8

"Then the he-goat [Alexander] became very great. And **when he was strong, the great horn was broken** [he died at the height of power]...." Alexander's rule over Medo-Persia, which had begun in 330 BC, lasted for only seven years. His reign was cut short by his death in Babylon on June 13, 323 BC, at the young age of thirty-two.

Alexander's Empire Divided by Four Generals

"And in its place there came up the appearance of **four horns** [Alexander's generals] toward the four winds of the heavens."

Upon the death of Alexander, joint rule was established under the regency of Craterus and Perdiccas on behalf of Philip III Arrhidaeus (Alexander's half-brother) and the newborn son of Alexander and Roxana (Alexander's Persian wife). Perdiccas, who soon gained sole power, appointed Alexander's generals as satraps over various parts of the empire. When Perdiccas was assassinated in 321 BC, the generals began to compete for supremacy, and turmoil gripped the empire for the next two decades. After the Battle of Ipsus in 301 BC, the empire was split into four regions with Seleucus ruling Mesopotamia and Persia, Ptolemy ruling Egypt and Palestine, Cassander ruling Macedon and Greece, and Lysimachus ruling Thrace and Bithynia.

Only *two* of the four who divided Alexander's empire emerged as powers which shaped the history of the ancient Mediterranean region. These two notable ones became "**the king of the south**" and the "**king of the north**"; their wars and intrigues are described in the detailed prophecy in Daniel 11.

The Two "Notable Ones" of Daniel 11

The King of the South: Ptolemy I Soter—
King of Egypt (305-283 BC)

"And the **king of the south** [Ptolemy I Soter] **shall be strong**. And **one of his princes** [Seleucus I Nicator], even he [Seleucus] shall overcome him [Ptolemy] and have dominion. His kingdom shall be a great kingdom [Syria, Babylon and Media]" (Dan. 11:5).

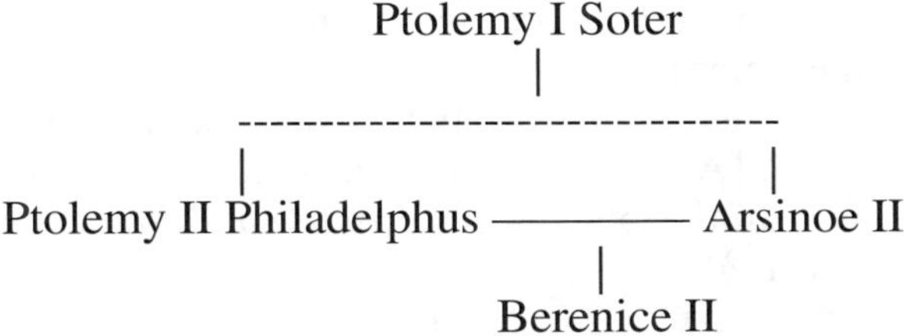

The King of the South Makes a League With the King of the North

Ptolemy II Philadelphus—King of Egypt (285-246 BC)

"And after some years [63 years] **they** [Ptolemy II Philadelphus of Egypt and Antiochus I Theos of Syria] **shall join themselves together** [form a league], for the king's daughter of the south [Berenice II, daughter of Ptolemy II Philadelphus] shall come to the king of the north [Antiochus II

Theos] to make an alliance. But she shall not keep her position of power. Nor shall he [Ptolemy II Philadelphus] stand, nor his authority. But she shall be given up [Berenice II and her infant son were murdered]—with those who brought her in, and he who begat her, and he who made her strong in these times" (verse 6).

The King of the South Attacks the King of the North

Ptolemy III Euergetes—(Benefactor) King of Egypt (246-221 BC)

"But out of **a branch of her roots** [Berenice II's father, Ptolemy II Philadelphus] **one shall stand up** [Ptolemy III Euergetes (Benefactor), brother of Berenice II] in his place [in the stead of her father], who shall come against the army of the king of the north [Seleucus II Callinicus, son of Antiochus II] and shall enter into his stronghold And he shall act against them **and shall prevail**. And he shall also carry their gods captives with their molten images into Egypt, and with their precious vessels of silver and of gold [the Third Syrian War, or the War of Berenice II, 246-241 BC]. And he shall refrain from attacking the king of the north for some years [Seleucus II died in 226 BC]. So the king of the north shall come into the kingdom of the king of the south, but shall return into his own land" (verses 7-9).

The King of the North Retaliates—Daniel 11:10-19

Antiochus III, the Great—King of Syria (223-187 BC)

"**But his sons** [Antiochus III and Seleucus III, the sons of Seleucus II] **shall mobilize** and shall gather a multitude of great forces. And **one of them** [Antiochus III] **shall certainly come** and overflow, and pass through [the first Palestinian campaign of Antiochus III]. And he [Ptolemy IV Philopater] will carry on [return to Egypt] and do battle, even to his fortress [raising an army of seventy-thousand men]" (verse 10).

"And the king of the south [Ptolemy IV Philopater] shall be in a rage and shall come out and fight with him [Antiochus III], even with the king of the north who will raise a great multitude, but the multitude shall be given into his hand [Ptolemy IV's]" (verse 11).

"And the multitude shall be carried away, and his [Ptolemy IV's] heart shall be lifted up. And he [Ptolemy IV] shall cast down tens of thousands [at the Battle of Raphia, 217 BC], but he shall not prevail" (verse 12).

"For the king of the north [Antiochus III] shall return [Antiochus III renewed the war twelve years later in 205 BC] and shall send out a multitude greater than the former, and at the end of some years [two years after renewing the war] shall come with a great army and with much equipment" (verse 13).

"And in those times there shall stand up [Antiochus III allied himself with Philip of Macedon and conquered Phoenicia and Syria] many against the king of the south [Ptolemy V Epiphanes, a child]. Also, the violent among your people [literally, sons of the oppressors: i.e., apostate Jews who defied laws and justice] shall rise up to establish the vision [of a free and independent Judah], but they shall fall [at the hand of Antiochus IV Epiphanes, for they indirectly helped to establish Antiochus IV through their support of his father, Antiochus III]" (verse 14).

"So the king of the north [Antiochus III] shall come, and cast up a siege mound, and take a fortified city. And the forces of the south [Ptolemy V] shall not hold out, nor his chosen people [who fled], nor shall there be any strength to withstand" (verse 15).

"But he [Antiochus III] who comes against him [Ptolemy V] shall do according to his own will, and none shall stand before him. And **he** [Antiochus III] **shall stand in the glorious land** [Palestine], **with destructive power in his hand** [foreshadowing his son, Antiochus IV, who continued his destructive ways]" (verse 16).

"He [Antiochus III] also shall set his face to enter with the strength of all his kingdom, and shall make an agreement with him; so he shall do [Antiochus III made a treaty with Ptolemy V]. And he shall give him [Ptolemy V, who was only age 12] the daughter of women [Cleopatra, daughter of Antiochus III, who was only 11 years of age] to destroy the kingdom, but she shall not stand by his side [she sided with her husband], nor be for him [her father, Antiochus III]" (verse 17).

"After this he [Antiochus III] shall turn his face to the isles [the coastlands or maritime countries of Asia Minor] and shall capture many. But a prince [the Roman General Lucius Scipio] shall put an end to his [Antiochus III's] insolence; and will turn his insolence back upon him" (verse 18).

"Then he [Antiochus III] shall turn his face to the fortresses of his own land. **But he shall stumble and fall**, and shall not be found [Antiochus III was defeated by General Scipio and was killed at the temple of Belus in 187 BC]" (verse 19).

The King of the North Plunders the Temple in Jerusalem—Daniel 11:20

Seleucus IV Philopater—King of Syria (187-175 BC)

"Then shall stand up in his [Antiochus III's] place one who will send out **an exacter of taxes** [his son Seleucus IV, brother of Antiochus IV] in the glory of the kingdom [the land of Palestine]. But within a few days he shall be destroyed [Seleucus was poisoned by his tax collector Heliodorus], not in anger, nor in battle" (Dan. 11:20).

During the twelve years that Seleucus IV reigned, the empire gradually regained strength. Seleucus IV sent Heliodorus, his exactor or tax collector, to "pass through the glorious land (cp. vv. 16, 41; 8.9) … [and] plunder the temple…. See 2 Macc. 3.4" (Bullinger, *The Companion*

Bible, p. 1203). Not long afterward, Seleucus died at the hands of Heliodorus, and the throne passed to his brother, Antiochus IV. It was Antiochus IV who invaded Jerusalem and polluted the Temple in 167 BC, causing the daily sacrifices to cease. As noted earlier, Antiochus IV was a *type* of the coming Antichrist. His defilement of the Temple was only a forerunner of the prophesied "abomination of desolation."

The rise and fall of the Antichrist are also discussed in Daniel 8, which provides additional insight into the events that will take place in Jerusalem and the Middle East in the years leading to the return of Christ.

Daniel 8:9-26

> "And **out of one of them** [one of the four divisions of Alexander's empire, verse 8] **came forth a little horn** [the Antichrist], **which became very great**, toward the south and toward the east and toward the glorious land [the land of Israel]. And it became great, even to the host of heaven. And it cast down some of the host and of the stars to the ground, and trampled upon them. Yea, he magnified himself, even to the Prince of the host, **and the daily sacrifice** [at a future temple in Jerusalem] **was taken away by him**, and the place of His sanctuary was cast down. And the host was given to it together with the daily sacrifice because of transgression, and it cast down the truth to the ground. And it practiced and prospered" (Dan. 8:9-12).

Daniel 8:9 states that the Antichrist will expand south toward the Persian Gulf, east toward India and west toward the nation of Israel, thus indicating that he **rises from the north**. This conclusion is supported by the prophecy in Daniel 11 concerning the **king of the north** who will rise at the time of the end. As in Daniel 11, the prophecy in Daniel 8 describes him as skilled in the use of subtlety and pretense.

> "And in the latter time of their kingdom [the time of the end], when the transgressors have come to the full, **a king, fierce of countenance** [mighty presence] **and understanding dark sentences** [skilled in dissimulation], **shall stand up**. And his power shall be mighty, **but not by his own power** [Satan will empower him]. And he shall destroy marvelously, and shall prosper [succeed] and do his own will, and **destroy the mighty and the holy people** [bringing the Great Tribulation upon the people of Israel]. And also through his cunning he shall cause craft to prosper in his hand. And he shall magnify himself in his heart, and in time of security shall destroy many. He also shall **stand up against the Prince of princes** [Christ, the King of

> kings]. **But he shall be broken without a human hand** [not by human strength, but by divine power]. And the vision of the evening and the morning which was told is true. But you shall shut up the vision, for it belongs to many days to come [the time of the end]" (Dan. 8:23-26).

The prophecies of both Daniel 8 and Daniel 11 reveal that the Antichrist will **come to power in the years immediately preceding the return of Jesus Christ** and will fight against Christ at His coming. The future fulfillment of the two prophecies is also confirmed by Jesus' words in Matthew 24 concerning the "abomination that brings desolation." These words were spoken two centuries after the invasion of Jerusalem by Antiochus IV Epiphanes, leaving no room to identify him as the "little horn" of Daniel eight—except in *type*. Indeed, the pollution of the Temple by Antiochus IV in 167 BC was a *foreshadowing* of the devastation that will take place in Jerusalem at the hands of the future Antichrist. The terrible distress that will strike the people of Israel when he sets up the "abomination of desolation" will surpass the holocaust that the Jews suffered during World War II.

> "For then **shall there be great tribulation, such as has not been from the beginning of the world until this time**, nor ever shall be again" (Matt. 24:21).

At this time of indescribable suffering, Christ will return to deliver the remnant of Israel. He will reign in Jerusalem as King of kings and Lord of lords, and all will acknowledge Him as the Messiah. That is the glorious future that lies beyond the prophecies of the end-time Antichrist.

Bibliography

"Achaemenes." *Encyclopedia Britannica*, 2006. Encyclopedia Britannica Premium Service. 28 May 2006. www.britannica.com/eb/article-9003515

Amadon, Grace. "The Crucifixion Calendar," *Journal of Biblical Literature*, Vol. LXIII, 1944, pp. 188-189.

_______. "The Jewish Calendar in the Fifth Century B.C." Adventist Heritage Center, James White Library, Andrews University. No date given.

_______. "Ancient Jewish Calendation—The Problem I." Adventist Heritage Center, James White Library, Andrews University. No date given.

_______. "Ancient Jewish Calendation—The Problem II." Adventist Heritage Center, James White Library, Andrews University. No date given.

_______. "Ancient Jewish Calendar Construction I." Adventist Heritage Center, James White Library, Andrews University. No date given.

_______. "Ancient Jewish Calendar Construction II." *The Ministry*, April 1944. Adventist Heritage Center, James White Library, Andrews University.

_______. "Ancient Jewish Calendation." *Journal of Biblical Literature*, LXI, Part IV, 1942.

_______. Register of the Grace Amadon Collection. Collection 154, November 2002. Adventist Heritage Center, James White Library, Andrews University.

Anstey, Rev. Martin. *The Romance of Bible Chronology,* Vol. 1. London, 1913.

Armstrong, Herbert W. *The Autobiography of Herbert W. Armstrong*, Vol. 1, pp. 338-339.

"Artaxerxes I." *Encyclopedia Britannica.* 2006. Encyclopedia Britannica Premium Service. 28 May 2006. www.britannica.com/eb/article-9009673

"Artaxerxes I Longimanus." *Encyclopedia Britannica.* 1911 Chronology (see article "Nehemiah").

"Artaxerxes II Mnemon." *Encyclopedia Britannica*. 2006. Encyclopedia Britannica Premium Service. June 2006. www.britannica.com/eb/article-9009674

"Artaxerxes III." *Encyclopedia Britannica*. 2006. Encyclopedia Britannica Premium Service. June 2006. www.britannica.com/eb/article-9009675

"Arses." *Encyclopedia Britannica*. 2006. Encyclopedia Britannica Premium Service. June 2006. www.britannica.com/eb/article-9009644

Biblia Hebraica Stuttgartensia. Stuttgart: Deutche Bibelstiflung, 1977.

Brown, Driver, Briggs. *Hebrew and English Lexicon of the Old Testament*. Oxford: Clarendon Press, 1906.

"Cambyses I." *Encyclopedia Britannica.* 2006. Encyclopedia Britannica Premium Service. 27 May 2006. www.britannica.com/eb/article-9018783

"Cambyses II." *McClintock and Strong's Chronology Cyclopedia of Biblical, Theological, and Ecclesiastical Literature*, Vol. III C-D, 1952, p. 49.

Cambyses II. *Finegan Chronology Handbook of Biblical Chronology*, 1998, pp. 178-181.

"Cambyses II." *Encyclopedia Britannica*. 2006. Encyclopedia Britannica Premium Service. 4 March 2006. www.britannica.com/eb/article-9018784

Cameron, George G. "Darius and Xerxes in Babylonia," *The American Journal of Semitic Languages and Literatures,* Vol. 58, 1941, pp. 314-325.

Clay, Albert T. *Business Documents of Murashu Sons of Nippur, Dated in the Reign of Darius II*, pages 1 to 54, plates 1 to 123. The University Museum Publications of the Babylonian Section, Vol. 2. Philadelphia: The University of Pennsylvania, 1912.

Cowley, A. E. *Aramaic Papyri of the Fifth Century B.C.* Oxford: Oxford University, 1923.

_______. *Jewish Documents of the Time of Ezra*, translated from the Aramaic by A. E. Cowley. New York: The Macmillan Co., 1919.

Cox, Bert. "A Study of Daniel 9:24-27," 2001. www.biblepath.org/6/index.html

Cross, F. M. Jr. "A Reconstruction of the Judean Restoration," *Journal of Biblical Literature*, Vol. 94, 1975, pp. 4-18; *idem*, *Int* 29 (1975), pp. 187-203.

"Cyrus I." *Encyclopedia Britannica.* 2006. Encyclopedia Britannica Premium Service. 27 May 2006. www.britannica.com/eb/article-9028432

"Cyrus II." *Encyclopedia Britannica*. 2006. Encyclopedia Britannica Premium Service. 4 March 2006. www.britannica.com/eb/article-9028433

Dankenbring, William F. "Daniel Nine Proves Jesus Is the Christ," *The Good News Magazine*, December 1965, pp. 9-11.

"Darius I." Behistun Inscription: Translation, Maps & Photos. www.livius.org/be-bm/behistun/behistun03.html

"Darius I." *Encyclopedia Britannica*. 2006. Encyclopedia Britannica Premium Service. 4 March 2006. www.britannica.com/eb/article-9028433

"Darius II Ochus." *Encyclopedia Britannica*. 2006. Encyclopedia Britannica Premium Service. June 2006. www.britannica.com/eb/article-9028779

"Darius III Codommanus." *Encyclopedia Britannica*. 2006. Encyclopedia Britannica Premium Service. June 2006. www.britannica.com/eb/article9028780

Dugger, A. N. *The Bible Home Instructor*. The Church of God Seventh Day. Stanberry, MO, 1919-1920.
"Calendar." *Encyclopedia Britannica*, 14th Ed., 1929-1933.

"Chronology." *Encyclopedia Biblica*, Vol. I. New York, 1899.

Eusebius. *Chronici Canones*. Translated into Latin by Jerome. Edited by J. K. Fotheringham. London: Humphrey Milford, 1923.

Faulstich, E. W. *Bible Chronology and the Scientific Method*. Spencer, Iowa: Chronology Books, 1990.

_______. *History, Harmony & the Hebrew Kings*. Spencer, Iowa: Chronology Books, 1986.

Ferguson, James. *An Astronomical Lecture, on Eclipses of the Sun and Moon, the True Year of Our Savior's Crucifixion, the Supernatural Darkness at That Time, and the Prophet Daniel's Seventy Weeks*. Bristol: S. Farley, 1775.

_______. *Ferguson's Astronomy, Explained Upon Sir Isaac Newton's Principles. With notes, and supplementary chapters by David Brewster*. 2 vols. Edinburgh: John Ballantyne and Co., 1811.

Finegan, Jack. *Handbook of Biblical Chronology: Principles of Time Reckoning in the Ancient World and Problems of Chronology in the Bible*. Hendrickson, 1998.

Fotheringham, J. K. "Calendar Dates in the Aramaic Papyri from Assuan," Monthly Notices of the Royal Astronomical Society, Vol. 69, 1908-1909, pp. 12-20.

_______. "Note on the Regnal Years in the Elephantine Papyri," ibid., pp. 446-448.

_______. "A Reply to Professor Ginzel on the Calendar Dates in the Elephantine Papyri," ibid., Vol. 71, 1911, pp. 661-663.

Franklin, Carl D. "Historical Evidence of the 19-Year Intercalation Cycle, Part I," 2002.

_______. "The Reigns of the Persian Kings in the Chronicle of Eusebius," 2006. An Analysis of *Praepar. Evang*. 10.10.4, *Eusebius Werke*, Vol. 8.1, p. 591, as recounted by Finegan.

_______. "Comparative Dates for the Reign of Cambyses II," 2006.

_______. "A Chronology of Historic and Prophetic Events From the Prophet Jonah to Jesus Christ," January 2001.

_______. "A Study of the 70-Year Cycles of Jeremiah and the 70-Weeks Prophecy of Daniel 9:24-27 in Relationship to the Sabbatical Cycles," April 2006.
_______. "The Two *Jehovahs* of the Psalms," June 1994.

_______. "Notes on the Dating of the Persian Kings According to Edwin M. Yamauchi," July 2006. Based on his book *Persia and the Bible*.

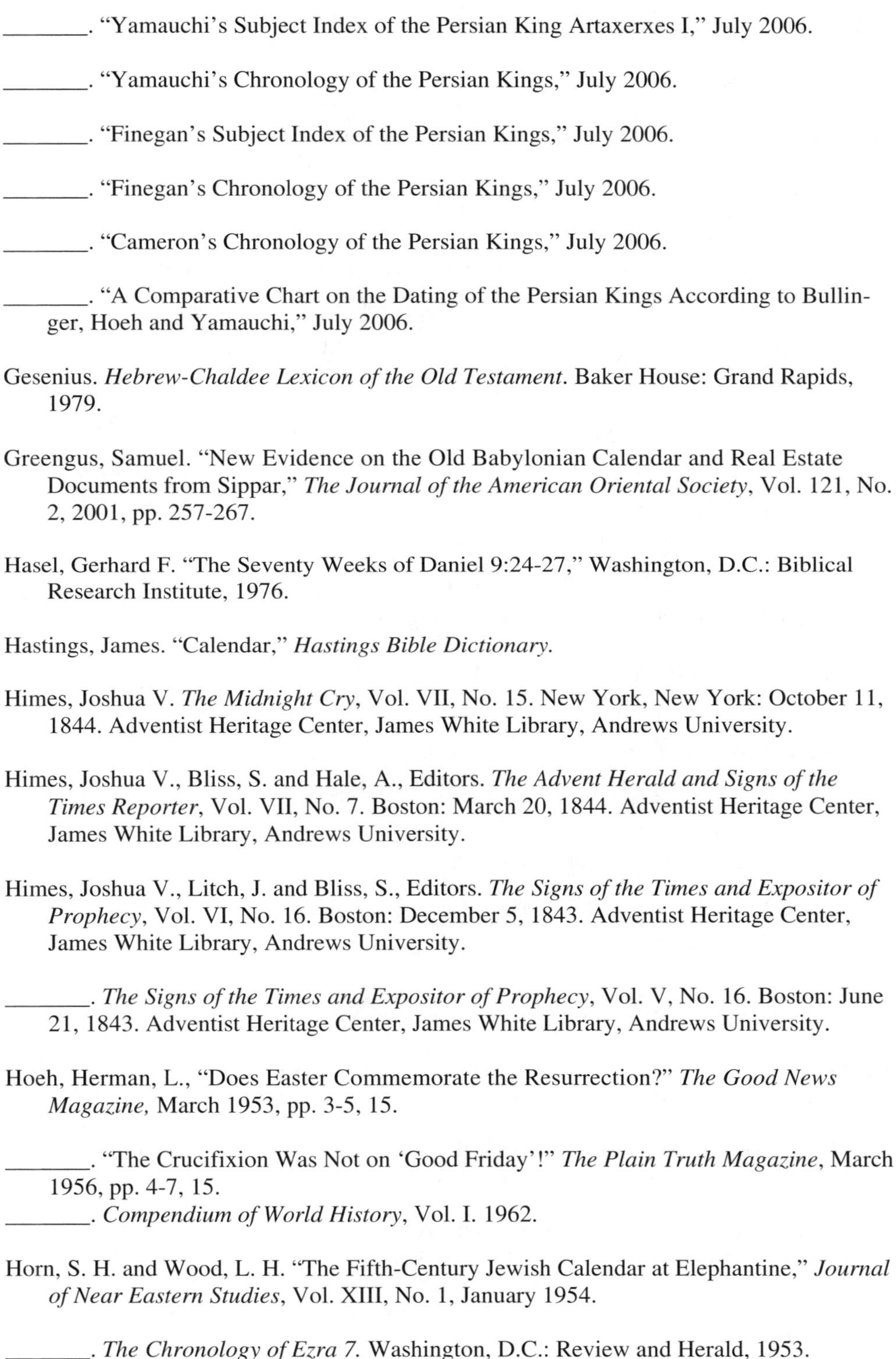

_______. "Yamauchi's Subject Index of the Persian King Artaxerxes I," July 2006.

_______. "Yamauchi's Chronology of the Persian Kings," July 2006.

_______. "Finegan's Subject Index of the Persian Kings," July 2006.

_______. "Finegan's Chronology of the Persian Kings," July 2006.

_______. "Cameron's Chronology of the Persian Kings," July 2006.

_______. "A Comparative Chart on the Dating of the Persian Kings According to Bullinger, Hoeh and Yamauchi," July 2006.

Gesenius. *Hebrew-Chaldee Lexicon of the Old Testament*. Baker House: Grand Rapids, 1979.

Greengus, Samuel. "New Evidence on the Old Babylonian Calendar and Real Estate Documents from Sippar," *The Journal of the American Oriental Society*, Vol. 121, No. 2, 2001, pp. 257-267.

Hasel, Gerhard F. "The Seventy Weeks of Daniel 9:24-27," Washington, D.C.: Biblical Research Institute, 1976.

Hastings, James. "Calendar," *Hastings Bible Dictionary*.

Himes, Joshua V. *The Midnight Cry*, Vol. VII, No. 15. New York, New York: October 11, 1844. Adventist Heritage Center, James White Library, Andrews University.

Himes, Joshua V., Bliss, S. and Hale, A., Editors. *The Advent Herald and Signs of the Times Reporter*, Vol. VII, No. 7. Boston: March 20, 1844. Adventist Heritage Center, James White Library, Andrews University.

Himes, Joshua V., Litch, J. and Bliss, S., Editors. *The Signs of the Times and Expositor of Prophecy*, Vol. VI, No. 16. Boston: December 5, 1843. Adventist Heritage Center, James White Library, Andrews University.

_______. *The Signs of the Times and Expositor of Prophecy*, Vol. V, No. 16. Boston: June 21, 1843. Adventist Heritage Center, James White Library, Andrews University.

Hoeh, Herman, L., "Does Easter Commemorate the Resurrection?" *The Good News Magazine,* March 1953, pp. 3-5, 15.

_______. "The Crucifixion Was Not on 'Good Friday'!" *The Plain Truth Magazine*, March 1956, pp. 4-7, 15.

_______. *Compendium of World History*, Vol. I. 1962.

Horn, S. H. and Wood, L. H. "The Fifth-Century Jewish Calendar at Elephantine," *Journal of Near Eastern Studies*, Vol. XIII, No. 1, January 1954.

_______. *The Chronology of Ezra 7.* Washington, D.C.: Review and Herald, 1953.

Jewish Encyclopedia. New York: Judaica Press, Inc., 1905.

Encyclopedia Judaica. New York: Judaica Press, Inc., 1995.

Jones, Floyd Nolen. *The Chronology of the Old Testament.* 2004.

Jonsson, Carl Olof., "The 20th Year of Artaxerxes." www.freeminds.org/doctrine/cojonsson.htm

Jordan, James B. *Biblical Chronology Newsletter*, Vol. 3, No. 2, February 1991. www.biblicalhorizons.com/biblical-chronology/3_02/

_______. *Biblical Chronology Newsletter*, Vol. 3, No. 3, March 1991. www.biblicalhorizons.com/biblical-chronology/3_05/

_______. *Biblical Chronology Newsletter*, Vol. 3, No. 4, April 1991. www.biblicalhorizons.com/biblical-chronology/3_04/

_______. *Biblical Chronology Newsletter*, Vol. 3, No. 5, May 1991. www.biblicalhorizons.com/biblical-chronology/3_05/

_______. *Biblical Chronology Newsletter*, Vol. 8, No. 3, March 1996. www.biblicalhorizons.com/biblical-chronology/8_03/

_______. *Biblical Chronology Newsletter*, Vol. 8, No. 4, April 1996. www.biblicalhorizons.com/biblical-chronology/8_04/

_______. *Biblical Chronology Newsletter*, Vol. 8, No. 5, May 1996. www.biblicalhorizons.com/biblical-chronology/8_05/

_______. *Biblical Chronology Newsletter*, Vol. 8, No. 6, June 1996. www.biblicalhorizons.com/biblical-chronology/8_06/

_______. *Biblical Chronology Newsletter*, Vol. 8, No. 7, July 1996. www.biblicalhorizons.com/biblical-chronology/8_07/

_______. *Biblical Chronology Newsletter*, Vol. 8, No. 8, August 1996. www.biblicalhorizons.com/biblical-chronology/8_08/

Josephus, Flavius. *Antiquities of the Jews*; *Wars*. "Complete Works of Josephus"; Grand Rapids: Kregel, 1981

Kitto, John. *The Court of Persia: Viewed in Connexion with Scriptural Usages*. London: The Religious Tract Society. No date given.

Knobel, E. B. "Note on the Regnal Years in the Aramaic Papyri from Assuan," Monthly Notices of the Royal Astronomical Society, Vol. 69, 1908-1909, pp. 8-11.

Kraeling, Emil G. *The Brooklyn Museum Aramaic Papyri*. 2 vols. New York: The Brooklyn Museum, 1953.

Kroll, Paul. "The Key To The Crucifixion Date," *The Good News Magazine*, April-May 1966, pp. 9-10, 18-20.

Lindo, E. H. *A Jewish Calendar for Sixty-Four Years*. London: Thompson, 1838.

Martin, Dr. Ernest L. *The Star of Bethlehem*. Published in 1996. www.askelm.com/books/book003.htm

________. *The Teachings of Pentecost.* Published in 1983. www.askelm.com/doctrine/d050501.htm

McFall, Leslie. "Was Nehemiah Contemporary with Ezra in 458 BC?" Dr. McFall's home page may be found at www.btinternet.com/~lmf12/

Meeus, Jean. *Astronomical Tables of the Sun, Moon and Planets*, 2nd ed. Willmann-Bell, Inc, 1995.

Olmstead, A. T. *History of the Persian Empire*. Chicago: University of Chicago Press, 1948.

Owens, John Joseph. *Analytical Key to the Old Testament*, Vol. 2.

_______. *Analytical Key to the Old Testament*, Vol. 3.

Parker, Richard A., Dubberstein, Waldo H. *Babylonian Chronology 626 BC to AD 75*. Providence: Brown University Press, 1956.

Poebel, Arno. *The Babylonian Expedition of The University of Pennsylvania, Series A: Cuneiform Texts*, edited by H. V. Hilprecht, Volume VI, Part 2. *Legal and Business Documents from the time of The First Dynasty of Babylon, Chiefly from Nippur*. Philadelphia: 1909.

Porten, Bezalel. *Archives from Elephantine: The Life of an Ancient Jewish Military Colony.* Berkeley: University of California Press, 1968.

_______. *Jews of Elephantine and Arameans of Syene (Fifth Century BCE): Fifty Aramaic Texts with Hebrew and English Translations.* Edited and newly translated by Bezalel Porten in collaboration with Jonah C. Greenfield. Jerusalem: 1974.

Price, James D. "The Fabulous Prophecies of the Messiah," 1995. www.infidels.org/library/modern/james_price/proph- response.html

_______. "The Syntax of the Masoretic Accents in the Hebrew Bible," *Studies in the Bible and Early Christianity,* Vol. 27. Lewiston, NY: The Edwin Mellen Press, 1990.

_______. *A Concordance of the Hebrew Accents in the Hebrew Bible*. Lewiston, NY: Mellen Biblical Press, 1995.

Ptolemy (Claudius Ptolemaeus). *The Almagest*. Translated by R. Catesby Taliaferro. "Great Books of the Western World," Vol. 16. Edited by John Maynard Hutchins and Mortimer J. Adler. Chicago: Encyclopedia Britannica, Inc., 1952. Pp. VI1-XIV, 1-478. Appendix A.

Rawlinson, Sir George. "Clio," Herodotus' Book I, July 2006.

Sachs, A. J. and Hunger, H. *Astronomical Diaries and Related Texts from Babylonia, Vol. I: Diaries from 652 to 262 BC.* Vienna: Österreichischen Akademie der Wissenschaften, 1988.

Sayce, A. H. and Cowley, A. E. *Aramaic Papyri Discovered at Assuan.* 79 pp. and facsimiles of the papyri. London: Alexander Moring, Ltd., 1906.

_______. *Records of the Past: Series 1 and 2* (12 vols., 1875-1899). *The Egibi Tablets*, Vol. 11. Translated by Theophilus Goldridge Pinches. www.brainfly.net/html/rop.html

Seutonius. J. C. Rolfe, ed. James Loeb Classical Library. London, 1914.

Shea, William H. "When Did the Seventy Weeks of Daniel 9:24 Begin?" Washington, D.C.: Biblical Research Institute, 1976.

Suren-Pahlav, Shapour. "Cyrus the Great's Cylinder: Transliteration & Translation of the Text," CAIS-SOAS (The Circle of Ancient Iranian Studies), 1998. www.cais-oas.com/CAIS/History/hakhamaneshian/Cyrus-the-great/cyrus_cylinder.html

Thiele, Edwin R. *The Mysterious Numbers of the Hebrew Kings.* Chicago: The University of Chicago Press, 1951.

"Teispes." *Encyclopedia Britannica.* 2006. Encyclopedia Britannica Premium Service. 27 May 2006. www.britannica.com/eb/article-9071563

Ussher, Archbishop. *Annales Veteris et Novi Testament: The Annals of the World.* 1658.

Vanhoye, Albert. *The Jubilee Year in the Gospel of Luke.* Theological Historical Commission, 1997.

Waltke, Bruce K. and M. O'Connor. *An Introduction to Biblical Hebrew Syntax.* Winona Lake, IN: Eisenbrauns, 1990.

Wigram, George V. *The Englishman's Hebrew Concordance of the Old Testament.* Hendrickson, 2001.

Williamson, H. G. M. "The Historical Value of Josephus' Antiquities XI," *The Journal of Theological Studies*, April 1977, pp. 49-66.

Wright, Rev. J. Stafford. "The Date of Ezra's Coming to Jerusalem." Tyndale Lecture Series, January 1947. Westminster, London.

"Xerxes I." *Encyclopedia Britannica.* Encyclopedia Britannica Premium Service. 28 May 2006. www.britannica.com/eb/article-9077684

Yamauchi, Edwin M. "The Reverse Order of Ezra/Nehemiah Reconsidered," *Themelios* 5.3, 1980, pp. 7-13.

_______. *Persia and the Bible.* Grand Rapids: Baker Book House, 1990.

Appendix D

The Calculated Hebrew Calendar: The Foundation of God's Weekly Sabbath And Annual "Appointed Times"

For centuries, the entire world has followed the common Roman (Gregorian) Calendar. Mainstream "Christians" peg their popular (albeit unbiblical) holidays to this calendar—New Year's Day, Christmas, Halloween, Easter, etc. Moreover, in the "Christian" world, the week revolves around their *chosen* day of worship, Sunday. Amazingly, today's "Christianity" operates in utter ignorance of the true weekly Sabbath (Saturday, the seventh day of the week) and the *biblical festivals* commanded by God in the Old Testament—which, as can be easily proven, are *still binding* on Christians (for a thorough study on this vital topic, please request our free book *Occult Holidays or God's Holy Days—Which?*).

These biblical festivals and high days are, essentially, God's "appointed times." Both the weekly Sabbath and the annual holy days occur on specifically appointed days or dates. The Sabbath, for example, always falls on the seventh day of the weekly cycle, as set from creation. This can still be seen even in the Gregorian Calendar, which rightly places Saturday as the seventh day of the week. Similarly, God's holy days fall on specific *days* of specific *months*. For instance, Passover always falls on the evening of the 14th *day* of the first *month*.

But Passover (as well as God's other "appointed times") cannot be determined by simply following the Gregorian Calendar. How, then, does one seeking to genuinely obey God go about determining *when* to keep His high days? How does a month begin, according to Scripture? When is the "first month" of the year, according to God? The answer is found in understanding God's Sacred Calendar, or the *Calculated Hebrew Calendar* (CHC).

Theologians have for centuries devised various liturgical calendars. Even among those who recognize the validity of the Old Testament holy days, numerous "calendar systems" have flourished. While such calendar schemes purport to proclaim God's high days, they have proven to be complex, confusing and contradictory to Scripture. Yet we know that God Himself is not the author of such confusion (I Cor. 14:33). Rather, it is the misguided schemes of men that cause confusion.

In order to understand the importance of the Calculated Hebrew Calendar, we need to ask one fundamental question: Did God *leave it to men* to devise their *own* calendars in order to observe the Sabbath and holy days on the days of *their choosing*? Indeed, if God has *not* provided clear, definitive directions on the observance of what *He* considers to be *holy time*, then any calendar scheme men might devise would, by default, be acceptable before God. But such a proposition is absurd, and suggests that God is weak, indecisive, and has no real plan. But if God *did give definite instructions*—commandments, laws and statutes—in His Word concerning *when* to observe His Sabbath and festivals, then are we not obligated to follow those instructions?

Of the God Who created the entire universe, Scripture says: " '**To whom then will you compare Me, or who is My equal?**' says the Holy One. '**Lift up your eyes on high, and behold, Who has created these *things*, Who brings out their host by number? He calls them all by names by the greatness of His might**, for He is strong in power; not one fails. Why do you say, O Jacob, and O Israel you speak, "My way is hidden from the LORD and my cause is disregarded by my God?" Have you not known? Have you not heard, that the everlasting God, the LORD, the Creator of the ends of the earth, does not grow weak nor weary? **And His understanding no one can fathom**' " (Isa. 40:25-28).

Since God is creator of the entire universe—all the stars and galaxies, which He calls by number—He knows how it functions. After all, He created *time* and the *astro-mathematics* by which the entire universe has functioned since the beginning of creation, and will continue to function throughout the ages into eternity. Thus, the Almighty is the only one Who can **provide mankind with a *fully accurate* method** of determining the "appointed times" He has ordained and commanded. No man has that ability—*only* God. In fact, no man or group of men has ever been able to devise a calendar that is as accurate as the Calculated Hebrew Calendar—not even NASA or the U. S. Naval Observatory, with all of their hi-tech computerized equipment.

Since no man can correctly determine the "appointed times" of God, He alone had to make this knowledge known through divine *revelation*. Indeed, God revealed His method of accurately *calculating* the Sacred Calendar to the Levites and the Aaronic priesthood of ancient Israel. This is why we find in Leviticus 23 the *specific dates* commanded for the **Passover** and the **Feast of Unleavened Bread** (with holy days on the 15th and 21st days of the first month); the proper count to Pentecost—using seven complete weeks, each ending on a weekly Sabbath, plus one day for the **Day of Pentecost**; the **Feast of Trumpets** on the first day of the seventh month; the **Day of Atonement** on the 10th day of the seventh month; the **Feast of Tabernacles** (with a single high day on the 15th day of the seventh month); and, finally, the eighth-day festival called the **Last Great Day** (falling on the 22nd day of the seventh month).

But having these preset dates is not enough to establish *precisely* when God's high days are to be observed. *When* is the first month of the year? *How* do we determine the beginning of the seventh month? Again, this information is not a part of any man-made calendar, such as the Gregorian Calendar. It can only be found by following the Calculated Hebrew Calendar.

Various sightings of the "new moon" crescent fall short of a complete method for determining the Sacred Calendar. Moreover, the *mathematical formula* for determining such calendar dates is not found in the

Bible. What we do find, however, is that God gave the *formula* and the *authority to calculate* His high days to the Levitical priesthood—and to no one else. Indeed, God clearly designated the priests in Leviticus 23 to proclaim the appointed feasts: "These *are* the appointed feasts of the LORD, holy convocations which you [the priests] shall proclaim in their appointed seasons" (Lev. 23:4).

This is why the apostle Paul wrote, "What then *is* the advantage of the Jew, or what *is* the profit of circumcision? Much in every way. Primarily, in that they were entrusted with the **oracles of God**" (Rom. 3:1-2). The "oracles" of God were given to the Levitical/Aaronic priests within the Jewish nation, and consist of the entire Old Testament *and* the methods of calculating the Hebrew calendar. Accordingly, the prophet Malachi wrote that "**the priest's lips should keep** [guard, preserve, have charge over] **knowledge**, and [that] *the people* should seek the Law at his mouth; for he is the messenger of the LORD of hosts" (Mal. 2:7). (Importantly, the "oracles" do *not* include the Jews' "oral law." Over time, Jewish rabbis perverted the trust God had placed in them by *falsely* claiming that their humanly-devised "oral traditions" were also given by God.)

Indeed, the Calculated Hebrew Calendar is not something to be devised according to the whims and traditions of men. It is in fact *set by God*—and has been preserved for us to this day.

The Weekly Seventh-day Sabbath Cycle

To begin, we must first examine God's weekly seventh-day Sabbath cycle—which is *foundational* to His entire Sacred Calendar. Did God leave the choice to *men* to select one day in seven as a day to worship Him? Or, in the beginning, did God specially *appoint* the *seventh day* as His Sabbath, specifically blessing and sanctifying the *seventh* day?

According to the scriptural account, He indeed did! He specifically designated the *seventh* day of the repeating seven-day cycle as the Sabbath. We have the record in Genesis chapters one and two. From the beginning, we find that **God continuously counts seven days in a never-ending sequence, and that the seventh day is always the weekly Sabbath**. There are *no exceptions* in the entirety of the Bible. Therefore, Sunday (or any other day) can never be God's weekly Sabbath, because He has created *only* the seventh day to be holy. Moreover, *no man* has the authority to make *any* day holy!

The account in Genesis chapter one gives us the record of the creation of the earth (actually the renewing of the earth) in six days. Each day is numbered and designated by the phrase "the evening and morning" in describing a whole day—a 24-hour day. Each day is counted in sequence with no gaps, partial days, or uncounted days.

In Genesis chapter two we have the record of God's creation of the *first* Sabbath day—the seventh day: "And by *the beginning of* the seventh day God finished His work which He had made. And He rested on the seventh day from all His work which He had made. And **God BLESSED the seventh day and SANCTIFIED it** [set it apart] **because on it He rested from all His work which God had created and made**" (Gen. 2:2-3). Thus, God's Sabbath cannot fall on *any other* day of the week, and no man has the authority to change it. Notice also that the Sabbath is independently reckoned by counting the days in a *continuous* seven-day sequence. As we will see, this day-by-day reckoning of the weekly cycle is *separate from* the reckoning of the days, months and years of the sacred CHC. The seven-day weekly cycle never varies and has *never been changed* by God. In fact, there is not a single passage in the Bible indicating that time has ever been "lost" or not counted—not a day, week, month or year has ever gone missing! God accounts for all time!

***The Exodus and the Sabbath*:** During the Exodus from Egypt, God revealed the seventh-day weekly Sabbath to the children of Israel by the giving of manna (Ex. 16). In this account, beginning on the morning of the first day of the week, God sent manna from heaven for the children of Israel to eat each day. For the first five days of the seven-day week, He sent only the portion for each particular day. God specifically commanded them not to gather more than what was to be eaten for each day. Those who disobeyed and gathered more found that the extra manna bred worms and stank, making it unfit to eat.

However, on the sixth day, God commanded the children of Israel to gather *twice* as much as they did on each of the first five days. This two-day supply was for the sixth day *and* the seventh-day Sabbath. God also commanded them not to go out to gather manna on the seventh day, because He would not send it. Notice God's reaction when some disobeyed and went out on the Sabbath morning to look for manna: "And it came to pass *that some* of the people went out on the seventh day in order to gather, but they did not find *any*. And the LORD said to Moses, 'How long do you refuse to keep My commandments and My laws? See, because **the LORD has given you the Sabbath** [God determines the Sabbath—not man], therefore He gives you the bread of two days on the sixth day. Let each one stay in his place. Do not let any one go out of his place on the seventh day.' So the people rested on the seventh day" (Ex. 16:27-30).

For forty years God consistently sent manna six days a week—with a double portion on the sixth day—but He never sent manna on the seventh-day Sabbath. The seven-day weekly cycle *remained unchanged* for the entire forty-year period.

To help Israel always remember that it was God Who fed them for those forty years, He commanded that Aaron gather an *omer* of manna be kept before the Lord as a witness of what God had done: "And Moses said, 'This *is* the thing which the LORD has commanded, "Fill an omer of it to be kept for your generations, so that you may see the bread with which I have fed you in the wilderness, when I brought you out from the land of Egypt." '

And Moses said to Aaron, 'Take a pot and put an omer full of manna in it, and lay it up before the LORD to be kept for your generations.' As the LORD commanded Moses, so Aaron laid it up before the testimony to be kept. And the children of Israel ate manna forty years until they came to a habitable land. They ate manna until they came into the borders of the land of Canaan" (Ex. 16:32-35).

Later, after the Ark of the Covenant was made, the *omer* of manna was put inside the ark along with the tables of stone (on which God had written the Ten Commandments) and the rod of Aaron that budded (Heb. 9:4). At the end of forty years, after the children of Israel entered the Promised Land, the manna ceased the day after they had eaten of the grain of the land (Josh. 5:12). However, **the continuous counting of the seven-day cycle has remained unchanged**.

It is essential to understand that God correlates all time—days, months and years—with His created seven-day cycle, with the Sabbath *always* being the seventh day of the week. **The seven-day weekly cycle is the *foundation* of all time on earth. There is absolutely no exception to the day-by-day count of seven consecutive days**. This seven-day cycle has been repeated perpetually from creation until now, and will likewise continue eternally into the age of the new heavens and new earth: " 'For as the new heavens and the new earth, which I will make, shall remain before Me,' says the LORD, 'so will your seed and your name remain. And it shall come to pass, that from one month to another, and **from one Sabbath to another**, shall all flesh come to worship before Me,' says the LORD" (Isa. 66:22-23).

God's Seven-day Cycle Unbroken

At no time has God ever mentioned or even hinted in Scripture that the seventh-day weekly Sabbath is to be reckoned by any other method than by a *continuous* counting of seven days as established from creation. This fact is supported by God establishing the weekly Sabbath as a *perpetual covenant*: "You shall keep the Sabbath therefore, for it *is* holy to you. Everyone that defiles it shall surely be put to death, for whoever does *any* work on it, that soul shall be cut off from among his people. Six days may work be done, but on the seventh day *is* the Sabbath of rest, holy to the LORD. Whoever does *any* work on the Sabbath day, he shall surely be put to death. Therefore the children of Israel [the church is spiritual Israel] shall **keep the Sabbath, to observe the Sabbath throughout their generations *as* A PERPETUAL COVENANT. It *is* a sign between Me and the children of Israel forever**; for in six days the LORD made the heavens and the earth, and on the seventh day He rested, and was refreshed" (Ex. 31:14-17).

When God gave the Ten Commandments, the Fourth Commandment was the Sabbath command. Notice how this command reflects a *continuous counting* of days in the seven-day cycle from creation: "Remember the Sabbath day to keep it holy. **Six days you shall labor and do all your work.**

But the seventh day *is* the Sabbath of the LORD your God. In it you shall not do any work, you, nor your son, nor your daughter; your manservant, nor your maidservant, nor your livestock, nor the stranger within your gates; **for *in* six days the LORD made the heaven and the earth, the sea, and all that *is* in them, and rested the seventh day. Therefore the LORD blessed the Sabbath day and sanctified it**" (Ex. 20:8-11). God also commanded that the Sabbath was to be kept from sunset to sunset (Lev. 23:32).

In the New Testament we find that Jesus and His disciples kept the weekly Sabbath. As "God manifested in the flesh," Jesus proclaimed that He is "Lord of the Sabbath" (Mark 2:27-28); as Lord God of the Old Testament, He was the one Who had *created time*, beginning with the continuous seven-day cycle leading to the seventh-day Sabbath. He is the one Who created the cyclical seven-day Sabbath count.

Contrary to what some religionists claim, time has *never* been lost. God—"with Whom there is no variation, nor shadow of turning" (James 1:17)—has continually upheld the vital seven-day cycle. While numerous religions have designated various days as "holy days" or "Sabbaths," such proclamations are null and void before God. **All self-proclaimed human decrees or calendar schemes have absolutely no effect upon God's divinely ordained seven-day cycle—nor do they alter His seventh-day Sabbath**.

Today, in most of the world and in nearly every language, the seventh-day Sabbath is known as *Saturday* on the Roman Civil Calendar. In spite of the fact that Europe utilizes a calendar that has been reconfigured to make *Sunday* appear to be the seventh day of the week, God is not bound by this calendar arrangement devised by men and sanctioned by the Roman Catholic Church. The European calendar notwithstanding, the seventh-day Sabbath of God, as commanded in the Bible, is still designated on the Roman Calendar as *Saturday* (though it appears as the sixth day on today's European calendar). Man's attempt to make it appear that *Sunday* is the seventh day of the week does nothing to change the true seventh-day Sabbath as commanded by God throughout Scripture. For thousands of years, the Jews' observance of the seventh-day Sabbath has been and continues to be living proof of this fact. While scattered into all parts of the world, the Jews have never lost the correct day for the Sabbath. (The weekly Sabbath is reckoned from sunset to sunset wherever one may live on the earth. For more information on the Sabbath, you may request our booklet *Which Day is the True Christian Sabbath.*)

The Calculated Hebrew Calendar

The Sacred Calendar of God is called the *Calculated Hebrew Calendar* (CHC). As a solar/lunar calendar, the CHC bases its years on the sun and utilizes the phases of the moon to determine the beginning of months. Importantly, the CHC *retains* God's continuous, cyclical count of the seven-day week to which the months and years must conform. The CHC is in harmony with and includes the counting of the days of the week (which are reckoned each day from "sunset to sunset"). In other words, God's reckoning and calculating of the months and years is entirely separate from—*but runs parallel to*—the weekly cycle.

On the fourth day of creation, God set the *positions* of the sun and moon (and the stars), which form the basis of the calculations of the CHC as a means of establishing days, months and years. "And God said, 'Let there be lights in the firmament of the heavens to divide between the day and the night [days are first], and let them be for signs, and for appointed seasons [the annual feasts], and for days [the annual holy days] and years [including the seventh-year land Sabbath and Jubilees every fifty years]; and let them be for lights in the firmament of the heavens to give light upon the earth.' And it was so. And God *had* made two great lights, the greater light to rule the day and the lesser light to rule the night; and *God had made* the stars *also*. And **God set them** [in their exact positions] **in the firmament of the heavens** to give light upon the earth, and to rule over the day and over the night, and to divide between the light and the darkness. And God saw that *it was* good. And the evening and the morning were the fourth day" (Gen. 1:14-19).

From Genesis chapters seven and eight, we are able to determine that at the time of the Flood each month contained *thirty* days. The Flood began "**in the second month, on the seventeen day of the month**.... And the waters prevailed upon the earth a hundred and fifty days ... and at the end of the **hundred and fifty days** the waters had gone down. And **in the seventh month, on the seventeenth day of the month,** the ark rested upon the mountains of Ararat" (Gen. 7:11, 24; 8:3-4). From these passages we can conclude that, *from the beginning*, each month had 30 days. This indicates that a year must have had 12 months of 30 days each, thus making 360 days in a year.

After the Flood in 2367 BC to the final exile of the Jews to Babylon in 585 BC, a total of 1782 years, there were various astronomical events by which God directly altered the arrangement of the heavenly bodies within the solar system—including the sun, moon and earth. As a result, the orbit of the earth around the sun was changed enough to *lengthen* the solar year from 360 days to 365¼ days. In approximately 800 BC, the last astronomical event found recorded in the Bible occurred in the days of King Hezekiah of Judah, when the shadow on the sundial was moved backward by 10 degrees.

These astronomical events were beginning to alter the way the sun and moon would keep time. Notice this intriguing quote by the Russian scholar Immanuel Velikovsky, from his 1950 book *Worlds in Collision*: "All over the world [in numerous cultures] we find that there was at some [ancient] time the same calendar of 360 days [per year], and that at some later date, about the seventh century before the present era ... a series of catastrophes occurred that changed the axis and the orbit of the earth and the orbit of the moon; and [we further find that] the ancient year, after going through a period marked by disarranged seasons, settled into a 'slow-moving year' *(Seneca)* of 365 days, 5 hours, 48 minutes, 46 seconds, [with] a lunar month being equal to 29 days, 12 hours, 44 minutes, 2.7 seconds, mean synodical period." Here, Velikovsky verifies from history what Genesis suggests, that there has been a *change* from a 360-day year (with 30-day lunar months) to an odd 365¼-day year with months averaging 29.53 days.

With these accumulated changes in the astronomical position of the earth in relationship to the sun, the earth's orbit was elongated causing 5¼ days to be added to the solar year. It also affected the movement of the moon, reducing it's orbit around the earth from 30 days to 29.53 days. After these changes, *which God caused to happen*, it was necessary for Him to reveal the *new* calculations to the Aaronic priesthood in order to keep the CHC accurate and maintain the "appointed times" in their seasons.

We have direct calendrical proof that God did indeed update the Levitical/Aaronic priesthood with new calculations for the Sacred Calendar after these astronomical events. From the destruction of Jerusalem and the First Temple, the Jews were exiled into many of the countries in the Middle East, with the majority of them living in Babylon. After the 70-year exile, some of the Jews returned to Judea to rebuild the city and the temple under the leadership of Zerubbabel, the governor, and Joshua, the high priest. The fact that they kept the Passover and the Feast of Unleavened Bread after the completion of the Second Temple **shows that the priests determined these festival dates using the updated calculations God had given to them before the exile**.

Some years later, before the city of Jerusalem was completely rebuilt, these calculations were preserved by Ezra the priest. In order to return the Jewish people to the true worship of God, Ezra established the Great Assembly of 120 priests. It was Ezra, with the help of these priests, who was responsible for the canonization of the Old Testament into the form we have today. At the same time, Ezra also formed what later became known as the "Calendar Court," which was responsible for properly calculating and proclaiming the festivals and holy days in their seasons as God had commanded in Leviticus 23. From that time until the destruction of the temple in 70 AD, the priests of the Calendar Court faithfully calculated the Sacred Calendar and proclaimed the "feasts of the Lord in their seasons."

During the time of Christ, the High Priest and president of the Sanhedrin was called *Nasi*, and was in charge of the calculations for the CHC. The Nasi had a lineage going back to Ezra, who traces his line back to Hilkiah, the High Priest who was the father of Jeremiah the prophet. They had all inherited a full knowledge of the CHC, with all of its God-given rules for the proper calculation of the high days.

The Nasi's, still of priestly lineage, continued to rule beyond Jerusalem from just after the time of Christ up to Hillel II in the 300s AD. Thus, we have a central calendar authority invested in a single family of the Aaronic line, going from the middle 300s AD back to Ezra, and then back to Hilkiah.

The popular idea that Hillel II "invented" the CHC with its various rules of calculation is contrary to the records of history, both in the Bible and those histories that have been accurately maintained by the priests and Levites within the Jewish community. Hillel II, as the last of the great sages, used his office of Nasi to absolutely guarantee that the knowledge of the CHC and its methods of calculation would not be lost. He made sure this priestly knowledge—withheld from the general populace until his day—was imparted worldwide to all Jews (and thus to the world). Hillel's motive was simply this: He was concerned that continued Roman persecution might compromise (or even eliminate) the Jews' observance of the holy days at the proper times as commanded by God.

The Jewish people and the early New Testament Christians were scattered far and wide throughout many nations—from the Middle East to the Atlantic and the British Islands in the west; to Europe, Scythia and Parthia in the north; from Babylon and Persia to India in the east; and from Egypt and North Africa to Ethiopia in the south. Therefore, because of this scattering, *direct visual sighting* of the "new moon" (the first visible crescent) for determining the beginning of a month as seen from the narrow geographical strip of the holy land and Jerusalem was no longer accurate. Why? Because the new moon does not appear on the same day in these distant places of the world.

However, the calculations God gave to the priests and Levites to accurately reckon the festivals made it possible for the holy days to be observed *at the same time* worldwide. Furthermore, with the CHC, the high days could be precisely determined years in advance. The discussion of the ancient rabbis in the tractate *Rosh Hashanah* offers historical evidence that the Sacred Calendar at the time of Christ and the apostle Paul was *calculated*, with all the necessary rules to keep festival observance accurate throughout time. In fact, the calculations of the CHC can be used to determine festival dates for any year into the future, as well as to accurately calculate such dates back in time to the 800s BC.

Today, even with the advent of "modern astronomy" and its super-telescopes coupled to high-speed supercomputers, no one has been able to improve on the CHC. Indeed, the CHC that God has given to the Aaronic priesthood (which has been preserved by Orthodox Jews for us today) is more accurate in calculating the festivals and holy days of God than any modern method. And it should be, because God ordained it.

The Calculated Hebrew Calendar Is Accurate for us Today

We need to know whether or not the CHC—as it is currently calculated, and has been calculated for thousands of years by the Levitical priesthood—is in fact the God-ordained method we should use today to determine when God's holy days should be kept. If it is, and we can prove it, then we should not tamper with it. It is just that simple.

***Simple Proof of the Accuracy of the CHC*:** According to the CHC, on the night of the beginning of the 15th day of the first month (Nisan), the first day of the Feast of Unleavened Bread, *and* on the night of the beginning of the 15th day of the seventh month (Tishri), the beginning of the Feast of Tabernacles, *there is a full moon.* Anyone can observe the moon on those two nights and see that it is full. Personally, I have done this for 51 years and the moon has always been full. **This is simple proof of the accuracy of the CHC.**

***Two Major Additional Proofs*:** In the *Harmony of the Gospels* and in the *Faithful Version* of the Bible (see the front section, "Other Works by the Author"), we present detailed scriptural and calendrical information about the *birth* and *death* of Jesus Christ. This information clearly proves that God used *only* the CHC in fulfilling His prophecies about these two most important biblical events. These two proofs, noted below, are also covered in detail in chapters *one* and *three*, respectively, of this book.

***Proof Number One*:** Paul writes of the "appointed time" of Jesus' birth: "Now then, I say, for as long a time as the heir is a child, he is no different from a servant, *although* he be lord of all; but he is under guardians and stewards until **the time appointed beforehand by the father**…. But when **the** [appointed] **time for the fulfillment came, God sent forth His own Son, born of a woman**…" (Gal. 4:1-2, 4; see chapter one).

***Proof Number Two*:** In his epistle to the Romans, Paul again writes that Jesus' death occurred at the "appointed time" of God: "For even when we were without strength, **at the appointed time Christ died for the ungodly**" (Rom. 5:6; see chapter three). We find in the book of Revelation that this "appointed time" of Jesus' death had been predetermined from the foundation of the world, as Christ is "the Lamb of God slain from *the* foundation of the world" (Rev. 13:8).

On what "appointed day" did Jesus die? **It was the Passover day, Nisan 14, in 30 AD, according to the CHC**—April 5 according to the Gregorian Calendar. Furthermore, the CHC shows that this day was in the middle of the week—the fourth day, Wednesday. This made it possible for Jesus to be in the tomb for *exactly* three days and three nights, and be raised from the dead toward the end of the weekly Sabbath—just as He had prophesied!

Why is it important that God fulfilled these two central prophetic events on the exact day He said? THEY PROVE THAT GOD'S WORD IS TRUE AND THAT HE FULFILLED THESE EVENTS ON THE EXACT DAY HE HAD "APPOINTED" BEFOREHAND—FROM THE FOUNDATION OF THE WORLD! Moreover, all of the prophesied details of events related to these days were fulfilled! Not one word failed!

These key events were fulfilled on the *exact* days foretold by prophecy thousands of years before. This means the timetable God used to accomplish these prophecies was predetermined by the CHC. Thus, the CHC—

with all of its rules and postponements—is the *only* calendar designed, ordained and authorized by God for the observance of His Sabbaths and holy days. **All other calendar schemes of men are null and void.** No one should allow himself or herself to be deceived into rejecting the CHC in order to follow calendar schemes of men!

If you would like additional information on this subject, please request our Calculated Hebrew Calendar Pack. It contains detailed written studies; four 90-minute DVDs; a book on how to calculate the Hebrew Calendar; and a CD that contains the mathematical formula for calculating the feasts and holy days of God. For those interested in purchasing a book on God's Sacred Calendar, Arthur Spier's revised third edition of *The Comprehensive Hebrew Calendar, 1900-2100 AD* may be obtained from Feldheim Publishers. You may e-mail them at sales@feldheim.com or order by calling 1-800-237-7149.

Appendix E

Numeric Patterns Relating to The Appointed Times of the Messiah

The Numbers *Four* and *Five* and the Passover

The scope of the God-given, sacred Calculated Hebrew Calendar (CHC) goes well beyond its primary purpose of accurately determining the weekly and monthly cycles and the annual "appointed times" or festivals. Not only can it be used to calculate forward into the future to know exactly when the festivals of God are to be kept, it can also be used to calculate backwards in time with pinpoint accuracy (to at least the 800s BC) to determine any appointed time of the past. Furthermore, because the CHC was designed by God and is registered in the heavens themselves, there are multitudes of unique "numeric patterns" that find their origins only in the sacred calendar. We will examine those that pertain to the Passover and Pentecost.

As can be seen in the chart on the following page, the *middle day* of the creation week is day *four*. God *set* the "appointed seasons" or "appointed times" on day *four*. The material creation was finished on the 4th day—with the sun, moon and stars ordained for *four* things: 1) signs, 2) seasons, 3) days, and 4) years (Gen. 1:14-19). The 4th commandment—"Remember the Sabbath to keep it holy"—was given to man at creation. The are *four* accounts of Jesus' life and ministry: **Matthew**, *Son of David and King*; **Mark**, *The Suffering Servant*; **Luke**, *The Perfect Man*; and **John**, *The Only Begotten Son of God*. The Gospels and Acts are the 4th division of *The Holy Bible In Its Original Order*.

As we view the chart, day *four* has been highlighted in the creation week. Next, in 30 AD, in the month of Nisan—the first month of the year, CHC, or April, Roman Calendar (RC)—the Passover fell on the 4th day of the week, Nisan 14. On this day, Jesus was 1) betrayed into the hands of sinners; 2) falsely accused, tried and convicted; 3) beaten and scourged beyond recognition; and 4) crucified unto death—the *four* major components to His sacrifice.

In Exodus 12:3, God commanded the children of Israel to select the lamb for the Passover on the 10th day of Nisan according the CHC. They were to keep it *four* days until the beginning of the 14th day, which began after sunset ended the 13th. Moreover, in the year of the Exodus, the Passover was also in the middle of the week—on the 4th day.

Likewise, Jesus, the Passover Lamb of God, was selected by God on the 10th day of the first month (John 12:23-33). In the chart, the *actual count* of the four days is indicated with small numbered circles. Again, *after* the Passover day, there were *four* more days (also indicated by numbered

Creation Week

Day 1	Day 2	Day 3	Day 4	Day 5	Day 6	Day 7
1	2	3	**4** God set the earth, moon and sun for the appointed times on the 4th day of wk.	5	6	7

Nisan 30 AD

Day 1	Day 2	Day 3	Day 4	Day 5	Day 6	Sabbath
				1	2	3
4	5	6	7	8	9	10 Selection of Passover lamb **Actual Count** **Grace Count** ① [1]
11 ② [2]	12 ③ [3]	13 Lambs slain right after sunset of 13th ④ [4]	**14 PASSOVER** **Grace Count** △1 **Heb. 2:9** **4th day of week** [5]	15 △2 ① **Actual Count**	16 △3 ②	17 △4 ③
18 Wave Sheaf Day △5 Jesus Ascends ④ to the Father	19 **Grace** **Rom. 4:24-25; 5:1-2; Zech. 4:7** **4+4=8**	20	21	22	23	24
25	26	27	28	29	30	

Sivan—7th Week Count to Pentecost

Day 1	Day 2	Day 3	Day 4	Day 5	Day 6	Day 7
1 Day 43	2 Day 44	3 Day 45	4 Day 46	5 Day 47	6 Day 48	7 Day 49
8 Sivan 8 Day after the 7th Sabbath Day 50 **Pentecost**						

Pentecost 50 Days = 5X10

Pentecost on 8th day after 7th day of the 7th week

Pentecost on 8th of Sivan 2X4=8

8 - New Beginnings - church began on Pentecost - New Beginning

Resurrection on Pentecost - New Beginning

5 = GRACE

circles) to the Wave Sheaf Offering Day, when Jesus ascended to the throne of God to present Himself as the perfect sacrifice for the sins of the world. Counting the four days before and after the Passover, we have 4 + 4 = 8. *Eight* is the biblical number for a new beginning. Indeed, the day of Jesus' acceptance by the Father did mark a new beginning.

The number five is the number of *grace*—and there are two counts of *five* associated with Jesus' last Passover and crucifixion. Beginning with the 10th day (indicated on the chart as day "1" in the small square), there are exactly *five* days including the Passover day itself. This fulfills Hebrews 2:9, that Jesus, "by the **grace** of God," tasted death for all mankind. The second count of *five* (indicated by numbered triangles) starts with the Passover Day and goes to the Wave Sheaf Offering Day. Indeed, it was by the *grace* of God that Jesus was accepted as the ultimate sacrifice for the sins of man (Rom. 4:24-25; 5:1-2). Thus, we have 5 + 5 — or *double* grace (Zech. 4:7).

Now examine the chart of *Sivan* (the third month, CHC, or May, RC) and the 7th week of the count to Pentecost. Here we find a combination of several numbers. *Pentecost* (meaning to "count fifty") is reckoned by counting seven complete weeks, each week ending in a Sabbath. Then, adding one day, "the day after the seventh Sabbath," is the day of Pentecost (Lev. 23:15-16). Thus, 7 x 7 = 49 + 1 = 50. Moreover, the number 50 can also be derived as 5 x 10, or *grace magnified*. Pentecost was 10 days after Jesus' final ascension—when the Holy Spirit was *graciously* given (Acts 2).

Because Pentecost is the day *after* the final Sabbath in the seven-week count, it is an *8th day*. The number *eight* symbolizes *new beginnings*. Interestingly, when Passover falls on the 4th day of the week, Pentecost is always on *Sivan 8*. The New Testament Church *began* on Pentecost, Sivan 8. Finally, the first resurrection is pictured by the day of Pentecost. It is most probable that the first resurrection will occur on Sivan 8—a *new beginning* for all the saints as immortal spirit beings.

Additional Numeric Patterns Relating to The Appointed Times of the Messiah

By Dwight Blevins

It is often said that the things of God begin and conclude from the basis of the Genesis account. Beginning in Genesis, a pattern thread and timeline of linkage was set in motion—one which moves forward through the Scriptures, demonstrating that the timing of all the major events of the life, ministry, death and resurrection of Jesus Christ had been calculated and predetermined from the foundation of the world. This fact is boldly stated in Revelation 13:8, and verified by Jesus' reference to "this hour" in John 12:27. The Passover day, Wednesday, day *four* of the week, Nisan 14, 30 AD, was that precise "hour" in history, determined long before when God positioned the "clock hands of time"—the sun, moon and stars. It was that moment in history that the countdown began, on the 4th day of creation (Gen. 1:14-19).

Without the precise calculations of the CHC, we would have no way of accurately following God's plan and road map of the many intricate steps which outline the "appointed times" of the Messiah. Indeed, the calculated times of God's annual Sabbaths (His "appointed times") validate that Jesus was the Messiah, while the events of Jesus' life in turn validate the accuracy of the calendar methods used to declare and fulfill the prophecies concerning His life, ministry, death and resurrection.

The seven-day creation account is flagged by the 4th day wherein the sun, moon and stars are ordained to *set* the seasons or "appointed times." This fourth day sets up a 4-3 division of the week—4 days followed by 3. This same 4-3 symmetry is displayed by the seven annual Sabbaths. The Feast of Trumpets, the 4th annual Sabbath, is the first day of the 7th month, *Tishri*, CHC (the month September, RC). This Holy Day is the *pivotal* high day of God's plan, and accordingly occupies the central position.

According to the calculations of the CHC, the Feast of Trumpets can only fall on four days of the week—days two, three, five or seven. It cannot fall on the other three days of the week—one, four or six. Again, we see the division of seven at the 4-3 mark.

On the one hand, it appears that Jesus was both born and resurrected on the 7th day of the week. On the other hand, His ministry both began and ended on Wednesday, the 4th day. Thus, Jesus' ministry spanned 44 months and four days—from Wednesday, the day of Atonement, 26 AD, until the Wednesday Passover of Nisan 14, 30 AD. Moreover, just as Jesus was selected as the Lamb of God on the Sabbath, Nisan 10, 30 AD, perhaps He was baptized by John on the Sabbath, Tishri 6, 26 AD—*four* days before Atonement, and *four* days before He began His 40-day fast and confrontation with Satan in the wilderness.

If this was the case, it means that from Jesus' baptism until the final hours of His confrontation with Satan was a span of 44 days. And, if Jesus was baptized four days before Atonement—"And lo, a voice from heaven said, 'This is My Son, the Beloved, in Whom I have *great* delight" (Matt. 3:17)—this follows the same pattern of God's voice from heaven four days before His final Passover (John 12:27). This was 44 months after His ministry began. Hence, we have a double validation of Jesus' selection and recognition by God the Father—i.e., "glorified" twice, but separated by a period of 44 months.

The 44 days at the outset of Jesus' ministry correspond to a similar period at the end of His ministry—the 44 days from Jesus' crucifixion to His ascent from the Mt. of Olives on Thursday, Iyar 27, 30 AD, 10 days before Pentecost. Between these two 44-day "bookends" was His ministry spanning 44 months and four days (the 3.5 years of Jesus' ministry translates into 44 months when you realize that two of the years were leap years, which adds one month of thirty days to each of the two years).

As noted earlier, the Wave Sheaf Offering Day began the 50-day count to Pentecost, which in Jesus' day fell on Sivan 8 (4 + 4). Pentecost is also the 8th day—the day *after* the final Sabbath in the 49-day count. Thus, Pentecost is associated with 50 and 8.—*Dwight Blevins*

As you can see, these few numeric patterns marking out the "appointed times" of Jesus' life, ministry, death and resurrection—as pictured by day four, the Passover, and the Day of Pentecost—demonstrate the accuracy and marvelous structure of the "appointed times" of the Messiah with the Calculated Hebrew Calendar. Absolutely none of these numeric patterns originate in the Roman Calendar. To cover the multitude of other numeric patterns pertaining to the Calculated Hebrew Calendar and the remaining feasts of God—including their methods of calculation, varied patterns and frequencies—would require an entire book (and that book would, of necessity, also include the numeric patterns of the diatonic musical scale). All of these numerical patterns demonstrate and confirm the greatness of God in His creation of the heavens and the earth, and in His awesome purpose for mankind. Perhaps Dwight Blevins could write such a book, as he alone, as far as I know, understands these fantastic numeric patterns. One final note: Dwight is also a harp maker.—*Fred R. Coulter*

Appendix F

An Overview of God's Annual Holy Days

The Scriptures teach that there are *seven* annual holy days or festivals ordained by God to be observed as special commanded convocations. These high days portray—in a step-by-step manner—God's entire plan of salvation for mankind. Moreover, the observance of these holy convocations is a sign between God and His people.

God's annual holy days were observed by Israel during Old Testament times—primarily as festivals acknowledging God's deliverance and physical blessings. The issue of sin and redemption was only dealt with superficially, utilizing rituals that pointed to a future reality. The deeper, spiritual meaning of these feasts would become clear only after Jesus' first coming.

In the New Testament, we find that Christ's entire ministry was centered around the spiritual meaning of God's holy days. The New Testament apostolic Church faithfully observed these annual feasts and holy days. Moreover, the Scriptures reveal that they will be observed by all mankind after the return of Christ (see Zech. 14:18-19).

As the holy days are annual Sabbath days, they may fall on any day of the week (except Pentecost, which always falls on a Sunday). When a holy day falls on a weekly Sabbath, the special observance of the holy day takes precedence. God's feasts and holy days are to be observed from sunset to sunset (Lev. 12:32) in accordance with the *Calculated Hebrew Calendar* as preserved by the Levitical Jews (Rom. 3:2).

The seven annual holy days are as follows (as listed in Leviticus 23):

Feast or Holy Day	**Scriptural Date of Observance**
1) Passover *	14th day of the first month (Nisan, or Abib)
2) Unleavened Bread (7 days)	15th through 21st days of the first month; the first and last days are high days
3) Pentecost	counted annually **
4) Trumpets	1st day of the seventh month (Tishri)
5) Atonement	10th day of the seventh month
6) Tabernacles (7 days)	15th through 21st days of the seventh month; only the first day is a high day
7) Last Great Day	22nd day of the seventh month

*Passover, which is actually a festival *event* (Ex. 34:25), is not a *high day*. It is observed on the *evening* of the 14th.

**Fifty days are counted, beginning with the first day of the week during the Days of Unleavened Bread. The feast is observed on the fiftieth day, which always falls on the first day of the week (Sunday).

God's Holy Day Plan for Mankind

Feasts	Old Testament	New Testament
Passover	God "passed over" the firstborn of Israel, sparing them from death; judgment on the gods of Egypt (Ex. 12-13). Passover is based on God's covenant promises to Abraham (Gen. 15).	God's love revealed as grace (Eph. 2:4-10). Jesus, the Lamb of God (John 1:29), our Passover (I Cor. 5:7), sacrificed for the sins of all mankind. Remission of sin is through His blood (Rom. 3:24-25; 5:1-2). The New Covenant is through Jesus' body and blood (Matt. 26:26-28).
Feast of Unleavened Bread	God led the children of Israel out of Egypt and into the Promised Land (Ex. 12-13). Israel ate the "bread of affliction" (Deut. 16:3). God fulfilled his covenant promise to Abraham (Gen. 15:14-16).	Christians are unleavened in Christ (I Cor. 5:7-8), overcome sin by the power of the Holy Spirit (Acts 1:8), and walk in newness of life (Rom. 6:4)—keeping the commandments of God (I John 3:22). Saints are the spiritual seed of Abraham (Gal. 3:29), and must be separate from this world, typed by Egypt (John 17:14).
Feast of Firstfruits (Pentecost)	Israel received the Law at Mt. Sinai (Ex. 20-23); Old Covenant ratified between God and Israel (Ex. 24:6-8). A festival celebrating the firstfruits of the grain harvest (Ex. 23:16; 34:22).	Christians are the firstfruits of God's plan of salvation (James 1:18; Rev. 14:4). On Pentecost, the Church received the Holy Spirit (Acts 2). Through His Spirit, God writes His Law on our hearts (Heb. 8:10; 10:16; Gal. 2:20).
Day of Trumpets	Memorial of the sounding of trumpets for war (Jer. 4:19; Ezek. 7:14; Joel 2:1).	Points to the end-time Day of the Lord, organized around 7 "trumpet plagues" (Joel 2:1; Rev. 8-9, 11:15). Christ and the saints return to the earth from the sea of glass at the 7th trumpet (Rev. 10:7; 15:2). God's final triumph over Satan and all evil (Rev. 11:15).
Day of Atonement	With special animal sacrifices, the High Priest atoned for the sins of Israel (Lev. 16). These rituals were *prototypical*, pointing to Jesus' future role as both High Priest and ultimate sacrifice (Heb. 9:8-14, 23-28; 10:1-6).	Christ's sacrifice applied to all people of the world. Saints as spirit beings are "at one" with God the Father and Jesus Christ. Satan removed and bound (Rev. 20:1-3).

Feasts	Old Testament	New Testament
Feast of Tabernacles	Memorial of Israel's temporary sojourn in the wilderness (Lev. 23:43). As festival of "ingathering" (Ex. 23:16; 34:22), celebrated the fullness of the annual harvest.	Points to the temporary nature of this age, as the saints "tabernacle" in anticipation of the Kingdom of God—the millennial reign of Christ and the saints (Rev. 20:4). Pictures the fullness of the "harvest" of all mankind into God's kingdom (Luke 10:2; Heb. 8:11). Jesus, who once "tabernacled" with man, now dwells by God's Spirit in the saints (Gal. 2:20). Saints to put off this physical "tabernacle" for an immortal spirit existence (II Cor. 5:1-4).
Last Great Day	The bounty of God's blessings on Israel. Lev. 23:36, 39 calls this feast the "eighth day." The Hebrew root for eight means "to be fat"—as in plentiful. In the Old Testament, the number eight is generally associated with a "new beginning."	Points to the post-millennial period, including: 1) the 2nd resurrection as an opportunity for salvation for *all* who have lived and died; 2) the final judgment of the wicked via the lake of fire; 3) the fullness of the new heavens and new earth; 4) the coming of the New Jerusalem to earth and God dwelling with mankind; 5) the *new beginning* of God's plan for eternity. See Rev. 20-22.

List of All the Commanded Holy Days and Feasts of God from 5 BC to 105 AD

The dates of the Calculated Hebrew Calendar are coordinated with the Julian Calendar

Year	Passover	Unleavened Bread (First)	Unleavened Bread (Last)	Pentecost	Feast of Trumpets	Day of Atonement	Feast of Tabernacles	Last Great Day
5 BC	MAR 22 WED	MAR 23 THU	MAR 29 WED	MAY 14 SUN	SEPT 2 SAB Jesus' Birth	SEPT 11 MON	SEPT 16 SAB	SEPT 23 SAB
4 BC	APR 11 WED	APR 12 THU	APR 18 WED	JUNE 3 SUN	SEPT 22 SAB	OCT 1 MON	OCT 6 SAB	OCT 13 SAB
3 BC	MAR 30 SAB	MAR 31 SUN	APR 6 SAB	MAY 19 SUN	SEPT 10 TUE	SEPT 19 THU	SEPT 24 TUE	OCT 1 TUE
2 BC	MAR 19 WED	MAR 20 THU	MAR 26 WED	MAY 11 SUN	AUG 30 SAB	SEPT 8 MON	SEPT 13 SAB	SEPT 20 SAB
1 BC	APR 7 WED	APR 8 THU	APR 14 WED	MAY 30 SUN	SEPT 18 SAB	SEPT 27 MON	OCT 2 SAB	OCT 9 SAB
1 AD	MAR 28 MON	MAR 29 TUE	APR 4 MON	MAY 22 SUN	SEPT 8 THU	SEPT 17 SAB	SEPT 22 THU	SEPT 29 THU
2 AD	APR 15 SAB	APR 16 SUN	APR 22 SAB	JUNE 4 SUN	SEPT 26 TUE	OCT 5 THU	OCT 10 TUE	OCT 17 TUE
3 AD	APR 4 WED	APR 5 THU	APR 11 WED	MAY 27 SUN	SEPT 15 SAB	SEPT 24 MON	SEPT 29 SAB	OCT 6 SAB
4 AD	MAR 24 MON	MAR 25 TUE	MAR 31 MON	MAY 18 SUN	SEPT 4 THU	SEPT 13 SAB	SEPT 18 THU	SEPT 25 THU
5 AD	APR 13 MON	APR 14 TUE	APR 20 MON	JUNE 7 SUN	SEPT 24 THU	OCT 3 SAB	OCT 8 THU	OCT 15 THU
6 AD	APR 2 FRI	APR 3 SAB	APR 9 FRI	MAY 23 SUN	SEPT 13 MON	SEPT 22 WED	SEPT 27 MON	OCT 4 MON
7 AD	MAR 21 MON	MAR 22 MON	MAR 28 MON	MAY 15 SUN	SEPT 1 THU	SEPT 10 SAB	SEPT 15 THU	SEPT 22 THU
8 AD	APR 9 MON	APR 10 TUE	APR 16 MON	JUNE 3 SUN	SEPT 20 THU	SEPT 29 SAB	OCT 4 THU	OCT 11 THU
9 AD	MAR 29 FRI	MAR 30 SAB	APR 5 FRI	MAY 19 SUN	SEPT 9 MON	SEPT 18 WED	SEPT 23 MON	SEPT 30 MON
10 AD	APR 16 WED	APR 17 THUR	APR 23 WED	JUNE 8 SUN	SEPT 27 SAB	OCT 6 MON	OCT 11 SAB	OCT 18 SAB
11 AD	APR 6 MON	APR 7 TUE	APR 13 MON	MAY 31 SUN	SEPT 17 THU	SEPT 26 SAB	OCT 1 THU	OCT 8 THU
12 AD	MAR 25 FRI	MAR 26 SAB	APR 1 FRI	MAY 15 SUN	SEPT 5 MON	SEPT 14 WED	SEPT 19 MON	SEPT 26 MON
13 AD	APR 14 FRI	APR 15 SAB	APR 21 FRI	JUNE 4 SUN	SEPT 25 MON	OCT 4 WED	OCT 9 MON	OCT 16 MON
14 AD	APR 2 MON	APR 3 TUE	APR 9 MON	MAY 27 SUN	SEPT 13 THU	SEPT 22 SAB	SEPT 27 THU	OCT 4 THU
15 AD	MAR 22 FRI	MAR 23 SAB	MAR 29 FRI	MAY 12 SUN	SEPT 2 MON	SEPT 11 WED	SEPT 16 MON	SEPT 23 MON
16 AD	APR 10 FRI	APR 11 SAB	APR 17 FRI	MAY 31 SUN	SEPT 21 MON	SEPT 30 WED	OCT 5 MON	OCT 12 MON
17 AD	MAR 31 WED	APR 1 THU	APR 7 WED	MAY 23 SUN	SEPT 11 SAB	SEPT 20 MON	SEPT 25 SAB	OCT 2 SAB
18 AD	MAR 19 SAB	MAR 20 SUN	MAR 26 SAB	MAY 8 SUN	AUG 30 TUE	SEPT 9 THU.	SEPT 13 TUE	SEPT 20 TUE
19 AD	APR 7 FRI	APR 8 SAB	APR 14 FRI	MAY 28 SUN	SEPT 18 MON	SEPT 27 WED	OCT 2 THU	OCT 9 THU

Year	Passover	Unleavened Bread (First)	Unleavened Bread (Last)	Pentecost	Feast of Trumpets	Day of Atonement	Feast of Tabernacles	Last Great Day
20 AD	MAR 27 WED	MAR 28 THU	APR 3 WED	MAY 19 SUN	SEPT 7 SAB	SEPT 16 MON	SEPT 21 SAB	SEPT 28 SAB
21 AD	APR 14 MON	APR 15 TUE	APR 21 MON	JUNE 8 SUN	SEPT 25 THU	OCT 4 SAB	OCT 9 THU	OCT 16 THU
22 AD	APR 4 SAB	APR 5 SUN	APR 11 SAB	MAY 24 SUN	SEPT 15 TUE	SEPT 24 THU	SEPT 29 TUE	OCT 6 TUE
23 AD	MAR 24 WED	MAR 25 THU	MAR 31 WED	MAY 16 SUN	SEPT 4 SAB	SEPT 13 MON	SEPT 18 SAB	SEPT 25 SAB
24 AD	APR 12 WED	APR 13 THU	APR 19 WED	JUNE 4 SUN	SEPT 23 SAB	OCT 2 MON	OCT 7 SAB	OCT 14 SAB
25 AD	APR 2 MON	APR 3 TUE	APR 9 MON	MAY 27 SUN	SEPT 13 THU	SEPT 22 SAB	SEPT 27 THU	OCT 4 THU
26 AD	MAR 22 FRI	MAR 23 SAB	MAR 29 FRI	MAY 12 SUN	SEPT 2 MON	SEPT 11 WED	SEPT 16 MON	SEPT 23 TUE
27 AD	APR 9 WED	APR 10 THU	APR 16 WED	JUNE 1 SUN	SEPT 20 SAB	SEPT 29 MON	OCT 4 SAB	OCT 11 SAB
28 AD	MAR 29 MON	MAR 30 TUE	APR 5 MON	MAY 23 SUN	SEPT 9 THU	SEPT 18 SAB	SEPT 23 THU	SEPT 30 THU
29 AD	APR 16 SAB	APR 17 SUN	APR 23 SAB	JUNE 5 SUN	SEPT 27 TUE	OCT 6 THU	OCT 11 TUE	OCT 18 TUE
30 AD	APR 5 WED Jesus' Death	APR 6 THU	APR 12 WED	MAY 28 SUN	SEPT 16 SAB	SEPT 25 MON	SEPT 30 SAB	OCT 7 SAB
31 AD	MAR 26 MON	MAR 27 TUE	APR 2 MON	MAY 20 SUN	SEPT 6 THU	SEPT 15 SAB	SEPT 20 THU	SEPT 27 THU
32 AD	APR 14 MON	APR 15 TUE	APR 21 MON	JUNE 8 SUN	SEPT 25 THU	OCT 4 SAB	OCT 9 THU	OCT 16 THU
33 AD	APR 3 FRI	APR 4 SAB	APR 10 FRI	JUNE 24 SUN	SEPT 14 MON	SEPT 23 WED	SEPT 28 MON	OCT 5 MON
34 AD	MAR 22 MON	MAR 23 TUE	MAR 29 MON	MAY 16 SUN	SEPT 2 THU	SEPT 11 SUN	SEPT 16 THU	SEPT 23 THU
35 AD	APR 11 MON	APR 12 TUE	APR 18 MON	JUNE 5 SUN	SEPT 22 THU	OCT 1 SAB	OCT 6 THU	OCT 13 THU
36 AD	MAR 30 FRI	MAR 31 SAB	APR 6 FRI	MAY 20 SUN	SEPT 10 MON	SEPT 19 WED	SEPT 24 MON	OCT 1 MON
37 AD	MAR 20 WED	MAR 21 THU	MAR 27 WED	MAY 12 SUN	AUG 31 SAB	SEPT 9 MON	SEPT 14 SAB	SEPT 21 SAB
38 AD	APR 7 MON	APR 8 TUE	APR 14 MON	JUNE 1 SUN	SEPT 7 MON	SEPT 16 WED	SEPT 21 MON	SEPT 28 MON
39 AD	MAR 27 FRI	MAR 28 SAB	APR 3 FRI	MAY 17 SUN	SEPT 7 MON	SEPT 16 WED	SEPT 21 MON	SEPT 28 MON
40 AD	APR 15 FRI	APR 16 SAB	APR 22 FRI	JUNE 5 SUN	SEPT 26 MON	OCT 5 WED	OCT 10 MON	OCT 17 MON
41 AD	APR 3 MON	APR 4 TUE	APR 10 MON	MAY 28 SUN	SEPT 14 THUR	SEPT 23 SAB	SEPT 28 THU	OCT 5 THU
42 AD	MAR 24 SAB	MAR 25 SUN	MAR 31 SAB	MAY 13 SUN	SEPT 4 TUE	SEPT 13 THU	SEPT 18 TUE	SEPT 25 TUE
43 AD	APR 12 FRI	APR 13 SAB	APR 19 FRI	JUNE 2 SUN	SEPT 23 MON	OCT 2 WED	OCT 7 MON	OCT 14 MON
44 AD	APR 1 WED	APR 2 THU	APR 8 WED	MAY 24 SUN	SEPT 12 SAB	SEPT 21 MON	SEPT 26 SAB	OCT 3 SAB
45 AD	MAR 20 SAB	MAR 21 SUN	MAR 27 SAB	MAY 9 SUN	AUG 31 TUE	SEPT 9 THU	SEPT 14 TUE	SEPT 21 TUE

Appendix F

Year	Passover	Unleavened Bread (First)	Unleavened Bread (Last)	Pentecost	Feast of Trumpets	Day of Atonement	Feast of Tabernacles	Last Great Day
46 AD	APR 8 FRI	APR 9 SAB	APR 15 FRI	MAY 29 SUN	SEPT 19 MON	SEPT 28 WED	OCT 3 MON	OCT 10 MON
47 AD	MAR 29 WED	MAR 30 THU	APR 5 WED	MAY 21 SUN	SEPT 9 SAB	SEPT 18 MON	SEPT 23 SAB	OCT 30 SAB
48 AD	APR 15 MON	APR 16 TUE	APR 22 MON	JUNE 9 SUN	SEPT 26 THU	OCT 5 SAB	OCT 10 THU	OCT 17 THU
49 AD	APR 5 SAB	APR 6 SUN	APR 12 SAB	MAY 25 SUN	SEPT 16 TUE	SEPT 25 THU	SEPT 3O TUE	OCT 7 TUE
50 AD	MAR 25 WED	MAR 26 THU	APR 1 WED	MAY 17 SUN	SEPT 5 SAB	SEPT 14 MON	SEPT 19 SAB	SEPT 26 SAB
51 AD	APR 14 WED	APR 15 THU	APR 21 WED	JUNE 6 SUN	SEPT 25 SAB	OCT 4 MON	OCT 9 SAB	OCT 16 SAB
52 AD	APR 3 MON	APR 4 TUE	APR 10 MON	MAY 28 SUN	SEPT 14 THU	SEPT 23 SAB	SEPT 28 THU	OCT 5 THU
53 AD	MAR 23 FRI	MAR 24 SAB	MAR 30 FRI	MAY 13 SUN	SEPT 3 MON	SEPT 12 WED	SEPT 17 MON	SEPT 24 MON
54 AD	APR 10 WED	WED 11 THU	APR 17 WED	JUNE 2 SUN	SEPT 21 SAB	SEPT 30 MON	OCT 5 SAB	OCT 12 SAB
55 AD	MAR 31 MON	APR 1 TUE	APR 7 MON	MAY 25 SUN	SEPT 11 THU	SEPT 20 SAB	SEPT 25 THU	OCT 2 THU
56 AD	MAR 19 FRI	MAR 20 SAB	MAR 26 FRI	MAY 9 SUN	AUG 30 MON	SEPT 8 WED	SEPT 13 MON	SEPT 20 MON
57 AD	APR 6 WED	APR 7 THU	APR 13 WED	MAY 29 SUN	SEPT 17 SAB	SEPT 26 MON	OCT 1 SAB	OCT 8 SAB
58 AD	MAR 27 MON	MAR 28 TUE	APR 3 MON	MAY 21 SUN	SEPT 7 THU	SEPT 16 SAB	SEPT 21 THU	SEPT 28 THU
59 AD	APR 16 MON	APR 17 TUE	APR 23 MON	JUNE 10 SUN	SEPT 27 THU	OCT 6 SAB	OCT 11 THU	OCT 18 THU
60 AD	APR 4 FRI	APR 5 SAB	APR 11 FRI	MAY 25 SUN	SEPT 15 MON	SEPT 24 WED	SEPT 29 MON	OCT 6 MON
61 AD	MAR 23 MON	MAR 24 TUE	MAR 30 MON	MAY 17 SUN	SEPT 3 THU	SEPT 12 SAB	SEPT 17 THU	SEPT 24 THU
62 AD	APR 12 MON	APR 13 TUE	APR 19 MON	JUNE 6 SUN	SEPT 23 THU	OCT 2 SAB	OCT 7 THU	OCT 14 THU
63 AD	APR 1 FRI	APR 2 SAB	APR 8 FRI	MAY 22 SUN	SEPT 12 MON	SEPT 21 WED	SEPT 26 MON	OCT 3 MON
64 AD	MAR 21 WED	MAR 22 THU	MAR 28 WED	MAY 13 SUN	SEPT 1 SAB	SEPT 10 MON	SEPT 15 SAB	SEPT 22 SAB
65 AD	APR 8 MON	APR 9 TUE	APR 15 MON	JUNE 2 SUN	SEPT 19 THU	SEPT 28 SAB	OCT 3 THU	OCT 10 THU
66 AD	MAR 28 FRI	MAR 29 SAB	APR 4 FRI	MAY 18 SUN	SEPT 8 MON	SEPT 17 WED	SEPT 22 MON	SEPT 28 MON
67 AD	APR 17 FRI	APR 18 SAB	APR 24 FRI	JUNE 7 SUN	SEPT 28 MON	OCT 7 WED	OCT 12 MON	OCT 19 MON
68 AD	APR 4 MON	APR 5 TUE	APR 11 MON	MAY 29 SUN	SEPT 15 THU	SEPT 24 SAB	SEPT 29 THU	OCT 6 THU
69 AD	MAR 25 SAB	MAR 26 SUN	APR 1 SAB	MAY 14 SUN	SEPT 5 TUE	SEPT 14 THU	SEPT 19 TUE	SEPT 26 TUE
70 AD	APR 13 FRI	APR 14 SAB	APR 20 FRI	JUNE 3 SUN	SEPT 24 MON	OCT 3 WED	OCT 8 MON	OCT 15 MON
71 AD	APR 3 WED	APR 4 THU	APR 10 WED	MAY 26 SUN	SEPT 14 SAB	SEPT 23 MON	SEPT 29 SAB	OCT 5 SAB
72 AD	MAR 21 SAB	MAR 22 SUN	MAR 28 SAB	MAY 10 SUN	SEPT 1 TUE	SEPT 10 THU	SEPT 15 TUE	SEPT 22 TUE

Year	Passover	Unleavened Bread (First)	Unleavened Bread (Last)	Pentecost	Feast of Trumpets	Day of Atonement	Feast of Tabernacles	Last Great Day
73 AD	APR 9 FRI	APR 10 SAB	APR 16 FRI	MAY 30 SUN	SEPT 20 MON	SEPT 29 WED	OCT 4 MON	OCT 11 MON
74 AD	MAR 30 WED	MAR 31 THU	APR 6 WED	MAY 22 SUN	SEPT 10 SAB	SEPT 19 MON	SEPT 24 SAB	OCT 1 SAB
75 AD	MAR 20 MON	MAR 21 TUE	MAR 27 MON	MAY 10 SUN	AUG 31 THU	SEPT 9 SAB	SEPT 14 THU	SEPT 21 THU
76 AD	APR 6 SAB	APR 7 SUN	APR 13 SUN	MAY 26 SUN	SEPT 17 TUE	SEPT 26 THU	OCT 1 TUE	OCT 8 TUE
77 AD	MAR 26 WED	MAR 27 THU	APR 2 WED	MAY 18 SUN	SEPT 6 SAB	SEPT 15 MON	SEPT 20 SAB	SEPT 27 SAB
78 AD	APR 5 WED	APR 16 TUE	APR 22 WED	JUNE 8 SUN	SEPT 26 SAB	OCT 5 MON	OCT 10 SAB	OCT 17 SAB
79 AD	APR 5 MON	APR 6 TUE	APR 12 MON	MAY 30 SUN	SEPT 16 THU	SEPT 25 SAB	SEPT 30 THU	OCT 7 THU
80 AD	MAR 24 FRI	MAR 25 SAB	MAR 31 FRI	MAY 14 SUN	SEPT 14 MON	SEPT 13 WED	SEPT 18 MON	SEPT 25 MON
81 AD	APR 11 WED	APR 12 THU	APR 18 WED	JUNE 10 SUN	SEPT 22 SAB	OCT 1 MON	OCT 6 SAB	OCT 13 SAB
82 AD	APR 1 MON	APR 2 TUE	APR 8 MON	MAY 26 SUN	SEPT 12 THU	SEPT 21 SAB	SEPT 26 THU	OCT 3 THU
83 AD	MAR 21 FRI	MAR 22 SAB	MAR 28 FRI	MAY 11 SUN	SEPT 1 MON	SEPT 10 WED	SEPT 15 MON	SEPT 22 MON
84 AD	APR 9 FRI	APR 10 SAB	APR 16 FRI	MAY 30 SUN	SEPT 20 MON	SEPT 29 WED	OCT 4 MON	OCT 11 MON
85 AD	MAR 28 MON	MAR 29 TUE	APR 4 MON	MAY 22 SUN	SEPT 8 THU	SEPT 17 SAB	SEPT 22 THU	SEPT 29 THU
86 AD	APR 17 MON	APR 18 TUE	APR 24 MON	JUNE 11 SUN	SEPT 28 THU	OCT 7 SAB	OCT 12 THU	OCT 19 THU
87 AD	APR 6 FRI	APR 7 SAB	APR 13 FRI	MAY 27 SUN	SEPT 17 MON	SEPT 26 WED	OCT 1 MON	OCT 8 MON
88 AD	WED 26 WED	MAR 27 THU	APR 2 WED	MAY 18 SUN	SEPT 6 SAB	SEPT 15 MON	SEPT 20 SAB	SEPT 27 SAB
89 AD	APR 13 MON	APR 14 TUE	APR 20 MON	JUNE 7 SUN	SEPT 24 THU	OCT 3 SAB	OCT 8 THU	OCT 15 THU
90 AD	APR 2 FRI	APR 3 SAB	APR 9 FRI	MAY 23 SUN	SEPT 13 MON	SEPT 22 WED	SEPT 27 MON	OCT 4 MON
91 AD	MAR 23 WED	MAR 24 THU	MAR 30 WED	MAY 15 SUN	SEPT 3 SAB	SEPT 12 MON	SEPT 17 SAB	SEPT 24 SAB
92 AD	APR 9 MON	APR 10 TUE	APR 16 MON	JUNE 3 SUN	SEPT 20 THU	SEPT 29 SAB	OCT 4 THU	OCT 11 THU
93 AD	MAR 29 FRI	MAR 30 SAB	APR 4 FRI	MAY 19 SUN	SEPT 9 MON	SEPT 18 WED	SEPT 23 MON	SEPT 30 MON
94 AD	MAR 19 WED	MAR 20 THU	MAR 26 WED	MAY 11 SUN	AUG 30 SAB	SEPT 8 MON	SEPT 13 SAB	SEPT 20 SAB
95 AD	APR 8 WED	APR 9 THU	APR 15 WED	MAY 31 SUN	SEPT 19 SAB	SEPT 28 MON	OCT 3 SAB	OCT 10 SAB
96AD	MAR 26 SAB	MAR 27 SUN	APR 2 SAB	MAY 15 SUN	SEPT 6 TUE	SEPT 15 THU	SEPT 20 TUE	SEPT 27 TUE
97 AD	APR 14 FRI	APR 15 SAB	APR 21 FRI	JUNE 4 SUN	SEPT 25 MON	OCT 4 WED	OCT 9 MON	OCT 16 MON
98 AD	APR 4 WED	APR 5 THU	APR 11 WED	MAY 27 SUN	SEPT 15 SAB	SEPT 24 MON	SEPT 29 SAB	OCT 6 SAB
99 AD	MAR 25 WED	MAR 26 THU	APR 1 WED	MAY 19 SUN	SEPT 5 THU	SEPT 14 SAB	SEPT 19 THU	SEPT 26 THU

Appendix F

Year	Passover	Unleavened Bread (First)	Unleavened Bread (Last)	Pentecost	Feast of Trumpets	Day of Atonement	Feast of Tabernacles	Last Great Day
100 AD	APR 11 SAB	APR 12 SUN	APR 18 SAB	MAY 31 SUN	SEPT 22 TUE	OCT 1 THU	OCT 6 TUE	OCT 13 TUE
101 AD	MAR 31 WED	APR 1 THU	APR 7 WED	MAY 23 SUN	SEPT 11 SAB	SEPT 20 MON	SEPT 25 SAB	OCT 2 SAB
102 AD	MAR 21 MON	MAR 22 TUE	MAR 28 MON	MAY 15 SUN	SEPT 1 THU	SEPT 10 SAB	SEPT 15 THU	SEPT 22 THU
103 AD	APR 10 MON	APR 11 TUE	APR 17 MON	JUNE 4 SUN	SEPT 21 THU	SEPT 30 SAB	OCT 5 THU	OCT 12 THU
104 AD	MAR 29 FRI	MAR 30 SAB	APR 5 FRI	MAY 19 SUN	SEPT 9 MON	SEPT 18 WED	SEPT 23 MON	SEPT 30 MON
105 AD	APR 16 WED	APR 17 THU	APR 23 WED	JUNE 8 SUN	SEPT 27 SAB	OCT 6 MON	OCT 11 SAB	OCT 18 SAB

Bibliography

Apostolic Constitutions—Didascalia Apostolorum, Book V

Dio's Roman History. James Loeb Classical Library. London, 1957

Edersheim, Alfred. *The Life and Times of Jesus the Messiah*

Finegan, Jack. *Handbook of Biblical Chronology*. Princeton University Press, 1964

Fox, Everett. *The Schocken Bible—Vol. I, The Five Books of Moses*. New York: Schocken Books, 1995

Josephus, Flavius. *Antiquities of the Jews*; *Wars*. "Complete Works of Josephus"; Grand Rapids: Kregel, 1981

Kudler, M., with E. Mickler. *Solar and Lunar Eclipses of the Ancient Near East*. Neukirchen-Bluyn: Verlas Butson & Bercker Kevelaer, 1971

Lietzmann, Hans. *A History of the Early Church*. New York: World Publishing, 1953

Martin, Dr. Ernest L. *The Star of Bethlehem.* Published in 1996; available at www.askelm.com/books/book003.htm

________. *The Teachings of Pentecost.* Originally published in 1983; found at www.askelm.com/doctrine/d050501.htm

Moffat, James. *The Bible—A New Translation.* New York: Harper & Row, 1954

Robertson, A. T. *Word Pictures in the New Testament.* Nashville: B & H Publishing Group, 2000

Seutonius. J. C. Rolfe, ed. James Loeb Classical Library. London, 1914

Talmud (*Sukkah*). London: Soncino Press, 1934

The Modern Language Bible: The New Berkeley Version in Modern English. Grand Rapids: Zondervan, 1969

Unger, Merrill. *Unger's Bible Dictionary*. Chicago: Moody Press, 1988

Vanhoye, Albert. *The Jubilee Year in the Gospel of Luke.* Theological Historical Commission, 1997

Velikovsky, Immanuel. *Worlds in Collision*, 1950

Waltke, Bruce K. and M. O'Connor. *An Introduction to Biblical Hebrew Syntax.* Winona Lake, Ind.: Eisenbrauns, 1990